Capacity Assessment and the Law

Kelly Purser

Capacity Assessment and the Law

Problems and Solutions

 Springer

Kelly Purser
Faculty of Law
Australian Centre for Health Law Research
Queensland University of Technology
Brisbane, Queensland
Australia

ISBN 978-3-319-54345-1   ISBN 978-3-319-54347-5   (eBook)
DOI 10.1007/978-3-319-54347-5

Library of Congress Control Number: 2017937582

Printed on acid-free paper

This Springer imprint is published by Springer Nature
The registered company is Springer International Publishing AG
The registered company address is: Gewerbestrasse 11, 6330 Cham, Switzerland

I would like to express my immense appreciation to Lyn and Bruce Purser. Without them, this would not have been possible. This book is dedicated to them as a token of my gratitude for their continuous love and support.

Preface

My interest in the area of capacity assessment in the testamentary and decision-making context arose from my time in legal practice as an estate planning practitioner. A situation arose whereby a client's capacity needed to be assessed. Attempts were made to speak to the client's general practitioner, who avoided all mediums of communication, that is, until after the amended will had been signed. It was at this time that the general practitioner said that the client lacked capacity to execute the will but did retain capacity to make financial decisions and, further, that the refusal to become involved in the capacity assessment resulted from a fear of inclusion in potential future litigation. There is a remarkable amount of trust necessarily being placed in the professionals conducting these assessments, which leads to the question: What happens if those professionals are not comfortable with that role or do not possess the skill to do that trust justice, especially as it became increasingly apparent throughout this research that the disparate stakeholders are siloed within their particular disciplines? It was informative but also alarming to witness first-hand the impact that capacity assessments can have on the people being assessed, their families and carers, and on the legal and health professionals involved in conducting the assessments. It demonstrated the need for an innovative new approach to assessing capacity in the context of testamentary and substitute decision-making.

Experiences in practice inspired this work of research which syntheses and analyses the existing literature, including some of the best assessment models worldwide, to generate a new methodology and understanding of what capacity assessment best practice means, and the impact this can have on individual autonomy and personal sovereignty. The critical discussion of the relevant literature throughout this work demonstrates an awareness of the contextual environment helping to produce an erudite work contributing new knowledge to this area. A comparison of the assessment paradigms worldwide with a view to informing best practice has not previously been undertaken. The innovative use of a therapeutic jurisprudence lens through which to approach this analysis has likewise informed an original outcome. Accordingly, this work is useful for people within a number of disciplines including those involved in academia, policy and practice.

To this end, this work focuses on the process of the assessment itself and does not attempt to delve into jurisdictional intricacies. The ideal method is based on respect for individual autonomy and fundamental human rights and thus, in this regard, stands alone from the specific legal jurisdiction in which the person's capacity is assessed. That is, best practice for the assessment process should not be dictated by the specific legal requirements, instead ideally being informed by value for individual autonomy and locating the necessary balance between autonomy and protecting vulnerable people. The first chapter establishes the magnitude of the problem around satisfactorily assessing capacity in the specific context of testamentary and substitute decision-making. The second chapter introduces the therapeutic jurisprudence lens to be used in this work, before examining the nature of capacity more generally in Chap. 3. Chapter 4 examines the determination of testamentary capacity. The challenges faced in the process used to assess substitute decision-making capacity are the focus of Chap. 5. It is acknowledged that there is a paradigmatic shift taking place away from substitute towards supported decision-making. Nevertheless, substitute decision-making documents are still critically important in the estate planning landscape and feature at the medico-legal interface within this contextual environment. Chapter 6 is dedicated to assessing some of the best capacity assessment guidelines worldwide. Some suggested solutions to progress the capacity assessment discourse through the adoption of therapeutic jurisprudence principles are then made in Chap. 7. Naturally, not everyone will agree with the arguments advanced here, but it is hoped that the novel approach taken and the original addition to the existing literature will progress the capacity assessment dialogue.

I would like to thank my friends, family and colleagues, especially those in the Australian Centre for Health Law Research, who have supported me in writing this work. Vicky Martin, Lisa Davis, Carrie Te Wani and Amy Cosby deserve a special mention for their time and assistance.

Brisbane, QLD, Australia   Kelly Purser

Contents

List of Abbreviations

ADL	Activities of daily living
ABA	American Bar Association
APA	American Psychological Association
CRPD	Convention on the Rights of Persons with Disabilities
FAI	Forensic Assessment Instrument
FCAI	Financial Competence Assessment Inventory
FCI	Financial Capacity Instrument
IADL	Instrumental activities of daily living
MacCAT-CR	MacArthur Competence Assessment Tool–Clinical Research
MacCAT-T	MacArthur Competence Assessment Tool–Treatment
MMSE	Mini-Mental State Examination
MoCA	Montreal Cognitive Assessment
TDS	Testament Definition Scale

Chapter 1
The Challenges Presented by the Assessment of Legal Capacity

1 Introduction

Decision-making autonomy is a fundamental human right. The law is concerned to ascertain an individual's capacity to make legal decisions because legal competency safeguards an individual's prerogative to make and manage his or her own testamentary, financial, property, personal and health care decisions, both inter vivos and on his or her death.[1] However, the primacy of individual autonomy must be, and is, counterbalanced by the need to protect vulnerable individuals, a growing concern confronting modern society.[2] The question is, how to satisfactorily achieve this equilibrium.

The assessment of legal capacity in the testamentary, financial and health decision-making context is the focus of this book. It provides a practical representation of the dichotomous nature of autonomy and protection. Assessments of capacity are characterised by this inherent dualism, with the assessor ultimately required to evaluate another's ability to make, understand and communicate decisions through the application of tests and/or processes.[3] Such determinations are incredibly complex, being practically, theoretically, methodologically and ethically challenging. The significance of such assessments cannot be under-estimated as a negative determination results not only in the removal of individual autonomy, but also potentially has emotional, social, relational, financial, legal and practical implications. Financial and health care decision-making capacity in particular is undergoing a paradigmatic shift, with the focus now turning towards supported decision-making. Increasing attention is likewise being paid to the assessment of testamentary capacity, especially as individual estates are growing in value. The increased size not only makes the estate more attractive to potential litigants, but

---

[1] Carney T (1997), p. 1; Devereux J and Parker M (2006), p. 54.
[2] Moye J and Marson DC (2007), p. 3.
[3] Carney T and Tait D (1991), p. 66.

also opens the actions of the legal, and possibly health, professionals involved in capacity assessments to growing scrutiny.

Ensuring the satisfactory assessment of legal capacity is essential. However, significant problems exist impeding the implementation of consistent, transparent and accurate assessments. Society is ageing and the numbers of mentally disabling conditions impacting cognition are growing. These are two factors informing the environment in which legal and health professionals are increasingly being required to assess the testamentary and decision-making capacity of individuals.[4] Two disparate, although often well-intentioned, professions are being forced to play in a playground with the same equipment but without necessarily knowing how to use that equipment, or even what the rules governing their play are. The call for capacity assessment guidelines is not new, but despite the best intentions of all involved, a consistent assessment paradigm has not been developed. What is consistently being developed is a multitude of different sets of guidelines, nationally and internationally, each differing slightly from the others in best practice process. This is distinct from necessary differences in the law and its application which are obviously going to be jurisdiction specific. The array of available guidelines is resulting in confusion about how the professions should collaborate when assessing issues pertaining to legal capacity. The outcome is the implementation of ad hoc, inconsistent and opaque assessment paradigms. Paradigms which are then further modified by individual practitioners, both legal and health, to suit their own skill sets rather than the specific capacity being assessed which serves to highlight the challenges presented by a lack of adequate training in this area.

Miscommunication and misunderstanding about roles and responsibilities when conducting capacity assessments further impact the relationship between legal and health professionals.[5] Health professionals are assessing notions of clinical capacity and applying those concepts to the question of legal capacity, the proverbial square peg in a round hole. Legal practitioners, while assessing legal capacity, do not always have the skills from their training to be able to satisfactorily assess the increasingly complex effect of various mentally disabling conditions on that specific legal capacity. Both legal and health practitioners have different exposure to assessing capacity which will inform their practice. Junior practitioners or those in, for example, rural or remote areas may not have the need to assess capacity often but if, and when, they do often lack access to guidance as to how to conduct the assessments. Further, accessing 'experts' to conduct the assessment can be difficult, if 'experts' are even appropriate as assessors in the particular circumstances. Given the significant ramifications of losing legal capacity, the lack of a consistent, transparent and accurate assessment process is legally, medically and ethically concerning—not only for the individuals who are having their capacity assessed but also for the practitioners who are conducting the assessments.[6]

---

[4]Moye J and Marson DC (2007), p. 3; Marson D (2016), p. 12.
[5]Squires B and Barr F (2005), p. 34.
[6]Aw D et al. (2012), p. 226.

The impact on practitioners is twofold. Not only are there potential liability risks but there is also the concern that most practitioners have to do the best that the practitioner can for the individuals whose lives they come into contact with. This raises the interesting consideration of the impact of law on individuals and whether that interaction has a positive or negative influence on that particular individual's life. To this end, the principles of therapeutic jurisprudence, a relatively little known doctrine originating in the United States of America, are relevant. This is because the doctrine promotes principles of fundamental importance to this problem. For example, the consequences incompetency labelling can have on an individual and how a negative label can, in effect, be a self-fulfilling prophecy. Thus, because a person has been labelled incompetent for one decision, the risk is that they will be thought to lack capacity for all decisions, even if that original assessment was incorrect. The label then becomes a self-fulfilling prophecy wherein few or no attempts are made to heighten a person's capacity to make decisions in relation to different areas, or even the same area at a different time (where relevant). The assessment process itself is vitally important to the law having a therapeutic effect on individuals. To this end little to no research has been carried out exploring the perceptions and experiences of those who have been assessed. Further, more research is needed into how the process can be improved to be more accessible to these individuals who may be experiencing very strong emotions in regard to both their specific mentally disabling condition, but also in having to undergo a capacity assessment where third parties will determine whether they retain the ability to make a legally recognised decision.

In response to these challenges, this book considers the dilemma of a lack of a satisfactory model to assess testamentary and decision-making capacity, the relationship between legal and health professionals in this context, and ways in which to try and progress the dialogue around capacity assessment. First, the challenges facing legal and health professionals when assessing capacity will be explored. The nature of capacity generally will then be discussed before focussing on issues that can arise in the assessment of testamentary and decision-making capacity. Approaches adopted in Australia, the United Kingdom and the United States of America will be outlined before making suggested recommendations for the development of a capacity assessment methodology incorporating proposed guidelines and general principles. The conundrum of how to better assess capacity is explored within a proposed framework of therapeutic jurisprudence, a novel approach to capacity assessment which may be one way in which to generate new ideas to begin to advance the capacity assessment discourse.

2 Terminology

First, though, a note on terminology. For the purposes of this book, testamentary capacity concerns the ability of an individual to determine what will happen to his or her property after his or her death. Decision-making capacity refers to an individual's ability to make financial and/or lifestyle/health decisions, and the enduring documents appointing substitute decision-makers in the event that the individual in question can no longer make those decisions. Capacity, generally, is the physical or mental ability of an individual to undertake an action or make a decision.[7] Capacity is used in both a legal and a health setting and it is the definition of *legal capacity* and its distinction from the medical concept that is of critical importance.[8] The interchangeable use of the terms competency and capacity has resulted in a terminological mélange compounded by the legal and/or medical context in which the assessment is conducted.[9] The legal practitioner is concerned with whether the individual has the legal ability to make the decision. A health professional assesses fluctuations in physical and mental abilities. Some literature, especially in the United States of America, attempts to distinguish between competency and capacity by classifying competency as a legal construct (although recognising that the legal profession can, and does, seek the aid of health professionals to make such determinations) and capacity as a medical concept which differentiates between an individual who is able to make their own decisions, no matter how reasonable or otherwise they may appear, and one who cannot.[10]

Recent literature has reiterated the problems presented by the terminological confusion between legal and medical competency/capacity.[11] Sabatino and Wood suggest that the concept of incapacity may be a legal fiction because the theoretical determination is treated as a fact no matter what the practical situation or implications.[12] This again represents a difference of approach in thinking between legal and health professionals. This is because an individual's legal capacity will necessarily have to be defined to determine whether that individual is legally able to make the decision they wish to make if their capacity is in issue. Sabatino and Wood do not separate the terms into legal competency and medical capacity instead labelling the concepts as legal capacity (or incapacity) and medical or de facto capacity (or incapacity).[13] They note the reasoning behind this, stating that although the traditional formulation was to identify competency/incompetency as the legal concept and capacity/incapacity as the medical notion that this brings with it the 'historical baggage' associated with each term.[14] The term competency, they contend, is also representative of an all or nothing approach when assessing the

---

[7]Falk E and Hoffman N (2014), p. 853.

[8]Shulman KI et al. (2005), p. 64.

[9]Appelbaum PS (2007), p. 1834; Dawson J and Kämpf A (2006), p. 310; Gunn MJ et al. (1999), p. 281.

[10]Moye J (1999), p. 488; Devereux J and Parker M (2006), p. 57; Sullivan K (2004), p. 131; Kitamura T and Takahashi N (2007), p. 578; Berg JW et al. (1995–1996), pp. 348–349.

[11]Sabatino CP and Wood E (2012), p. 35.

[12]Ibid.

[13]Ibid.

[14]Ibid.

legal notion.[15] It should be acknowledged that Sabatino and Wood are conceptualising competency/capacity in the specific contextual environment of the United States of America but their use of legal and medical capacity/incapacity can be adopted more broadly. This is because clearly delineating between the concepts of legal and medical competency/capacity is difficult, in part because assessing physical and mental acumen is relevant in assessing legal 'competency', and health practitioners are involved in assessing legal 'competency'. Further, practitioners tend not to make the distinction between competency as a legal notion and capacity as a medical construct. Therefore, any attempt at defining the terms within those parameters is more an academic exercise lacking any practical utility. This is now relatively well settled in the more recent literature.[16] Consequently, throughout this book the legal and medical constructs are distinguished, where possible, by use of the phrase *legal* or *medical* competency/capacity.

What is clear, however, is that terminological, definitional and methodological differences can create miscommunication and misunderstanding leading to tension between the legal and health professions. This then directly impacts the assessment process—what is being assessed, by whom and to what standard. This is exacerbated by the ad hoc individualistic implementation of assessment processes resulting from the lack of a consistent and accurate base assessment paradigm from which to begin. The practical impact of this is that it is not necessarily straightforward for a legal professional to seek the opinion of a health practitioner as to an individual's legal capacity, in any context. Nor is it easy for the health professional to provide such an opinion, and to present it in such a manner as to be useful to the legal practitioner and/or to any potential court proceedings. This creates yet another challenge to assessing capacity.

3   Challenges to Assessing Capacity

Despite the significance of both the assessment process determining an individual's ability to independently make decisions, and the outcome of such a process, the literature and practical guidance examining the medico-legal interface in the contextual environment of testamentary and decision-making capacity assessment is limited. This is especially evident when considering financial capacity and the effect the miscommunication and misunderstanding between the disciplines can have on capacity determinations. This section will examine some of the main challenges arising in the assessment of legal capacity, in addition to the terminological issues discussed above, before investigating the tension which underlies the relationship between legal and health professionals.

---

[15]Ibid.

[16]Moye J et al. (2013), pp. 159–160.

3.1   Mentally Disabling Conditions

Individuals can present with a mentally disabling condition which can impact, impair or eliminate the legal capacity necessary to understand and execute testamentary and/or substitute decision-making instruments. A problem arises when legal professionals are confronted with mentally disabling conditions that may not clearly present themselves. Consequently, the practitioner may not necessarily be aware that the individual is potentially legally incompetent. A diagnosis of a particular illness, such as Alzheimer's disease, should not, however, mean that incapacity is automatically assumed. Capacity may fluctuate and incapacity may be reversible with an appropriate treatment plan, including recognition of the effect that medications can have upon capacity.[17]

An understanding of the causes of incapacity is important in analysing the assessment process. This is because any evaluative scheme should be flexible enough to identify and respond to the nuances of each mentally disabling condition. Although the labels differ, highlighting again the interpretative problems evident in this context and the importance that can attach to the labelling of the mentally disabling condition, it is suggested that the general categories for mentally disabling conditions are similar. That is, mentally disabling conditions can be broadly categorised as: developmental/intellectual disability; acquired brain injury; alcohol and drug-related diseases with the impact ranging from temporary to permanent; mental illness; and conditions impacting cognition such as dementia.[18] Thus, the genesis of disabling conditions can be mental, intellectual, physical or psychological. They are not necessarily easy to identify, hence the need for the capacity assessment process to be as unassailable as possible.

'Diseases of the aged' have been suggested as a mentally disabling condition.[19] However, it should be noted that ageing in and of itself is not an indicator of a lack of capacity. In fact, to presume that a certain age means that a person has lost capacity is to intrude upon that person's basic human rights. Prescription medications can also have a negative effect on capacity, compounding presently existing illnesses. Oftentimes legal professionals have inadequate experience to be able to precisely determine the effects of prescription medications on capacity.[20] Further, the impact on capacity of the illness, any comorbidities and the medications can be difficult to separate. This is significant because it is sometimes possible for practitioners to time the assessment for when the person is 'most' capable and/or to reduce medications in anticipation of having to conduct an assessment. To successfully do this, however, requires a good understanding of when this would be taking into account not only the capacity being assessed, but also the mentally disabling condition and the prescription medications.

---

[17]Dārziņš P et al. (2000), p. 4.
[18]Carney T and Keyzer P (2007), p. 255.
[19]Creyke R (1995), pp. 10–12.
[20]Frost M et al. (2015), p. 8.

The indicators of a mentally disabling condition can include acute depression, social withdrawal, lack of motivation, confusion, anxiety, inability to make decisions or pay attention, poor short term memory retention, acquired brain injury, organic brain injury, neurodegenerative diseases such as dementia, intellectual disability, manic depression, delirium or mental illnesses such as schizophrenia.[21] Individuals with mild cognitive impairment ('MCI') may exaggerate their impairments in functional tests because of depression. Consequently, untreated depression can have a severe impact on cognitive and functional abilities leading to an incorrect determination of legal capacity.[22]

Dementia related illnesses are especially significant to all interested 'stakeholders' given the expected increase in the number of people diagnosed with dementia worldwide. An understanding of how the different forms of dementia manifest themselves is essential.[23] Dementia is broadly defined as 'an acquired global impairment of memory, intellect and personality without impairment of consciousness'.[24] The term describes a large group of chronic degenerative neurological disorders that result in a progressive decline in cognition. These symptoms are characterised by a decline in memory, reasoning, communication skills, one or more cognitive abilities and the ability to perform tasks associated with daily living.[25] Behavioural symptoms of dementing illnesses can include paranoid delusions which can clearly have an impact on testamentary and decision-making capacity. People with dementia suffer severe confusion exacerbated by medications as well as by other acute illnesses, for instance, pneumonia. While fluctuating cognition may occur in the early stages of dementia, sufferers of moderate to severe dementia will not have lucid intervals. A 'lucid interval' is more likely to take place in 'psychotic psychiatric disorders, such as schizophrenia, manic depressive psychosis or severe depressive illness' rather than in dementing illnesses.[26] This highlights the importance of being aware of any comorbidities, a difficult task for a legal professional if the client does not inform them of this information.[27] Interesting also is the statement that individuals suffering from moderate to severe dementia cannot have lucid intervals—an important legal notion in establishing testamentary capacity in cases where the testator is thought to have moments of lucidity.

Most notable amongst the dementias is Alzheimer's disease, for which no definitive diagnostic tests exist.[28] It is thought to be a gradually progressive decline in capacity which can be compared to multi-infarct vascular dementia, a disease which can result in unpredictable loss of capacity. Alzheimer's disease is believed

---

[21]O'Neill N and Peisah C (2011), p. 3.

[22]Okonkwo OC et al. (2008), p. 656.

[23]Peisah C and Brodaty H (1994), p. 382; Liptzin B et al. (2010), p. 950.

[24]Peisah C and Brodaty H (1994), p. 382.

[25]Alzheimer's Australia (2009), p. 5.

[26]Berry G (2006), p. 2.

[27]*Sargent & Anor v Brangwin* [2013] QSC 306.

[28]Kawas CH (2003), p. 1056.

to have seven stages which include where there is: no decline in cognition (stage 1); very mild decline in cognition which can be referred to as the 'forgetfulness phase' (stage 2); mild decline in cognition or the 'early confusional phase' (stage 3); moderate decline in cognition or the 'late confusional phase' which can generally be identified through a carefully constructed clinical interview (stage 4); moderately severe decline in cognition or the 'early dementia phase' (stage 5); severe decline in cognition which is also referred to as the 'mid-dementia phase' (stage 6); and finally, very severe cognitive decline or the 'late dementia phase' (stage 7).[29]

Stages one–three do not normally affect capacity. Stage four is on the periphery whereas individuals in stages five to seven will not have capacity with no possibility of a 'lucid interval' in which to execute a valid testamentary or enduring document.[30] The difficulty of ascertaining which stage an individual is at again begs the question of how this is to be achieved by a legal professional without medical qualifications, especially when clients do not always see the relevance in disclosing such information to their lawyer. It should be noted that there are other types of dementia, for example, vascular dementia which 'results from vascular or circulatory lesions ... in the brain'[31] and dementia with Lewy bodies. This form of dementia is thought to be the second most common cause of dementia following Alzheimer's disease and can result in hallucinations.[32] Pick's disease, another form of dementia, can result in loss of capacity earlier than in other forms of dementia.[33]

Dementia obviously impacts legal capacity and its existence should provide warning signs to those involved with the individual in question. Assessing testamentary and decision-making capacity is challenging at the best of times, let alone when an individual suffers from mild-to-moderate dementia.[34] The statistics about the incidents of dementia make the significance of this particular mentally disabling condition all too clear. In fact, there is a fear that the world is facing a 'dementia epidemic' and the statistics are sobering.[35] It is estimated that 44 million people have been diagnosed with dementia worldwide, a figure that is believed will almost double by 2030.[36] Dementia cost an estimated $604 billion dollars worldwide in 2010 and it is only expected to increase exponentially in prevalence in the next 20 years as the 'baby boomer' generation begins to reach retirement age.[37]

So, for example, in Australia dementia is the second leading cause of death and the largest single cause of disability in people aged 65 years and older.[38] Over

---

[29]Sprehe DJ and Loughridge Kerr A (1996), p. 263.
[30]Ibid 263; Peisah C and Brodaty H (1994), p. 382.
[31]O'Neill N and Peisah C (2011), p. 3.
[32]Ibid.
[33]Peisah C and Brodaty H (1994), p. 382.
[34]Moye J et al. (2006), p. 78.
[35]Alzheimer's Australia (2009), p. 5.
[36]UK Government (2015).
[37]Lin SY and Lewis FM (2015), p. 237.
[38]Australian Bureau of Statistics (2009), pp. 2–3; Access Economics (2009), i.

320,000 Australians are living with dementia, including one in four Australians over the age of 85, highlighting the importance of the ageing population given the higher rates of dementia in that demographic. Over the last 10 years deaths resulting from dementia have increased approximately 137%. The increasing prevalence places an ever increasing emotional and financial burden not only on individuals, their families and friends, but also on government and policy makers, as well as the health and legal systems. It is estimated that nearly one million Australians will have dementia by 2050, with 7,500 Australians being diagnosed with the illness each week.[39] In 2015 over half of the residents in aged care facilities had been diagnosed with the illness.[40] Total expenses for health related care are estimated to increase by 3.5% from 2016–2017 to 2019–2020 reflecting both increased demand for services as well as an ageing population. It is projected that within the next 20 years dementia will become the third largest source of health and residential aged care spending, totalling approximately 1% of GDP,[41] with spending on dementia estimated to outstrip that on other health conditions by the 2060s, representing approximately 11% of the entire spending for the health and aged care sector.[42] However, other neurological illnesses cannot be lost in the focus on dementia. Parkinson's Disease, for example, is the second most common neurological disease in Australia. It is more common than both prostate and bowel cancer.[43]

In the United Kingdom there are currently 14.9 million people aged 60 years and over, more people in fact than those aged under 18 years.[44] By 2040 the number of people aged 60 years and over is expected to increase to 24.2%, or nearly one in four people. Dementia is one of the main causes of disability in later life and is the leading cause of death for women in the United Kingdom.[45] In 2014, 850,000 people were estimated to be living with dementia, which is expected to increase to in excess of 2 million people by 2051.[46] It is anticipated that one in three people over the age of 65 years will die with a form of dementia.[47] In the United Kingdom dementia costs approximately £26.3 billion per year, about double the cost of cancer which receives nearly 12 times as much funding.[48] Interestingly, people aged 55 years and over fear being diagnosed with dementia more so than any other disease, including cancer.[49] Another important related issue to the diagnosis of

---

[39]National Health and Medical Research Council (2014).

[40]Australian Institute of Health and Welfare (2016).

[41]Australian Bureau of Statistics (2009), pp. 2–3; Access Economics (2009), i.

[42]Ibid.

[43]Parkinson's Queensland (2015).

[44]AgeUK (2016), pp. 12–13.

[45]Ibid.

[46]Ibid.

[47]Ibid.

[48]Ibid.

[49]UK Government (2015).

dementia is the impact of loneliness, with 40% of people diagnosed with dementia feeling lonely and 34% not feeling that they are part of their community.[50] This is especially concerning when capacity is in question as it increases the vulnerability of the individual(s) in question. Increased vulnerability can then make the individual more open to all forms of abuse including undue influence, 'physical, sexual, psychological, emotional, financial and material abuse, abandonment, neglect and serious losses of dignity and respect', as well as them having an anti-therapeutic interaction with the law.[51]

In the United States of America, the growth of the ageing population is one of the most significant demographic trends in the history of that country, with the number of people aged 65 years and older expected to increase from 46 million to more than 98 million by 2060.[52] The number of people living with Alzheimer's disease could increase to approximately 14 million by 2050 with the ageing of the population, with one in nine people aged 65 years and over currently having been diagnosed with the illness.[53] This figure is expected to nearly triple by 2050.[54] It is estimated that dementia costs the United States of America between $157 billion and $215 billion each year and, in a similar statistic to Australia and the United Kingdom, more than either heart disease or cancer.[55] Alzheimer's disease has been identified as one of the costliest chronic diseases in the United States of America, with nearly one in every five Medicare dollars being spent on the disease and other dementias, with this figure also expected to increase to one in three by 2050.[56]

In considering some of the national and international responses to the challenge presented by dementia an extensive report, *Dementia: A Public Health Priority*, was produced in 2012 by the World Health Organisation in conjunction with Alzheimer's Disease International.[57] That dementia needs to be addressed on a multitude of levels including internationally, nationally, locally and more personally by family members was acknowledged in the report.[58] In the United Kingdom, the then Prime Minister, David Cameron, initiated a Prime Minister's Challenge on Dementia 2020, noting that: 'Dementia also takes a huge toll on our health and care services. With the ... predicted costs likely to treble to over £50 billion, we are facing one of the biggest global health and social care challenges—a challenge as big as those posed by cancer, heart disease and HIV/AIDs.'[59] Action has also

---

[50]Ibid.

[51]World Health Organization (2015), p. 74.

[52]Population Reference Bureau (2015).

[53]Ibid; Alzheimer's Association (2016).

[54]Alzheimer's Association (2016).

[55]Population Reference Bureau (2015).

[56]Alzheimer's Association (2016).

[57]World Health Organization, Alzheimer's Disease International (2012).

[58]Ibid 90.

[59]UK Government (2015).

commenced in the United States of America and in Australia.[60] In the United States, for example, then President Obama signed into law the National Alzheimer's Action Act which has resulted in the National Plan to Address Alzheimer's Disease (including its annual updates).[61] In Australia dementia is recognised as a national health priority area.[62]

What these statistics show, across three countries, is the significance of mentally disabling conditions, in this case dementia given its primacy in modern society, and the impact they are having. It is clear that society is seeing an increase in the effects of ageing, including dementia, in part as a result of the maturing baby boomer generation.[63] Such statistics should be drawing attention to the enormity of a determination of a loss of capacity and the process through which this is assessed. Surprisingly, however, especially given the increasing prevalence of mentally disabling conditions such as dementia, there is an unexpected lack of empirical research on the effects of mentally disabling conditions on, particularly, financial and decision-making capacity.[64]

As can be seen dementia related illnesses can have a significant and broad ranging impact, but especially on the ability to make a will, and to make financial transactions as well as health decisions. As noted above, how is a legal practitioner to understand if a client has been diagnosed with moderate to severe dementia if the information is not forthcoming, let alone the impact of this on the client's legal capacity? Furthermore, individuals can give the impression that they are functioning at a higher level than they actually are, making the collection of independent evidence a key concern in the assessment process.[65] For example, dementia sufferers can lack insight into the changes that are occurring thus being unable to accurately relate information relevant to the capacity assessment process.[66] In order to speak to third parties, however, authorities are required and the individual in question may potentially either lack the capacity to give such an authority or simply not want to. What this also highlights are the problems that can exist if the potentially incapable person is being subjected to abuse. Legal professionals are not trained to know this and it is questionable whether health professionals are trained to assess this in specific legal contexts. Indeed, it can be difficult for health professionals to diagnose mild-to-moderate dementia let alone its impact in a legal framework.

Compounding this, legal professionals generally have budgetary constraints which can restrict the amount of time spent with clients. Estates are also now increasingly worth one million dollars or more with the value of superannuation and

---

[60]For a comparison of each of the national plans see Lin SY and Lewis FM (2015).

[61]National Institute on Ageing (2012); Lin SY and Lewis FM (2015), p. 237.

[62]Department of Health (2016).

[63]Access Economics (2009), p. 5.

[64]Marson DC et al. (1996), pp. 667–668.

[65]Moye J et al. (2013), p. 163; Falk E and Hoffman N (2014), p. 856.

[66]Falk E and Hoffman N (2014), p. 856.

real estate, thus making them more litigable particularly given that society is becoming ever more litigious in nature.[67] It is a combination of these factors which means that the work of legal professionals when preparing wills and substitute decision-making documents will increasingly be scrutinised. It is therefore vital, especially when confronted with statistics such as these, to ensure that the systems in place for capacity assessments, as well as the relationship between legal and health professionals, are enhanced to provide protection not only for individual autonomy, but also for the legal and health professionals involved with its preservation or removal.

3.2   The Impact of Ageing

As evidenced by the above statistics society is ageing worldwide and although not the only cause, this is one of the main contributing factors to the growth and significance of capacity assessments. As stated above, it is important to note that ageing, in and of itself, is not indicative of a lack of capacity. One area where ageing and cognitive impairment is commonly thought to always intersect is dementia. This is because dementia is often believed to be an illness associated with ageing and the aged. However, the diagnosis of a dementing illness is not an inevitable part of ageing, nor is it restricted to people over the age of 60 years. For example, although uncommon, dementia can affect people in their forties or younger.[68] Nevertheless, ageing—both normal and pathologic - can have a considerable and detrimental impact upon an individual's mental and physical abilities. The risks of dementia, cognitive impairment, as well as medical and neurological diseases do increase with age.[69]

Although some cognitive functions, for example vocabulary, are resistant to ageing other capabilities, including reasoning and memory, do gradually decline as an individual ages.[70] Even 'normal' ageing can result in loss of day-to-day functioning which can increase the vulnerability of the individual in question and, although 'normal' age-related cognitive change does not impair an individual's capability to complete daily activities, subtle decline in complex functional abilities, such as the ability to drive, can occur.[71] The possible loss of decision-making autonomy can be permanent or temporary but either is a confronting prospect for both the individual and his or her family. Policy makers, governments and society more widely are increasingly becoming aware of the problems associated with

---

[67] Jourdan JB and Glickman L (1991), p. 415.

[68] Australian Health Ministers' Conference (2006), p. 2.

[69] Moye J and Marson DC (2007), p. 3; Harada CN et al. (2013), pp. 737–738; Moye J et al. (2013), p. 162.

[70] Harada CN et al. (2013), p. 738.

[71] Ibid.

ageing, including the challenges to the retention of individual autonomy. This is evidenced by the significant amount of increased attention being directed towards these issues.

The use and impact of terminology here is significant and indeed, is a running undercurrent in the capacity assessment discourse which has the ability to influence assessments. The phrase 'ageing tsunami' can often be heard. However, as will be seen with the discussion of therapeutic jurisprudence, this type of terminology presents its own challenges. By naming the ageing population as a 'tsunami', it is attaching a negative connotation to ageing—and there can be immense power in labels, especially negative labels.[72] It underestimates the contribution and positive impact of age, instead focusing on negative imagery. This can sway capacity assessments, especially as assessors will come from a variety of backgrounds with varying skill sets. Assessors may also be unaware of the relationship, or lack thereof, between ageing and capacity. Consequently, the effect of a negative label here may impact autonomy if indeed the assessor is not skilled or experienced enough to take this into account in any assessment being conducted.

3.3   Societal and Familial Perceptions

The notion of capacity is an invaluable social, as well as legal, construct.[73] Capacity is representative of autonomy and self-determination within familial and societal environments. If an individual is legally capable they possess the autonomy to make their own decisions. Both individual and communal perceptions of autonomous behaviour can affect the assessment of individual capacity and, in fact, whether professional assessment even takes place. For example, a potentially incapable person can be hidden behind family or communal support or can be open to abuse because of the traditional reluctance of the law to interfere in private matters. Family members may be either too reluctant or too eager to impose their own notions of independence and autonomy on the individual. This may be for either malevolent or benevolent reasons and can impact how the individual is able to function or how they see themselves. For example, elder abuse can have significant physical, psychological, emotional and financial consequences, consequences which may be exacerbated by, or in turn aggravate, reduced legal capacity. Although difficult to determine with any precision, it is estimated that the prevalence of elder abuse in middle to high income countries worldwide ranges from 2.2% to 14%.[74] Significantly, these figures exclude older adults with cognitive impairments despite this group being particularly vulnerable to abuse. For instance, it is estimated that psychological abuse of older adults with dementia ranges from

---

[72]Winick BJ (1996), pp. 54–55.

[73]Carney T (1997), p. 1.

[74]World Health Organization (2015), p. 74.

28% to 62% and physical abuse 3.5% to 23%.[75] Acknowledging the significance and impact of not only legal, but also societal and familial perceptions on capacity is fundamental to developing appropriate ways in which to assess legal capacity and progress the dialogue taking place.

3.4   The Legal and Medical Tension

The relationship between legal and health professionals is obviously of particular importance to facilitating satisfactory assessment regimes. The problem is whether the legal and health professionals are able to identify and assess the type and standard of legal capacity when the medical and legal notions are fundamentally different. So, while legal professionals see capacity more as a dualistic construct in that the person either has capacity to make the decision, execute the document or enter the transaction or they do not, health professionals see capacity more as a fluctuating variable existing within a continuum.[76] This can result in, and add to, confusion about what is actually being assessed, how, to what standard, and by whom. This dilemma is especially evident in practice where clarity about the type of capacity being assessed and to what standard would be the most beneficial. It also demonstrates the need to try and ascertain the legal capacity and match it to what health professionals need to assess in a clinical environment, such as examining memory and executive functioning when executing a will. This is difficult because legal professionals do not generally establish definitive criteria for what is needed to meet the legal test, for example the test for testamentary capacity. This can be frustrating for health professionals conducting clinical assessments who look for functional or operating abilities to establish whether the individual has the requisite capacity to meet the relevant legal standard.[77]

It is arguable that legal professionals do not understand the medical world and vice versa. Legal professionals have been censured for not having health professionals witness documents such as testamentary instruments where capacity was in issue.[78] They have also been criticised for abdicating responsibility for the assessments to health professionals, and for refusing to take instructions where there is any indication of impaired capacity, even if the indicia present do not warrant such a response.[79] Conversely, health practitioners have been criticised for not wanting to participate in capacity assessments because of uncertainty about the potential effects of such involvement.[80] Legal professionals arguably fail to adequately explain what is necessary to assess legal capacity, and in what format they want

---

[75]Ibid 75.

[76]Falk E and Hoffman N (2014), p. 854.

[77]Ibid.

[78]O'Connell v Shortland (1989) 51 SASR 337, 348.

[79]Queensland Law Society, Allens Linklaters, Queensland Advocacy Incorporated (2014), p. 13.

[80]O'Connell v Shortland (1989) 51 SASR 337, 348.

and/or need the assessment report. It is unreasonable on their part to assume that
health professionals understand what is being asked of them.

Historically, tension has existed between the legal and health professions, especially with the appearance of legal professionals in the professional lives of health
practitioners.[81] For example, the problems that have traditionally faced the medico-
legal community in the United States of America concerning capacity assessment
have been termed the five 'I's'. They are, the '*ignorance and irrelevance* of courtroom
testimony; psychiatric or psychological *intrusion* into essentially legal matters; and
insufficiency and incredibility of information provided to the courts'.[82] Additionally,
'paid by the case ... [clinicians] learn to provide the courts with the minimally
acceptable amount of information that can be obtained in the least possible time',[83]
that is, if the legal professional even seeks evidence about capacity, which they often
do not.[84] Grisso notes that the disenchantment of legal actors with the health community regarding capacity assessments is not surprising and that there has been a
concerted effort to improve assessment methodology, at least within the United States
of America.[85] A good example of this is the interdisciplinary guidelines produced by
the American Psychological Association and the American Bar Association.[86]

A legal professional has to be aware of the effect that a primary illness,
comorbidities and/or medications can have upon an individual. The law has a
significant and undeniable role to play in the assessment of the impact of these on
an individual's capacity. This is despite the preference of some health professionals
that no legal interference takes place.[87] Such health professionals generally desire
instead to be governed by their own ethical principles of respect, beneficence,
non-malfeasance, justice and fidelity.[88] What is important is the recognition of
the symbiotic relationship that exists between the legal and health professions.[89]
Despite capacity being a legal determination, legal professionals are often not
comfortable and are not trained to assess the medical construct of capacity which
is inherently linked to the legal notion of capacity.[90] This is evidenced by the

---

[81]Freckelton I (1999), p. 86.

[82]Grisso T (2003), p. 23.

[83]Ibid xiii.

[84]Darzins P et al. (2000), p. 3.

[85]Grisso T (2003), pp. 11–12.

[86]American Bar Association Commission on Law and Aging, American Psychological Associa-
tion Assessment of Capacity in Older Adults Project Working Group (2005); American Bar
Association Commission on Law and Aging, American Psychological Association and National
College of Probate Judges (2006); American Bar Association Commission on Law and Aging,
American Psychological Association Assessment of Capacity in Older Adults Project Working
Group (2008).

[87]Sales BD and Shuman DW (1996), p. 795.

[88]Ibid.

[89]Ibid 801.

[90]Standing Committee on Legal and Constitutional Affairs, Parliament of the Commonwealth of
Australia (2007), p. 112.

discussion of the effects of mentally disabling conditions, for example dementia, on legal capacity and legal notions such as lucid intervals. Conversely, health practitioners should have an awareness of the legal concepts they are being asked to evaluate. What this demonstrates is the opportunity and responsibility that the law and legal, as well as health, professionals have when entering the lives of individuals to assess their capacity. There is a real opportunity to ensure that each individual's interaction with the legal system is not anti-therapeutic.

One of the difficulties in reconciling legal with medical capacity when assessing legal competency with respect to, for example, dementia and the ability to make a will, is that there is no objective test by which to determine the diagnosis of dementia or sub-type of dementia against a specific decision at a specific point in time. That is, it is currently not possible to conclude that it is at a particular stage of a mentally disabling condition that the individual in question has lost legal capacity. Compounding the difficulties faced is the fact that legal professionals are not trained to be able to detect the effects of, for example, dementia and dementia sufferers can present very well socially. Consequently, this makes it problematic for legal professionals to know that there is an issue unless the individual chooses to disclose the information. Further, there is little recorded evidence detailing how legal professionals advise clients in these circumstances, let alone how they conduct assessments.[91]

The miscommunication and misunderstanding between the legal and health professions is, in part, caused by the different vocabularies used by each.[92] As noted, terminology has to be consistent both between and within the professions. The tangled nature of the terms 'competency' and 'capacity' is a case in point of the terminological confusion. Moye and Marson note that research in this area must recognise the importance of legal terminology and, vice versa, the legal profession must recognise the differing medical terminology.[93] This will require further interdisciplinary investigation of the relationship between legal and health professionals, including the assessment models employed and the impact of the terminology used on capacity determinations.[94]

Complicating this even further are the legal 'terms of art' such as 'lucid interval', 'testamentary capacity' and 'undue influence'.[95] These do not have exact medical equivalents.[96] For instance, most health practitioners confuse testamentary capacity with the absence of a psychiatric illness, and conflate capacity with undue influence. As a result, many reports obtained from health practitioners are unhelpful, instead tending to complicate an already challenging situation.[97] In another example of the

---

[91]Alzheimer's Australia (2006), pp. 18–19.
[92]Sales BD and Shuman DW (1996), p. 804.
[93]Moye J and Marson DC (2007), p. 3.
[94]Ibid.
[95]Sprehe DJ and Kerr AL (1996), p. 255.
[96]Ibid.
[97]Mullins P (1999), p. 5.

misapplication of cognitive assessments within the requisite legal framework, clinical research into judgment and decision-making has indicated that human decision-making is not necessarily consistent with notions of legal capacity because legal standards assume that individuals engage in rational decision-making.[98] Whilst admittedly human decision-making does not always accord with legal notions of capacity, allowances are able to be made at law for 'irrational decision-making', for example accepting that a testator has a right to be capricious and eccentric in the making of his or her will. However, a satisfactory explanation of what is required regarding the precise legal capacity in question is not always forthcoming from the legal profession to the health practitioner involved in the assessment. Consequently, the health professional may not fully comprehend what it is they are to assess, potentially compromising the validity of the assessment process.[99] Therefore, a legal professional requesting a health practitioner to evaluate, for example, testamentary capacity with a cover letter merely listing the elements required for testamentary capacity does not guarantee that the legal and health professionals are assessing the same thing. There is a need for the development, acceptance and implementation of a common language and framework that will improve both the consistency and accuracy of capacity assessments.[100]

Understanding the different approaches, training and thinking of the two professions will be fundamental in the development of any workable 'common' language. Falk and Hoffman's recent work on this is enlightening.[101] They note that legal professionals are transactionally focussed, that is, can the individual in question complete certain transactions such as executing this particular will or this particular enduring power of attorney? Whereas, a health practitioner thinks in terms of domains, that is, how is the individual performing in terms of domains such as memory, language, personality, and/or executive functioning?[102] They note that legal practitioners tend to be binary in their approach to capacity—does the individual have the ability to make the specific decision—while health professionals approach capacity in a continuous manner because clinically, capacities are variable, existing on continuums in which there are no black and white or yes/no answers.[103] Legal professionals are identified as having a 'conceptual template'. Assume for example the test for testamentary capacity—while conceptually and legally sound, such a standard does not set definite tests or link the tests to the abilities required. This can be contrasted to the approach of the health professionals who are operational, that is, have an understanding about which abilities are necessary to meet the legal standards.[104] Falk and Hoffman note, correctly, that

---

[98]Moye J et al. (2013), p. 167.
[99]Cockerill J et al. (2005), p. 55.
[100]Lai JM and Karlawish J (2007), p. 109.
[101]Falk E and Hoffman N (2014), p. 854.
[102]Ibid 861.
[103]Ibid 854.
[104]Ibid.

the operational abilities must meet the appropriate legal standard.[105] However, as well as often failing to understand the approach of the other profession, assessments are generally missing this link between the clinical notion of operational abilities and how these abilities connect to the legal standards necessary to have the requisite capacity at law to make the specific decision in question.

Health professionals should also refrain from offering an opinion as to the ultimate legal question.[106] Evidence from a health professional as to capacity is not conclusive and the court is free to accept, or reject, it as it sees fit. If accepting, there is then the question of the weight that will be attached to it. However, arguably, it is becoming more and more difficult for health professionals to refrain from offering such an opinion given that medical evidence is increasingly being relied upon to determine questions of legal capacity, especially as such determinations are outside the scope of traditional legal training. Nevertheless, reliance on health professionals may be problematic because there is a lack of empirical knowledge when assessing testamentary and decision-making capacity to ensure the accuracy of the assessment process.[107] Signs of cognitive impairment, whatever the underlying cause, are not always clearly apparent and legal professionals are not trained to recognise them even if they were. Even health professionals, who are trained to identify such issues, can have difficulty in recognising them. For example, an expert retained to undertake a capacity assessment may never have seen the individual before, and thus, not be cognisant of that person's personality and environment enough to be able to identify signs as to the existence of a cognitive impairment. Further, some health professionals conducting assessments may *not* have the requisite training to assess capacity because there is a need for better and increased training in cognitive specific diagnostic assessment processes which can then be used in the legal context. This is the case generally, but especially if those health professionals are being put forward as 'experts'.

As a corollary to this, legal environments can be intimidating, inducing health professionals to potentially venture beyond their expertise to offer an opinion.[108] As noted by Appelbaum and Roth, there is 'a danger that the clinician will abandon the uncertainties of the clinical perspective for the alluring rationality of legal thought'.[109] The very nature of the adversary system itself may help to explain the tension between the professions. It has been suggested that legal professionals exalt this as a tribute to 'process and participation' but to health professionals it can exemplify 'hostility and non-cooperation'.[110] Legal professionals working within this system may lack the understanding or have perhaps forgotten how formidable the legal system can be to those who are not used to it. This can be heightened when

---

[105]Ibid.

[106]Grisso T (2003), p. 7.

[107]Sales BD and Shuman DW (1996), p. 805; Lai JM and Karlawish J (2007), p. 101.

[108]Sales BD and Shuman DW (1996), p. 805.

[109]Appelbaum PS and Roth LH (1981), p. 1466.

[110]Sales BD and Shuman DW (1996), p. 804.

health professionals also appear to be concerned about becoming involved in litigation, either as a witness or as a defendant.[111]

In examining the actual evidence given about capacity, it seems that there is a traditional preference by the courts for evidence given by legal professionals over health professionals. For example, as was stated in the case of *Hawes v Burgess*,[112]

> the courts should not too readily upset, on the grounds of lack of mental capacity, a will that has been drafted by an experienced independent lawyer. If, as here, an experienced lawyer has been instructed and has formed the opinion from a meeting or meetings that the testatrix understands what she is doing, the will so drafted and executed should only be set aside on the clearest evidence of incapacity.[113]

The question is, however, what is 'clear evidence of incapacity' to a health practitioner may not be clear to a legal practitioner, or to a court. Further, with respect, just because a legal practitioner has been a lawyer for a long time does not mean that they have been engaging in best practice, or kept abreast of medical and/or legal developments. Such concerns were noted in *Re Ashkettle*[114] where it was acknowledged that such an opinion is worthless unless based on an appropriate assessment and correct information. This preference for legal evidence may also serve to fuel the tension between the professions. Such an inclination could arise, in part, because of the differing legal and medical standards and definitions, as well as some of the issues noted above—the lack of adequate training, and the misunderstanding and miscommunication between legal and health professionals which can result, for example, in reports from health professionals that the courts may not find helpful. This can be heightened when the assessment is retrospective as was the case in, for example, *Sargent v Brangwin*.[115] However, as noted by the then Chief Justice Dixon, 'a conflict of evidence on such a matter does not necessarily involve a conflict of veracity'.[116] In fact, it is essential that the clinical independence and skills of health practitioners be respected because their input in this area is vital.[117] The answer, in part, is to ensure that the quality of the evidence placed before the court is beyond reproach through adequate training for assessors and rigorous assessment paradigms.

---

[111]Standing Committee on Legal and Constitutional Affairs, Parliament of the Commonwealth of Australia (2007), p. 112.

[112][2013] WTLR 453 CA; EWCA Civ 74.

[113]Ibid.

[114][2013] WTLR 1331.

[115]*Sargent & Anor v Brangwin* [2013] QSC 306.

[116]*Middlebrook v Middlebrook* (1962) 36 ALJR 216, 172.

[117]Standing Committee on Legal and Constitutional Affairs, Parliament of the Commonwealth of Australia (2007), p. 111.

3.5 No Uniform Approach

Although instruments to assess decision-making capacity may have been developed there is no methodology for translating that information into unqualified determinations.[118] Therefore, presenting medical information in a format understandable and useable by the courts can be challenging, especially as the legal and health professions approach capacity from conceptually different frameworks. Interestingly, empirical data suggests that clinical capacity assessments can be influenced by the health practitioner's emotional state at the time of the determination.[119] The same could also be said about the effect of the emotional state of a legal professional involved in capacity assessments. Exacerbating this problem is the lack of relevant and useful information that can be given to health professionals about the legal requirements of capacity as opposed to the medical, that is, the *legal* reason they are conducting the assessment.[120]

Additionally, while statute and common law has defined decision-making capacity in some jurisdictions, the paradigm in which to conduct the assessments has not been stipulated.[121] Consequently, variations and discrepancies in approach are inevitable amongst both legal and health professionals. A uniform method to capacity assessment is to be preferred to an idiosyncratic, individualistic based approach.[122] This is because without a standard framework there is the risk that clinical assessments will continue to be 'a subjective and "highly unreliable enterprise"'.[123]

3.6 Education and Ongoing Training

As discussed, part of the tension between legal and health professionals when conducting capacity assessments is a fundamental misunderstanding about the nature of capacity and what is being assessed. This relates back to the training that each profession receives—both at a tertiary level but also continuing professional education that legal and health professionals receive throughout their careers. Capacity, and how to assess it, is generally not taught at tertiary level, for either profession. If taught, for example capacity issues were included as a core ethical component in the Australian medical curricula in 2001, it is questionable as to whether this training includes rigorous education in how to actually *assess*

---

[118]Kim SY et al. (2007), p. 38.
[119]Kornfeld DS et al. (2009), p. 471.
[120]Moye J et al. (2007), p. 597.
[121]See, for example, Kapp, M (2015), p. 165.
[122]Smyer MA (2007), p. 14.
[123]Sullivan K (2004), p. 135.

capacity.[124] Similarly, while education is accessible throughout continuing professional development, it then becomes a question of quality, exactly how available it is (for example to rural and remote practitioners), and whether it is something that health and legal professionals realise is important to their continuing professional development. Some commentators, however, believe that in most jurisdictions capacity can be assessed by health professionals and that the legal criteria is something that can just be taught to those health practitioners.[125] This statement, no matter whether in the context of consenting to treatment, preparing an advance care directive or assessing testamentary capacity, is indicative of the arrogance and ignorance that exists between the professions with each, on occasion, believing that it can carry out the functions of the other.

3.7 Cost

Expense is an additional issue associated with developing, implementing, conducting and maintaining an accurate, transparent and consistent capacity assessment regime.[126] Dārziņš, Molloy and Strang, writing from the perspective of health professionals, highlight the issue with respect to costs and charging for assessments, noting that legal professionals need to realise that doctors often have a limited understanding of legal notions of capacity.[127] Further, there is no easy method for health professionals to bill their patients which can be off-putting for many health professionals to either conduct the assessment or to even have the conversation which would be required before the assessment can take place. The pattern of rapid patient turnover that most medical practices engage in likewise prevents assessments of, and discussions about, a client's capacity. Even the most senior of health practitioners are not immune to these challenges, or necessarily aware of their limitations in the legal domain, all of which can culminate in unsatisfactory assessments.

Currently individuals pay for capacity assessments which can be expensive. In Australia, for instance, with these issues being echoed in the United Kingdom and the United States of America, it appears difficult for health professionals to charge for assessments.[128] There is currently no specific Medicare Benefits Schedule (Medicare being the publicly funded universal health care scheme run by the Australian Government, and which is augmented by private health care funds) item number for health professionals to discuss advance health care planning with their patients, or to undertake capacity assessments.[129] Thus, it will likely be a full-

---

[124]Parker M (2008), pp. 34–35.

[125]Kornfeld DS et al. (2009), p. 472.

[126]Dārziņš P et al. (2000), p. 139. See also Kim SYH and Caine ED (2002), p. 1322.

[127]Dārziņš P et al. (2000), pp. 3–4.

[128]Ibid.

[129]Dārziņš P (2007), pp. 3–4.

fee paying exercise, the cost of which may be prohibitive, certainly to access 'quality' assessments.

The issue of cost is further compounded by the question of geography with limited access to relevant services outside metropolitan areas, especially in rural and remote regions. This invokes criticism about the lack of incentives and interest for legal and health professionals to practise in these areas—not only contextually but also geographically.[130] Dārziņš' observation about the time allocated by a health professional to each patient is reflective of the demands also faced in legal practice.[131] The issue is whether time and budgetary constraints are restricting the satisfactory assessment of testamentary and decision-making capacity, which arguably they are. The current trend towards multidisciplinary team approaches developed in response to the discrepancies between single and interdisciplinary based approaches will only add to the potential costs for obtaining a capacity assessment.[132]

4 Conclusion

The problem is clear. The population worldwide is ageing and mentally disabling conditions are increasing in number. While the latter do not automatically occur as a result of the former, both are combining to contribute to the increasing need for capacity assessments both generally, and specifically, in the context of testamentary and decision-making capacity. 'Satisfactorily' assessing when a person has lost legal capacity is an ever-increasing concern facing a multitude of stakeholders including: the individual who stands to lose his/her autonomy; the families and carers of those individuals; governments and policy makers; the legal and health professionals conducting the assessments; and medico-legal insurers, especially as concerns around both legal and health practitioner liability grow. Given the complexity of presenting mentally disabling conditions, let alone when taking into account any comorbidities and the effects of medications, legal assessments must contain a cognitive determination. Such a determination, however, has to occur within a legal framework as the determination of the existence of capacity, or otherwise, is ultimately a legal decision.

The calls for a consistent approach to capacity assessment are not new, and yet the dialogue seems to be stalled. So, despite seemingly general consensus, there remains no rigorous process to assess testamentary and decision-making capacity.[133] Surprisingly, relatively scarce literature exists examining cognitive

---

[130]Standing Committee on Legal and Constitutional Affairs, Parliament of the Commonwealth of Australia, (2007), p. 112.
[131]Dārziņš P et al. (2000), pp. 3–4.
[132]Sullivan K (2004), p. 134.
[133]Carney T (1995), p. 518.

assessments of capacity within a legal framework to determine the impact of a specific mentally disabling condition on a particular legal capacity. However, this literature is steadily growing, especially around the assessment of financial capacity. Of concern, neither legal nor health professionals are trained to perform this specific function of capacity assessment, resulting in the unsatisfactory and ad hoc implementation of various methods tailored to suit individual practitioners, be they legal and/or health. This can have a detrimental impact on individual autonomy, ensuring that the individual's interaction with the legal system, and the legal as well as health professionals operating within that system, is anti-therapeutic.

Such an ad hoc approach is also increasingly exposing both legal as well as health professionals to the risk of litigation—either being included as the subject of, or as a witness in, a matter where the assessment and/or the decision is being challenged. These assessment methods are further plagued by two problems; terminological ambiguity and inadequate training for legal and health professionals resulting in a relationship characterised by miscommunication and misunderstanding. Additional challenges also arise because of cost, and familial as well as societal approaches. The standard applied is further dependent on the jurisdiction in which the assessment is being conducted, posing novel difficulties for assessors conducting assessments in different jurisdictions to the one he or she is familiar with. There is also an underlying tension between the legal and health professions in this context which is only exacerbating an already challenging situation. The need for flexibility in the assessment process is not denied but guidance is necessary to provide a consistent assessment platform from which to begin to help recognise and protect individual autonomy whilst promoting a positive experience for individuals with the law.

What is needed is work exploring the development of a transdisciplinary approach to capacity assessments. Such an approach has to be informed by relevant stakeholders. Interdisciplinary guidelines have been produced in the United States of America by the American Psychological Association and the American Bar Association, and in the United Kingdom by the British Medical Society and the Law Society. This is an admirable start to the development and implementation of sound assessment practises. Nevertheless, the legal and health professions continue to look inwardly which is threatening individual autonomy and creating potential professional liability issues. Instead, a reference baseline from which the necessary transdisciplinary approach to assessments can be conducted is needed. This book will now explore this, in particular, defining capacity in the legal and health domains with specific reference to testamentary and substitute decision-making. It will consider whether testamentary and decision-making capacity assessments can be conducted in such a way that promotes a consistent and accurate paradigm, what this process should include, and the impact of the relationship between legal and health professionals on assessments. This will be undertaken in an overarching framework of therapeutic jurisprudence which offers an innovative theoretical perspective to assessing legal capacity which may help further the capacity assessment discourse.

References

Access Economics (2009) Keeping dementia front of mind: incidence and prevalence 2009–2050. Alzheimer's   Australia.   http://www.fightdementia.org.au/common/files/NSW/ 2010NSWFront_of_Mind_Full_Report1.pdf. Accessed 1 Nov 2016

AgeUK (2016) Later in Life in the United Kindgom. http://www.ageuk.org.uk/Documents/EN-GB/Factsheets/Later_Life_UK_factsheet.pdf?dtrk=true. Accessed 1 Nov 2016

Alzheimer's Association (2016) 2016 Alzheimer's Disease Facts and Figures. http://www.alz.org/ facts/. Accessed 1 Nov 2016

Alzheimer's Australia (2006) Decision making in advance: reducing barriers and improving access to advance directives for people with dementia. Discussion Paper No 8, pp 18–19

Alzheimer's Australia (2009) Dementia: facing the epidemic. A Vision for a World Class Dementia   Care   System.   https://www.fightdementia.org.au/files/20090901_Nat_Sub_ DemFacingEpidemic.pdf. Accessed 1 Nov 2016

American Bar Association Commission on Law, Aging, American Psychological Association (2005) Assessment of Older Adults with Diminished Capacity: A Handbook for Lawyers. https://www.apa.org/pi/aging/resources/guides/diminished-capacity.pdf. Accessed 1 Nov 2016

American Bar Association Commission on Law and Aging, American Psychological Association (2008) Assessment of Capacity in Older Adults Project Working Group, Assessment of Older Adults with Diminished Capacity: A Handbook for Psychologists. https://www.apa.org/pi/ aging/programs/assessment/capacity-psychologist-handbook.pdf. Accessed 1 Nov 2016

American Bar Association Commission on Law and Aging, American Psychological Association, National College of Probate Judges (2006) Judicial Determination of Capacity of Older Adults in Guardianship Proceedings: A Handbook for Judges. https://www.apa.org/pi/aging/ resources/guides/judges-diminished.pdf. Accessed 1 Nov 2016

Appelbaum PS (2007) Assessment of Patient's competence to consent to treatment. N Engl J Med 357(18):1834–1840

Appelbaum PS, Roth LH (1981) Clinical issues in the assessment of competency. Am J Psychiatr 138(11):1462–1467

Australian Bureau of Statistics (2009) Australian Social Trends 4102.0 - Future Population Growth and Ageing. http://www.ausstats.abs.gov.au/ausstats/subscriber.nsf/0/4FABEA5D1AA59548 CA2575830015E7B0/$File/41020_populationprojections.pdf. Accessed 1 Nov 2016

Australian Health Ministers' Conference (2006) National Framework for Action on Dementia 2006–2010.   https://www.nhmrc.gov.au/_files_nhmrc/file/grants/apply/strategic/dementia_ attachmenta.pdf. Accessed 1 Nov 2016

Australian Institute of Health and Welfare (2016) Dementia. http://www.aihw.gov.au/dementia/. Accessed 1 Nov 2016

Aw D et al (2012) Advance care planning and the older patient. Q J Med 105(3):225–230

Berg JW, Appelbaum PS, Grisso T (1996) Constructing competence: formulating standards of legal competence to make medical decisions. Rutgers Law Rev 48(2):345–396

Berry G (2006) Testamentary Capacity & Undue Influence, Testamentary Capacity – Medical Aspects. In: Queensland Law Society Succession Law Conference, Brisbane, 27 October 2006

Carney T (1995) Judging the competence of older people: an alternative. Ageing Soc 15 (04):515–534

Carney T (1997) Introduction: competence. Int J Law Psychiatry 20(1):1–4

Carney T, Keyzer P (2007) Planning for the future: arrangements for the assistance of people planning for the future of people with impaired capacity. Queensland Univ Technol Law Justice J 7(2):255–278

Carney T, Tait D (1991) Guardianship dilemmas and care of the aged. Sydney Law Rev 13:61

Cockerill J, Collier B, Maxwell K (2005) Legal requirements and current practices. In: Collier B, Coyne C, Sullivan K (eds) Mental capacity, powers of attorney and advance health directives. Federation Press, Leichhardt

Creyke R (1995) Who can decide? Legal decision-making for others. Australian Government Publishing Service, Canberra

Dārziņš P (2007) Operationalising the Rational Cognitive Model of Decision-Making Capacity – Notes for Elder Law Conference. In: Queensland Law Society Elder Law Conference, Brisbane, 14 June 2007

Darzins P, Molloy DW, Strang D (eds) (2000) Who can decide? The six step capacity assessment process. Memory Australia Press, Adelaide

Dawson J, Kämpf A (2006) Incapacity principles in mental health laws in Europe. Psychol Public Policy Law 12(3):310–331

Department of Health (2016) Dementia. Available via Australian Government. https://agedcare. health.gov.au/older-people-their-families-and-carers/dementia. Accessed 1 Nov 2016

Devereux J, Parker M (2006) Competency issues for young persons and older persons. In: Freckelton I, Petersen K (eds) Disputes and dilemmas in health law. Federation Press, Leichhardt

Directions in Law and Aging. Springer, Berlin Heidelberg, pp 35–55

Falk E, Hoffman N (2014) The role of capacity assessments in elder abuse investigations and guardianships. Clin Geriatr Med 30(4):851–868

Freckelton I (1999) Doctors as witnesses. In: Freckelton I, Petersen K (eds) Controversies in health law. Federation Press, Leichhardt

Frost M, Lawson S, Jacoby R (2015) Testamentary capacity law, practice, and medicine. Oxford University Press, Oxford

Grisso T (2003) Evaluating competencies: forensic assessments and instruments. Perspectives in law and psychology, 2nd edn. Kluwer Academic/Plenum Publishers, New York

Gunn MJ et al (1999) Decision-making capacity. Med Law Rev 7(3):269–301

Harada CN, Natelson Love MC, Triebel KL (2013) Normal cognitive ageing. Clin Geriatr Med 29 (4):737–752

Jourdan JB, Glickman L (1991) Reasons for requests for evaluation of competency in a municipal general hospital. Psychosomatics 32(4):413–416

Kapp MB (2015) Evaluating decision making capacity in older individuals: does the law give a clue? Laws 4(2):164–172

Kawas CH (2003) Early Alzheimer's disease. N Engl J Med 349(11):1056–1063

Kim SY et al (2007) Determining when impairment constitutes incapacity for informed consent in schizophrenia research. Br J Psychiatry 191(1):38–43

Kim SYH, Caine ED (2002) Utility and limits of the mini mental state examination in evaluating consent capacity in Alzheimer's disease. Psychiatr Serv 53(10):1322–1324

Kitamura T, Takahashi N (2007) Ethical and conceptual aspects of capacity assessments in psychiatry. Curr Opin Psychiatry 20(6):578–581

Kornfeld DS, Muskin PR, Tahil FA (2009) Psychiatric evaluation of mental capacity in the general hospital: a significant teaching opportunity. Psychosomatics 50(5):468–473

Lai JM, Karlawish J (2007) Assessing the capacity to make everyday decisions: a guide for clinicians and an agenda for future research. Am J Geriatr Psychiatr 15(2):101–111

Lin SY, Lewis FM (2015) Dementia friendly, dementia capable, and dementia positive: concepts to prepare for the future. Gerontologist 55(2):237–244

Liptzin B et al (2010) Testamentary capacity and delirium. Int Psychogeriatr 22(6):950–956

Marson D (2016) Commentary: a role for neuroscience in preventing financial elder abuse. Public Policy Aging Rep 26(1):12–14

Marson DC et al (1996) Toward a neurologic model of competency: cognitive predictors of capacity to consent in Alzheimer's disease using three different legal standards. Neurology 46(3):666–672

Moye J (1999) Assessment of competency and decision making capacity. In: Lichtenberg PA (ed) Handbook of assessment in clinical gerontology. Wiley, Hoboken, pp 488–528

Moye J et al (2006) Neuropsychological predictors of decision-making capacity over 9 months in mild-to-moderate dementia. J Gen Intern Med 21(1):78–83

Moye J et al (2007) A conceptual model and assessment template for capacity evaluation in adult guardianship. Gerontologist 47(5):591–603

Moye J, Marson DC (2007) Assessment of decision-making capacity in older adults: an emerging area of practice and research. J Gerontol B Psychol Sci Soc Sci 62(1):3–11

Moye J, Marson DC, Edelstein B (2013) Assessment of capacity in an aging society. Am Psychol 68(3):158–171

Mullins P (1999) A practical guide to testamentary capacity. Evidence in Wills & Estates Litigation, Brisbane

National Health and Medical Research Council (2014) Boosting Dementia Research Initiative. https://www.nhmrc.gov.au/research/boosting-dementia-research-initiative. Accessed 1 Nov 2016

National Institute on Ageing (2012) Obama administration presents national plan to fight Alzheimer's disease. https://www.nia.nih.gov/newsroom/2012/05/obama-administration-pre sents-national-plan-fight-alzheimers-disease. Accessed 1 Nov 2016

O'Neill N, Peisah C (2011) Capacity and the law. Sydney University Press, Sydney

Okonkwo OC et al (2008) Awareness of deficits in financial abilities in patients with mild cognitive impairment: going beyond self-informant discrepancy. Am J Geriatr Psychiatr 16 (8):650–659

Parker M (2008) Patient competence and professional incompetence: disagreements in capacity assessments in one australian jurisdiction, and their educational implications. J Law Med 16 (1):25–35

Parkinson's Queensland (2015) Statistics. http://parkinsons-qld.org.au/pqi-research/statistics/. Accessed 1 Nov 2016

Peisah C, Brodaty H (1994) Dementia and the will-making process: the role of the medical practitioner. Med J Aust 161(6):381–384

Population Reference Bureau (2015) Population Bulletin, Vol. 70, No. 2. December 2015. http://www.prb.org/pdf16/aging-us-population-bulletin.pdf. Accessed 1 Nov 2016 Publishing Service

Queensland Law Society, Allens Linklaters, Queensland Advocacy Incorporated (2014) Queensland Handbook for Practitioners on Legal Capacity

Sabatino CP, Wood E (2012) The conceptualization of legal capacity of older persons in western law. In: Doron I, Soden AM (eds) Beyond elder law: new directions in law and aging. Springer, New York

Sales BD, Shuman DW (1996) The newly emerging mental health law. In: Wexler DB, Winick BJ (eds) Law in a therapeutic key: developments in therapeutic jurisprudence. Carolina Academic Press, Durham, p 795

Shulman KI, Cohen CA, Hull I (2005) Psychiatric issues in retrospective challenges of testamentary capacity. Int J Geriatr Psychiatry 20(1):63–69

Smyer MA (2007) Contexts of capacity: local and state variations in capacity assessment– commentary on assessment of decision-making capacity in older adults. J Gerontol B Psychol Sci Soc Sci 62(1):14–15

Sprehe DJ, Kerr AL (1996) Use of legal terms in will contests: implications for psychiatrists. J Am Acad Psychiatry Law 24(2):255–265

Squires B, Barr F (2005) The development of advance care directives in new South Wales. Australas J Ageing 24(S1):S30–S35

Standing Committee on Legal and Constitutional Affairs, Parliament of the Commonwealth of Australia (2007) Older People and the Law

Sullivan K (2004) Neuropsychological assessment of mental capacity. Neuropsychol Rev 14 (3):131–142

UK Government (2015) Policy paper: Prime Minister's challenge on dementia 2020. https://www.gov.uk/government/publications/prime-ministers-challenge-on-dementia-2020/prime-minis ters-challenge-on-dementia-2020. Accessed 1 Nov 2016

Winick BJ (1996) The side effects of incompetency labeling and the implications for mental health law. In: Wexler DB, Winick BJ (eds) Law in a therapeutic key. Carolina Academic Press, Durham

World Health Organization (2015) World Report on Ageing and Health. http://apps.who.int/iris/bitstream/10665/186463/1/9789240694811_eng.pdf?ua=1. Accessed 1 Nov 2016

World Health Organization, Alzheimer's Disease International (2012) Dementia: a public health priority. http://www.who.int/mental_health/publications/dementia_report_2012/en/. Accessed 1 Nov 2016

Cases

Hawes v Burgess [2013] WTLR 453 CA; EWCA Civ 74
Middlebrook v Middlebrook (1962) 36 ALJR 216
O'Connell v Shortland (1989) 51 SASR 337
Re Ashkettle [2013] WTLR 1331
Sargent & Anor v Brangwin [2013] QSC 306

Chapter 2
Therapeutic Jurisprudence

1 Introduction

A novel approach to examining capacity assessments and the relationship between the legal and health professionals involved in making the determinations is through the framework of therapeutic jurisprudence. Adopting a new lens through which to view capacity assessments may assist with progressing the dialogue, ultimately towards achieving the consistent, transparent and accurate approach that is necessary to successfully establish best practice. Therapeutic jurisprudence provides such a framework because it promotes participation, dignity and trust, all concepts which are vital to the recognition and protection—where possible—of personal autonomy when capacity is being assessed.[1] The doctrine was developed in the United States of America by Wexler and Winick in the early 1990s and has been widely influential in an expanding number of areas.[2] By way of a brief explanation, therapeutic jurisprudence analyses 'the extent to which substantive rules, legal procedures, and the roles of lawyers and judges produce therapeutic or anti-therapeutic consequences'.[3] The doctrine has a law reform as well as a scholarly agenda which intends to reflect society's evolving standards.[4] It originally concentrated upon mental health law, although it is steadily being extended to new legal domains, including testamentary capacity and substitute decision-making.[5] The extension of the doctrine to this environment is emergent and has not been explored in detail. However, it has been foreshadowed in literature from the United States of America, most notably by Champine.[6]

---

[1]Australian Law Reform Commission (2014), p. 13. See also Tyler TR (1996), pp. 9–11; Kapp MB (2003), p. 142.

[2]Slobogin C (1995), p. 193; Freckelton I (2008), pp. 580–581.

[3]Finkelman D and Grisso T (1996), p. 588.

[4]Winick BJ (1997), p. 200.

[5]Ibid 184. See also Perlin ML (2003), p. 171–175.

[6]For example, Champine PR (2003), p. 177.

© Springer International Publishing AG 2017
K. Purser, *Capacity Assessment and the Law*, DOI 10.1007/978-3-319-54347-5_2

It is of critical importance to examine the role of the law and its effect on people, including the legal and health professionals who assess capacity. Principles of therapeutic jurisprudence are useful in this area, not least because the prospect of being legally unable or incapable of making testamentary decisions or decisions regarding financial and/or lifestyle/health concerns can be distressing.[7] It is this distress which can cause further detriment to an individual's ability to function, potentially having a negative impact on the outcome of the assessment. In fact, therapeutic jurisprudence proponents acknowledge that testamentary documents, enduring powers of attorney and advance health directives help to empower people to plan for a future in which they may no longer be able to make their own decisions.[8] Therapeutic jurisprudence is likewise concerned with how the law is interpreted and applied in practice distinct from any theoretical and academic debates that may exist. Such an attitude is of fundamental importance when assessing the relationship between legal and health professionals when they are actually assessing an individual's capacity.[9] These factors all contribute to make therapeutic jurisprudence an innovative framework in which to re-evaluate the approaches to capacity assessment in modern society. This chapter will offer definitions for relevant terms, followed by an examination of therapeutic jurisprudence principles and an analysis of the limitations of the doctrine. The extension of these principles to testamentary and decision-making capacity will then be explored.

2 Definitions

Discussion surrounds the application of both the terms 'therapeutic', and 'therapeutic jurisprudence'.[10] The term 'therapeutic jurisprudence' is deliberately vague.[11] This ambiguity attracts questions concerning what the jurisprudence aims to accomplish and what falls within the ambit of 'therapeutic'. Therapeutic jurisprudence has been described as the study of 'the role of the law as a therapeutic agent, recognizing that substantive rules, legal procedures and lawyers' roles may have either therapeutic or anti-therapeutic consequences, and questioning whether such rules, procedures and roles can or should be reshaped so as to enhance their therapeutic potential'.[12] This should not, however, negatively impact on the principles of due process and/or natural justice. So, therapeutic jurisprudence is

---

[7]Winick BJ (1996–1997), p. 58.
[8]Winick BJ (1996a), pp. 54–55.
[9]Kapp MB (2003), p. 145.
[10]Freckelton I (2008), p. 576.
[11]Winick BJ (1997), p. 192.
[12]Perlin ML (2003), pp. 1047–1048; Wexler DB (1995), p. 231. See also Winick BJ (1997), p. 185; Slobogin C (1995), p. 194.

concerned with individuals retaining a measure of control and/or involvement in the decision-making process because it is thought that those individuals will then be more likely to positively benefit from its outcomes.

The doctrine is a normative approach intended to be of use in law reform which incorporates an interdisciplinary element.[13] It is a phenomenological legal methodology which encourages pragmatic thought, careful analysis and empirical research, and, significantly, it also promotes individual autonomy.[14] The potential therapeutic, or anti-therapeutic, impact of the law in the capacity assessment context is clear considering, for example, not only the effect it can have on the lives of individuals having their capacity assessed, as well as on the family members and carers of those individuals, but also in how it regulates and impacts the practice of legal and health professionals.[15]

Wexler, one of the doctrine's founders, has defended the equivocal definitions thought to plague therapeutic jurisprudence, stating that, 'as a mere lens or heuristic for better seeing and understanding the law ... therapeutic jurisprudence has ... opted not to provide a tight definition ... thereby allowing commentators to roam within the intuitive and common sense contours of the concept'.[16] Thus, while on the one hand exasperating to minds that search out definitional exactitude, it is thought by proponents of therapeutic jurisprudence that predetermined definitions may obscure issues which would otherwise have been identified, thus 'prematurely eclipsing' the potential scope, and therefore utility, of the doctrine.[17] Wexler further notes that it must be questioned whether any proposed definition is a legal and/or political imposition, or an academic concern driven and determined by researchers.[18] Instead, the ambit of the doctrine should be able to be contextually defined enabling it to respond to circumstantial drivers.[19]

Sanism is a therapeutic jurisprudence concept which is particularly relevant to testamentary instruments, but one which also requires definitional attention. It focuses on the reasons for an individual being found to lack capacity instead of, for example, the content of the decision or the transaction, hence its importance particularly to the area of testamentary capacity. Sanism has been described as 'an irrational prejudice of the same quality and character as other irrational prejudices that cause, and are reflected in prevailing social attitudes of racism, sexism, homophobia, and ethnic bigotry. ... It is based primarily on stereotype, myth, superstition, and de-individualization.'[20] It is an important concept because, given its general invisibility, sanism can unconsciously taint both legal jurisprudence, as

---

[13]Freiberg A (2003), p. 8; Winick BJ (1997), p. 185; Kapp MB (2003), pp. 4–5.

[14]Hall MA (2002–2003), pp. 466–467; Freckelton I (2008), p. 576; Freiberg A (2003), p. 8.

[15]Mark A Hall, 'Law, Medicine, and Trust' (2002–2003), p. 55 *Stanford Law Review* 463, 467.

[16]Wexler DB (1995), p. 221.

[17]Ibid.

[18]Ibid.

[19]Wexler DB (1995), p. 222; Slobogin C (1995), p. 196.

[20]Perlin ML (1992–1993), p. 669; See also Ellis HS (2003), p. 195.

well as professional practice. It is suggested by Ellis that 'a masked sanism which extends to economic status and social status has been overlooked in both the law of wills and the law of mental health'.[21] For example, Ellis hypothesises that a person of economic means has a greater chance of having his or her will probated even though he or she may have made eccentric bequests or disinherited certain potential beneficiaries. This is because, it is argued, financial wealth guarantees a corresponding degree of sanity.[22] Ellis suggests that 'money and social status certainly has not proven to make us any saner but with such assets we would be less likely to fall under the umbrella of paternalism because through the sanist eye we are seen as more capable'.[23] Other commentators, such as Perlin, have concurred that sanism can exist in trust and estate law.[24]

Pretextuality is a concept linked to sanism. It suggests critically reviewing expert evidence to avoid blindly adopting legal fictions, an important concern given the increasing use of expert evidence by courts in determining capacity issues. Pretextuality has been defined as when 'courts accept (either implicitly or explicitly) testimonial dishonesty and engage similarly in dishonest (frequently meretricious) decision-making, specifically where witnesses, especially expert witnesses, show a "high propensity to purposively distort their testimony in order to achieve desired ends"'.[25] That is, pretextuality can be seen as the excuse condoning legal fictions which are assumptions that obscure or manipulate the rules of law. Pretextuality can be empirical in nature wherein elements of popular phenomenon are automatically accepted as fact.[26] The concept of 'pretextuality' is particularly relevant when, for example, legal and health professionals can be placed under immense pressure by family members with a private agenda to achieve a desired outcome regarding a specific individual's capacity determination.

3 The Utility of Therapeutic Jurisprudence

As stated, therapeutic jurisprudence traditionally focused on mental health law in the United States of America.[27] One motivating factor behind this was empirical research which demonstrated that mental disabilities are the most negatively viewed of all the mentally disabling conditions.[28] However, the law and the actions of legal actors (which consists of legal professionals including members of the

---

[21]Ellis HS (2003), p. 200.
[22]Ibid.
[23]Ibid.
[24]Perlin ML (2003), pp. 171–172.
[25]Perlin M (2000), pp. 226–227. See also Ellis HS (2003), p. 195.
[26]Perlin ML (1992–1993), p. 635.
[27]Winick BJ (1996–1997), p. 57; Wexler DB (1995), p. 223.
[28]Perlin ML (2000), p. 1032.

judiciary) have the potential to be anti-therapeutic in any interaction with individuals with a disability, or even those who are vulnerable, in any context. Consequently, therapeutic jurisprudence principles have extended beyond the mental health law context. They are already able to be recognised in the testamentary and substitute decision-making environment to varying degrees, even if the notions which exist have not expressly been attributed to therapeutic jurisprudence. These principles will now be investigated.

3.1 *Incompetency Labelling and Individual Autonomy*

Incompetence is defined as 'cognitive impairment caused by physical trauma, organic brain disorder, or mental illness ...'.[29] Scholars of therapeutic jurisprudence encourage the exploration of the possible effects, including psychological and legal, of labelling a person as 'incompetent'.[30] This is because the labelling process can be a negative experience stripping a person of their autonomy and liberty.[31] There can be both legal and social disadvantages to incompetency labelling including psychological harm, stigmatisation, loss of credibility, increased vulnerability, as well as detrimental effects upon self-esteem, motivation and overall functioning.[32] Financial after-effects can also result from a label of incapacity. These are all consequences which have been inadequately analysed generally, let alone in the specific context of testamentary and substitute decision-making where the application of therapeutic principles is just beginning.[33] It should be noted that the labelling theory needs to be filtered in light of the particular mental disability.[34]

The potential therapeutic, or otherwise, effect of the law is often neglected in policy development. However, the ageing population is one issue which demands public policy consideration, thus giving rise to a tension which cannot be ignored.[35] For example, the increasing occurrence of dementia, especially amongst the aged, will also result in an increase in the number of capacity assessments being conducted. The current ad hoc approaches to assessing capacity call into question the accuracy of such determinations because assessments are currently predicated on individualistic approaches which are informed by the assessor's experiences and skills.[36] This, in turn, only serves to amplify the number of erroneously labelled

---

[29]Winick BJ (1996–1997), p. 66.

[30]Winick BJ (1996a), p. 18.

[31]Ibid 19–20.

[32]Ibid 20. See also Carney T (1995), p. 517.

[33]Winick BJ (1996a), p. 20.

[34]Perlin ML (1996), p. 63.

[35]Moye J and Marson DC (2007), p. 8. See also Moye J et al. (2013), pp. 161–162.

[36]Darzins P et al. (2000), p. 1.

individuals. Likewise, this also highlights the relationship not only between the legal and health professions, but also the public policy considerations in both identifying and responding to the need for a rigorous assessment process. This is so that individuals are not subjected to restrictions on the basis of vague definitions of capacity and unsatisfactory assessment processes.

The effects of labelling an individual as incompetent similarly raise the dualistic notions of autonomy and protection which may not always be in harmony. This is because protecting an individual's well-being may necessarily mean infringing upon their liberty. People are sometimes labelled as incompetent by the law in order to achieve certain outcomes, for example, a decision as to whether a person is able to make a will.[37] Winick hypothesises that the labelling process is paternalistic, resulting from the desire to protect people and benefit society.[38] However, an individual, and indeed others in society, can perceive such a 'paternalistic' action as 'offensive', amounting to an attack on 'dignity and personhood'.[39] Alternatively, it can be welcomed, even retrospectively, by the individual and those around the individual.[40] Consider, for example, Mabel. Until she reached her late 80s, Mabel consistently and adamantly stated that she would never be a 'burden' on her family and would enter a retirement village before becoming so. Mabel, now 94, wants to remain in her own home no matter the cost, the impact, or the 'burden'. Mabel collapses at home, is taken to hospital where an assessment is done, and she is deemed to have the capacity to make the decision to return home. However, Mabel does not like taking her medication and forgets to drink water without constant reminders, care that her family are not in a position, either financially nor time wise, to provide despite their best intentions to the contrary. Mabel is found by her 18 year old grandson collapsed on the floor and bleeding from where she hit her head when she fell 24 hours after returning home. Would Mabel want to stay at home despite the impact on those around her, given her repeated and persistent earlier statements that she did not want to be a 'burden'? Is the 'incompetent' label in this scenario one she would accept or even welcome? Further, which Mabel is being referred to—the one in her 80s or the one in her 90s? Is this a scenario in which a notion of 'practical paternalism' should apply? That is, what happens when the 94 year old woman, despite theoretically having capacity to make the decision to return home, practically can no longer look after herself? Could or indeed should such practical considerations, which can endanger the individual in question, overcome the paramountcy of the notion of individual autonomy?

Winick has argued that the paternalistic approach obstructs personal sovereignty and individual autonomy, but that it is done 'on the ground of beneficence'.[41] Nevertheless, it is arguable that respecting such individuals as adults who are

---

[37]Schopp RF (1996), pp. 727–728; Winick BJ (1996a), pp. 18–19.

[38]Winick BJ (1996a), p. 19.

[39]Winick BJ (1991), p. 17.

[40]Ibid.

[41]Ibid 18.

capable of making their own decisions rather than as 'incompetent subjects of our paternalism, pity, or even contempt' will have therapeutic outcomes.[42] Is this the case in the above scenario with Mabel? It should be noted that Winick wrote from an American perspective. In, for example, Australia and the United Kingdom, there appears to have been a policy move away from paternalism.[43] Taking this concept further, Parker argues that in democratic countries the law ensures that decision-making autonomy is outside the grasp of paternalism.[44]

One of the issues associated with incompetency labelling is the notion that it will become a self-fulfilling prophecy. That is, labelling a person as competent or incompetent will cause that person to then develop, or further develop, an image or persona of themselves that meets the label thus impeding his or her ability to act independently of the label that he or she has been given.[45] This concept needs to be examined with reference to testamentary and substitute decision-making given the importance of removing an individual's decision-making autonomy in this context. This is similar to the notion of the marker and the marked, whereby it is proposed that the incompetency label will encourage the marker to behave in a way that will induce the marked to act in a manner that will confirm the label.[46]

Winick admits that the self-fulfilling prophecy theory has been controversial, noting for example, the argument that some illnesses are correctly viewed as an illness and that in certain situations recognising the existence of an illness is a precondition to improvement.[47] Further, the incompetency label can imply a personal trait rather than a legal status. However, in this case the label could be self-executing. That is, if a person believes that they are incompetent then this could be debilitating, leading to depression and possibly prolonging the illness.[48] This again emphasises the relevance of incompetency labelling to testamentary and decision-making capacity, highlighting the question of who has the power to determine whether an individual is incapable of making their own decisions in this context.

Therapeutic jurisprudence also emphasises the psychological ramifications of 'the label' upon an individual. The removal of a person's decision-making autonomy means that the individual, in effect, can be likened to a child. This is because on the removal of his or her autonomous decision-making ability he or she becomes subject to the authority of others. He or she then, rightly, perceives events to no longer be within his or her control, instead being within the domain of the surrogate decision-maker.[49] This, as Winick states, could serve to exacerbate the situation

---

[42]Ibid 51.

[43]Cockerill J et al. (2005), p. 28.

[44]Parker M (2004), p. 485.

[45]Winick BJ (1996a), p. 21.

[46]Ibid 22–23.

[47]Ibid 24.

[48]Ibid 24–25.

[49]Ibid 26.

with the labelled 'incompetent' individual becoming increasingly frustrated, and thus possibly feeling increasingly helpless and defeated.[50] It is important to examine how the nature and the imposition of the 'label' influence feelings of self-worth.

The theory of 'learned helplessness' developed by Seligman is also of interest here. This is because it may be used to potentially refine any proposed standardised method of capacity assessment. In its early stages, this concept theorised that feelings of helplessness and hopelessness are pervasive when individuals have been subjected to constant negative (or positive) consequences.[51] Seligman revised his hypothesis based upon studies with human subjects. His reformulated model proposed that 'a perceived non-contingent relationship between . . . actions and . . . outcomes . . . leads people to believe that events are outside their control'.[52] These feelings are heightened by three factors: first, blaming the feeling of uncontrollability on internal causes (for example, lack of intelligence) rather than external reasons; secondly, global deficits; and thirdly, causes of failure are stable.[53] That is, it is the individual's belief that uncontrollability is a direct result of internal failings which leads to feelings of helplessness and hopelessness that then carry over into reality. Further, incompetency labelling may lead to diminution of self-esteem and reduced performance which can result in learned helplessness and exacerbate the situation.[54] The intrinsic, extrinsic and motivational systems identified by Deci, Hartmann's independent ego energy theory, and Robert White's effectance motivation premise, all parallel Seligman's learned helplessness concept.[55] The 'locus of control' is the relationship between perceptions of control, mood and feelings of psychiatric well-being.[56] Again, although these principles have been developed and discussed in different contexts to that of testamentary capacity and substitute decision-making, they reinforce the notion that it is vital to try and maintain decision-making autonomy for as long as possible.

The issue of 'law related psychological dysfunction', which examines the effects on individuals of interacting with the law, compares the real need, as opposed to the artificial use, of labels and possible mislabelling.[57] This emphasises the need for accuracy and consistency in capacity evaluations especially as the 'system' as it currently stands is equivocal. In assessing capacity, consideration also needs to be given to imposed political and moral judgments, or what Winick describes as 'descriptive concepts', given that people do not live in isolated environments. So, for example, given the growing incidence of dementia, decision-making autonomy

---

[50]Ibid 26–27, 35.
[51]Ibid 28.
[52]Ibid 29.
[53]Ibid.
[54]Ibid 30, 32.
[55]Ibid 33.
[56]Ibid 36.
[57]Ibid 36–37.

and protecting individuals who are unable to protect themselves is increasingly on the political agenda.

Justifications for incompetency labelling vary depending upon the legal context, and yet, assumptions exist that a label of a lack of capacity has the same meaning in each and every context.[58] The subsequent application of incorrect assessment and labelling processes can perpetually threaten an individual's independence and right to self-determination. This is because self-determination is only significant if an individual is able to make his or her own decisions. This is concerning because relatively cavalier attitudes towards the determination of an individual's capacity can prevail. Legal professionals, unaware of the intricacies of a particular illness, may incorrectly label an individual. Health professionals also need to fully understand the effect of the legal concepts and framework when conducting assessments in this context. The need for a specific and consistent method of evaluation exists to protect not only the individuals, but also the legal and health professionals who are involved in the making of these determinations. The American legal profession has been called upon to clarify the vague notions of capacity and context.[59] This also needs to occur elsewhere, such as in Australia and the United Kingdom. The law needs to recognise the increasingly problematic concept of capacity in an ageing society where medical innovation is able to prolong the body but, in many circumstances, not the mind. The current structures and procedures are amorphous and inadequate. Subjective social, moral, political, legal, medical and cultural elements all need to be considered when determining whether an individual is legally competent.[60]

3.2   The Dualistic Nature of Autonomy and Protection

Autonomy in the therapeutic jurisprudence context is the notion of individual 'self-determination within a sphere of personal sovereignty'.[61] That is, an individual will either retain complete control within the identified area of decision-making, thus having sovereignty, or a third party can intervene meaning the individual lacks discretion and thus sovereignty.[62] Assessments conducted in the testamentary and substitute decision-making environment can potentially remove an individual's ability to continue to make their own financial, including testamentary, and/or lifestyle/health decisions, thus removing their autonomy and ultimately their personal sovereignty. This embodies the, at times, dualistic notions of autonomy and protection. Preserving an individual's well-being will, on occasion, come at the

---

[58]Ibid 37.
[59]Ibid 46.
[60]Ibid.
[61]Schopp RF (1996), pp. 727–728.
[62]Ibid.

expense of that individual's decision-making autonomy requiring third party intervention.

Legal capacity is variable. It is time and decision specific.[63] This must be recognised in an assessment process given the severe implications of removing an individual's decision-making ability. The autonomy/protection dualism is heightened by the unsatisfactory assessment methods currently employed by the legal and health professions as well as the ambiguous terminology adopted. That both professions do not always necessarily understand what it is they are assessing can negatively impact the fine balance between autonomy and protection. Individual autonomy should be protected where possible, and where to do so does not cause harm to the individual. It is finding the correct balance that is so challenging.

One of the ways in which to accomplish this is to encourage the preparation of estate planning documents such as wills, enduring powers of attorney and advance health directives. The preparation of these documents being 'therapeutic' because they empower individuals to put legally recognised mechanisms in place for when they are no longer able to make those decisions themselves. Having this 'plan' can make people feel more in control, thus giving them a sense of certainty. However, as is well known, problems can exist with these documents. Vulnerable individuals may be exposed to abuse. Further, the preparation of such documents may cause familial infighting thus countering the therapeutic benefits of engaging with the process to start with. Taking the notion of 'therapeutic estate planning' to the extreme is the suggestion of, in effect, 'compulsory' future planning. That is, forcing individuals to implement measures while they are still legally competent for the times when they may not be. For example, upon the diagnosis of a mentally disabling condition such as dementia the individual would be required to prepare his or her will, enduring power of attorney and advance health directive. This clearly impinges upon decision-making sovereignty despite the aim of extending individual decision-making autonomy. However, the very notion of infringing upon sovereignty to protect decision-making autonomy, especially in this manner, is counter-intuitive. It is also unlikely to be successful in encouraging the therapeutic aspect of engaging with estate planning for a number of reasons, not least the autonomy (and policy) arguments.

Fairness and trust are symbiotic when presenting an individual with the knowledge that they may no longer have decision-making autonomy.[64] Traditionally, the legal/health professional—client/patient rapport exemplified a paternalistic relationship which arguably has been replaced with a rights oriented approach in the twenty-first century.[65] However, concerns have been raised that 'health care law lacked any developed vocabulary, analytical framework, or body of empirical information'.[66] This comment was made with reference to the existence of trust

---

[63] Attorney General's Department of New South Wales (2008), p. 27.
[64] Tyler TR (1996), p. 9.
[65] Hall MA (2002–2003), p. 469.
[66] Ibid.

in the relationship between health professionals and their patients. However, it is also pertinent to the relationship existing between legal professionals and their clients, especially in the testamentary and substitute decision-making context. An individual will trust a legal professional to draft a legally binding document. The same individual simultaneously places their trust in both the legal and health professions to satisfactorily assess their capacity. Therefore, trust *must* exist between the individual, and both the legal and health professionals, as well as between the professionals themselves. This is especially so when considering that when a substitute decision-maker assumes an active role, the principal is no longer able to guard their own interests, placing the substitute decision-maker in an immense position of power. The implications of this level of trust only serve to highlight the dualistic nature of autonomy and protection.

Interestingly, the increasing recognition of individual autonomy has produced a corresponding decline in the unquestioning trust placed in legal and health professionals. Indeed, trust was seen to be emblematic of an anachronistic and paternalistic system.[67] However, it is now being recognised that 'trust' has therapeutic benefits which cannot be ignored. The absence of trust could prevent individuals seeking out legal and medical assistance.[68] Even if sought, a lack of trust may likewise prevent individuals from then relying on the information given, perhaps to the individual's detriment. Therefore, although the twenty-first century has seen the rise of a rights based society, the fundamental element of trust has not completely abated, and nor should it be allowed to do so. Individuals are more educated and demand more of legal and health professionals, often seeking holistic approaches. Therapeutic jurisprudence offers a framework in which legal and health professionals can co-exist and supplement each other's expertise in this context. This is through an interdisciplinary approach designed to maximise trust. It is suggested that merging the principles of therapeutic jurisprudence with capacity assessments would result in an approach which would recognise the significance of the interaction between the individual, and both the legal and health professions.[69] Further, it promotes the strategic use of satisfactory assessment processes in an attempt to promote the balance of autonomy and protection.[70]

3.3   The Neutral Fact Finder

In therapeutic jurisprudence some emphasis is placed on the concept of the 'neutral fact-finder'. This concept was not developed with reference to testamentary and decision-making capacity determinations but is theoretically compatible with this

---

[67]Ibid 472.
[68]Ibid 478.
[69]Winick BJ (1998), p. 909.
[70]Ibid.

context. This is because the 'neutral fact-finder' notion focuses on issues of bias, honesty and expertise. It questions whether procedural safeguards can ensure neutral fact-finding or, in this context, satisfactory assessments of testamentary capacity and substitute decision-making.[71] The neutral fact-finder concept acknowledges that mental capacity can be determined by tests and interviews,[72] a theory which is employed in Canada through the use of a competency assessor system.[73] However, the adaptability of this system to testamentary and substitute decision-making capacity assessments has not been fully explored. From an American perspective, Tyler has observed that the capabilities of professional and judicial decision-makers should be evaluated. This is because American research has demonstrated that there have been errors in decision-making in the clinical context.[74] Such errors in decision-making can extend to decision-making when conducting capacity assessments. It would not be unreasonable to think that errors would also exist in other jurisdictions internationally. However, empirical evidence would need to be undertaken to determine this and the nature of any errors, if they were found to occur. Inaccuracies are to be expected when an already complex field is unnecessarily complicated even further by miscommunication and misunderstanding between the legal and health professionals involved in the determinations. Nevertheless, adapting the notion of a neutral fact finder to this context could be beneficial, beginning with the implementation of a satisfactory assessment process and guiding principles emphasising fairness, honesty and expertise.

3.4 The Least Restrictive Alternative

The comprehensive exploration of the term 'competency' within the American mental health law arena serves to highlight the limited investigation of the term in the testamentary and substitute decision-making context.[75] Any intervention by third parties should be no more restrictive than is absolutely necessary upon an individual's physical, mental, cultural and/or legal autonomy.[76] Further, ideally interference should only be as a last resort and have as little impact as possible on an individual's autonomy. This principle is representative of the importance of individuals maintaining their independence and so, has a role to play in both testamentary and decision-making capacity. Interestingly, in the United States of America the least restrictive alternative is both constitutionally and legislatively based.[77]

---

[71]Tyler TR (1996), p. 3.
[72]Ibid.
[73]Cockerill J et al. (2005), p. 49.
[74]Tyler TR (1996), p. 5.
[75]Ellis HS (2003), p. 195.
[76]Perlin ML (2000), p. 1015.
[77]Winick BJ (1997), p. 204; Perlin ML (2000), p. 1028.

4 Limitations of Therapeutic Jurisprudence

To thoroughly examine the application of therapeutic jurisprudence principles to testamentary and decision-making capacity assessments, it is first necessary to identify the limitations of the doctrine which exist. The five primary dilemmas facing therapeutic jurisprudence, as categorised by Slobogin in a leading article, include the identity dilemma, the definitional dilemma, the dilemma of empirical indeterminism, the rule of law dilemma and the balancing dilemma.[78] Although Slobogin has engaged in a critique of therapeutic jurisprudence, it is important to note that he nevertheless states that the doctrine is 'innovative and worthwhile', and that his remarks are intended to be 'constructive'.[79]

Before dealing with the five dilemmas identified by Slobogin, an initial critique that must be addressed is that therapeutic jurisprudence is 'overwhelmingly American'.[80] As stated, therapeutic jurisprudence initially developed within the American context, which has a constitutional framework. However, the absence of American constitutional constraints elsewhere, such as in Australia and the United Kingdom, is actually a positive because therapeutic jurisprudence can develop free from any constitutional restrictions. Consequently, the doctrine can potentially accomplish objectives not possible in the American context.[81]

4.1 The Identity Dilemma

The identity dilemma is concerned with whether the vague definitions of terms such as 'therapeutic' and 'well-being' prevent the doctrine from establishing an identity within modern jurisprudence.[82] Slobogin has contended that 'therapeutic jurisprudence should carve out a niche for itself by focusing its analysis on the impact of legal rules on the well-being of those they affect'.[83] This is what differentiates the identity dilemma from the definitional dilemma, that is, it is the lack of definitions that prevent the doctrine from establishing its own place in modern jurisprudence because absent a clear focus it is difficult to establish a clear identity.

In considering the term 'therapeutic', Slobogin has explored whether the term is intended to 'simply mean beneficial ... [or] beneficial in light of what behavioural science has to say about the effect of the law and why people behave the way they do ... [or] beneficial in the sense of improving the psychological or physical well-being of a person'.[84] He has proposed that therapeutic jurisprudence is 'the use of

---

[78]Slobogin C (1995), p. 195.
[79]Ibid 218.
[80]Magner E (1998), p. 127.
[81]Winick BJ (1997), p. 204.
[82]Slobogin, C (1995), p. 201.
[83]Ibid 218.
[84]Ibid.

social science to study the extent to which a legal rule or practice promotes the psychological and physical well-being of the people it affects'.[85] Wexler has conceded that this statement best represents his view of what the doctrine is.[86] On this point, Winick noted that it was a deliberate decision to leave the definition of therapeutic 'ambiguous and open to argument'.[87] To narrowly define the jurisprudence may be to restrict potential future avenues of valuable research.[88]

Ancillary to this is the question of, therapeutic for whom? Wexler has noted that conflict can arise where a law may be therapeutic for one individual but antitherapeutic for another.[89] His response has been that the aim of therapeutic jurisprudence is merely to highlight the issue, not to resolve it. Once the problem has been characterised it should be entrusted to the appropriate legal and/or political forum.[90] Take, for example, the situation where there is a 78 year old woman with borderline capacity who has been the victim of romance fraud on more than one occasion. Her daughter is extremely worried about her through no motive other than wanting the best for her mother. An assessment has occurred and it was determined that the elderly woman has lost financial capacity. A validly executed enduring power of attorney consequently comes into effect. Whilst this interaction could be seen to be therapeutic for the concerned daughter, the mother may not feel the same given the argument is, it is her money to do with as she sees fit, especially as her capacity was borderline. Arguably, however, it is 'therapeutic' for the mother who has stopped sending money to the perpetrators of the romance scam, even though the third party intervention infringed upon her autonomy. Thus, the questions arise, therapeutic in what sense and for whom? Here, once the problem has been identified, it does become the domain of the legal system, but it is also potentially a policy issue with the question as to funds and resources protecting against, for example, elder abuse, and in this case, romance fraud.

The identity dilemma also questions whether therapeutic jurisprudence is unique or reminiscent of other modern legal movements such as critical legal studies and the feminist movement. Winick has hypothesised that therapeutic jurisprudence is normative in nature whereas these movements are not.[91] Slobogin has acknowledged that therapeutic jurisprudence is arguably distinctive from other modern jurisprudences, but perhaps because of its diverse focus rather than its substance.[92] Therefore, the unrestrictive identity of therapeutic jurisprudence should not impede the successful implementation of its principles in the capacity assessment context.

---

[85]Ibid.
[86]Wexler DB (1995), pp. 223–224.
[87]Winick BJ (1997), p. 192.
[88]Wexler DB (1995), p. 221.
[89]Ibid 224.
[90]Ibid.
[91]Ibid 206.
[92]Slobogin C (1995), p. 200.

In fact, it may actually be beneficial because capacity determinations should be situational, reflecting the decision specific nature of capacity.

4.2   The Definitional Dilemma

Slobogin's second identified dilemma is the 'definitional dilemma'. This questions the lack of clearly articulated definitions, specifically, what is meant by the terms 'therapeutic' and 'well-being'. The question is how can the doctrine be applied, and evaluated, when such key terms lack clear definitional boundaries.[93] In addition to calling for clearly formulated definitions of the terms, Slobogin has postulated that outcome based measures should be identified, no matter whether the ultimate aspiration is individual autonomy, societal satisfaction or psychological well-being.[94] This would, arguably, enable the assessment of the impact of the jurisprudence in achieving its overarching goal of the law having a therapeutic effect rather than the more nebulous notions which currently exist.

Prior to Slobogin's identification of the definitional dilemma, Small questioned the applicability of therapeutic jurisprudence principles to areas outside mental health law.[95] He has also queried whether therapeutic jurisprudence principles are able to adequately address the multiplicity of issues enveloped by the banner of legal psychology.[96] Wexler has responded to Small's appraisal noting that therapeutic jurisprudence has started, and continues, to infiltrate and influence areas of law outside the mental health field, not least within the context of wills, enduing powers of attorney and advance health directives.[97] This is because anxiety and tension are not confined to mental health law and addressing the impact of the law on an individual is one of the primary concerns of therapeutic jurisprudence.[98] In fact, decision-making in the context of wills, enduring powers of attorney and advance health directives seems a natural extension for the principles of therapeutic jurisprudence given the inherent question of autonomy, and notions of labelling and self-fulfilling prophecies in this area. The law and legal actors have a role to play in facilitating the positive impact that a constructive interaction between individuals and the 'law' can have, and the vital role accurate, consistent and transparent capacity assessments have to play in this. Wexler has acknowledged the validity of Small's second critique, justifiably questioning whether Small is 'correct in pushing for a psychological jurisprudence that would be co-extensive with the area of legal psychology ... [because a] jurisprudence that encompasses the

---

[93]Ibid 201.

[94]Ibid 218.

[95]Small MA (1993), p. 699.

[96]Ibid.

[97]Wexler DB (1995), p. 227.

[98]Ibid.

whole of legal psychology might lose its explanatory or normative power'.[99]
Further, no jurisprudence does, nor can, claim to contend with all legal issues.[100]
It was never intended that therapeutic jurisprudence should be all-encompassing
and any attempt to assert such a claim may limit the doctrine's usefulness as a
forum in which to explore particular legal issues.

Slobogin himself has queried whether using the guise of autonomy to force an
individual to make a choice is not more anti-therapeutic than actually not making
the decision.[101] That is, is the choice not to make a decision but to leave the decision
to others, a valid exercise of autonomy? This raises the notion of the 'practical'
paternalism discussed above. Compelling an individual to make a decision may
likewise be more anti-therapeutic than the alternative given that the prospect of
choosing between multiple possibilities may be more upsetting than not making a
decision at all for some people.[102] Further, making a decision and then having to
deal with the repercussions can also be more distressing than not making a decision.
Consider an elderly widow who suffers from anxiety and generally does what all
her three children tell her, although she is concerned that child 3 is an alcoholic. She
executes a will and an enduring power of attorney appointing child 1 and child 2 but
not child 3 as executor and attorney respectively. In this scenario, child 3 may act in
such a way as to greatly upset both the widow and the familial harmony, for
example threatening to contest the will. In this case the exercise of the widow's
autonomy may be more anti-therapeutic for her even if the law has been used to
implement her decision-making ability and appoint trusted persons.

4.3   The Dilemma of Empirical Indeterminism

The questioning of how the therapeutic effect, or otherwise, of a law or action could
be evaluated when key terms have not been defined raises the third dilemma, that of
empirical indeterminism. Therapeutic jurisprudence relies upon empirical research
to assess hypotheses developed through the application of the doctrine's principles.[103] Slobogin has pinpointed two fundamental problems with relying on social
science research methodologies. First, social science does not easily lend itself to
the legal domain and qualitative and/or quantitative results in this context should
therefore be accepted critically.[104] Slobogin is correct given that qualitative and
quantitative research is not prolific in legal scholarship. Alternatively, if it is
utilised it is generally undertaken somewhat sparingly and seemingly without a

---

[99]Ibid 227. See also Winick BJ (1997), p. 190.

[100]Wexler DB (1995), p. 227.

[101]Slobogin C (1995), p. 201.

[102]Ibid 202.

[103]Ibid 204.

[104]Ibid 204, 218.

full understanding of the complexities associated with adopting an empirical methodology.[105] However, the purely doctrinal approach to legal research is changing with increasing usage of empirical methodologies being seen, and socio-legal research being conducted. This is facilitating the exploration of the effect of the law on and within society, both as a whole and on its members individually. Furthermore, those who have mastered the rigorous application of analytical skills to theoretical and practical problems, as required of a law graduate, should be able to successfully apply these skills to social science research.[106]

Winick has addressed this first problem arising from the dilemma of empirical indeterminacy.[107] He has noted that because therapeutic jurisprudence is reliant upon the 'tools' of social science, one of the inevitable consequences will be that the jurisprudence will be impacted by the challenges faced by that discipline.[108] However, he has further noted the utility of social science research in helping to resolve legal issues and that courts, as well as the legislature, are increasingly utilising empirical research in the making of laws.[109] Therefore, as with any research, the results of social science methodologies must be viewed critically, but this is not to say that they cannot augment traditional legal doctrinal analysis. Indeed, the adoption of empirical methodologies adds another dimension to traditional black letter legal scholarship.

The second problem that Slobogin has identified is that even if an infallible research paradigm is developed, often therapeutic jurisprudence is concerned with issues that are not easily answered. This can be compounded when considering the effect of the definitional dilemma in even being able to determine what issue it is that therapeutic jurisprudence is attempting to answer.[110] This observation is also correct. However, the problem of challenging and imprecise research questions is not limited to therapeutic jurisprudence. This is one of the many problems that face all practitioners, scholars, policy makers and members of society, especially as interdisciplinary approaches are increasingly being required to adequately answer questions which are not easily contained within the province of any one discipline.

4.4 The Rule of Law Dilemma

The rule of law dilemma is concerned with the role of legal actors and whether their actions are therapeutic or anti-therapeutic. Winick has noted that it is the suggestion that legal actors should ensure that their actions have beneficial consequences that

---

[105]Schuck PH (1989), p. 323.

[106]Zimring FE (1983), p. 455.

[107]Winick BJ (1996b), p. 657.

[108]Ibid.

[109]Winick BJ (1997), p. 196.

[110]Slobogin C (1995), pp. 207–208.

can give rise to the rule of law dilemma. Further, the fear is that by placing significant trust and authority in the hands of, for example, health practitioners, in this context by their being involved in the assessments of capacity, the process can 'produce abuse'.[111] This is because those who feel they are interpreting and applying the law can be seduced by that power, a notion which is easily applied in the context of determining whether an individual has or does not have legal capacity. As Slobogin has stated, if 'the therapeutic impact of a rule is mixed, an evaluation of the rule's value should consider not only the proportion of people who are likely to benefit from it but also the extent to which that proportion will be accurately identified ...'.[112] Therefore, consideration needs to be had for the cost in attaining individual therapeutic outcomes.

Slobogin likewise has noted that the quandary for therapeutic jurisprudence is how to assess whether the greatest good for the greatest number of people is derived from an individualistic approach where rules are applied on a case by case basis or whether a more fixed paradigm is necessary.[113] Winick has countered saying that therapeutic jurisprudence principles are not promoted at the expense of natural justice.[114] While it is important to note these concerns and to be able to adequately address them, the general law must obviously be malleable enough to be tailored to individual circumstances. This is especially necessary in a contentious area such as the assessment of legal capacity.

4.5 The Balancing Dilemma

The balancing dilemma considers how to assess whether the legal system, be it a law, practice or procedure is therapeutic given disparate factors.[115] For example, in the rivalry between autonomy and paternalism the latter should not automatically be viewed negatively, especially when considering this notion of 'practical paternalism'.[116] Winick has theorised that therapeutic jurisprudence contributes to the concept of 'balance' by promoting the previously relatively ignored issue of 'therapeutic dimension'.[117] However, Schopp believes that when a legal doctrine is designed to maximise therapeutic success, such effectiveness will come at a cost to personal liberty, and that the potential rivalry between liberty and therapeutic effectiveness is not satisfactorily addressed by the jurisprudence.[118] Slobogin has

---

[111]Winick BJ (1996b), p. 664.
[112]Slobogin C (1995), p. 218.
[113]Ibid 210.
[114]Winick BJ (1997), p. 203.
[115]Slobogin C (1995), p. 210.
[116]Ibid 218.
[117]Winick BJ (1997), p. 198.
[118]Schopp RF (1996), p. 725.

questioned why the focus on autonomy as the pre-eminent ideal should automatically override individual welfare noting that 'some Asian societies value allegiance to the family and the state over individual rights; perhaps it is more therapeutic to do so'.[119]

Slobogin has also questioned the ability of therapeutic jurisprudence to manage the balancing dilemma. His criticism, however, centres more on the lack of a specific framework reflecting his identified definitional dilemma and possibly the lack of clarity of assessment of the goals of therapeutic jurisprudence.[120] Nevertheless, arguably, one form or another of the 'balancing dilemma' is faced by all law, especially law reform, irrespective of the solidity of the framework underpinning it. The difference is that therapeutic jurisprudence aims to provide theoretical proposals supported by additional knowledge supplied by empirical research. Such an approach would be particularly useful in attempting to ensure accurate, consistent and transparent capacity assessment paradigms.

Therapeutic jurisprudence proponents argue that notions of what is 'therapeutic' and individual interests often converge. It is when this does not occur, however, that Slobogin has raised the issue of internal balancing.[121] Then again, the very definition of therapeutic jurisprudence indicates that its aims should not be achieved at the expense of policy considerations and natural justice.[122] Winick has emphasised that promoting therapeutic effects is a desirable outcome conditional upon 'other things being equal'[123] and that the doctrine 'does not suggest that therapeutic considerations should outweigh other normative values that law may properly seek to further. Rather, it calls for an awareness ... and ... a ... weighing of sometimes competing values'.[124] Further, as Slobogin himself has noted, these are concerns which confront society as a whole and not just the doctrine of therapeutic jurisprudence.[125] External balancing is also concerning for Slobogin.[126] Basically, he has espoused that proponents of therapeutic jurisprudence must recognise that if the doctrine is to retain credibility, it must not ignore the fact that while a law may be therapeutic for some, it may be anti-therapeutic for others.[127]

Overall Slobogin, as well as other commentators, have presented a valid critique of therapeutic jurisprudence which must be both acknowledged and addressed. Slobogin, however, admits that he is sympathetic to the principles espoused by the doctrine, concluding his critical analysis by stating that, 'therapeutic jurisprudence, carefully pursued, will help produce a critical psychology that will force

---

[119]Slobogin C (1995), p. 213.

[120]Ibid 211.

[121]Ibid.

[122]Perlin ML (2000), pp. 1047–1048; Wexler DB (1995), p. 231.

[123]Winick BJ (1997), p. 188.

[124]Ibid 191.

[125]Slobogin C (1995), p. 212.

[126]Ibid 216.

[127]Ibid.

policymakers to pay more attention to the actual, rather than the assumed, impact of the law and those who implement it'.[128] This is why therapeutic jurisprudence is a useful lens through which to view capacity assessments as well as the relationship between legal and health practitioners. It offers a fresh view of what is actually happening when these determinations are being made. This is of substantial theoretical, but also practical, significance to not only the individuals involved but also to the legal and health practitioners, judiciary, governing bodies, community stakeholders and policy makers.

5   Application to the Capacity Context

The literature examines the application of therapeutic jurisprudence to testamentary acts and familial protection as well as substitute decision-making, particularly advance care directives, in the United States of America. The doctrine's application in this contextual environment internationally, such as in Australia and the United Kingdom, has not been comprehensively explored. The preparation and effect of wills, enduring powers of attorney and advance health directives may have therapeutic or anti-therapeutic consequences as discussed.[129] As Winick has noted, promoting individual autonomy and self-determination is therapeutically beneficial because to deny such basic human rights, and needs, can exacerbate 'powerlessness, dependence, incompetence, and depression'.[130] Positive feelings, for example those of being competent, are linked to increasing internal motivation for good emotional and psychological health. This can then lead to positive interaction in other aspects of a person's life, thus providing further external motivators, such as a positive determination of legal capacity.[131]

The concept of the 'totality of circumstances' should also be considered when applying therapeutic jurisprudence principles in the testamentary and decision-making context. Admittedly, this concept was developed with reference to the validity of criminal justice waivers, but it can be extended to this setting. Traditionally, this concept focused on the three aspects of knowledge, intelligence and voluntariness.[132] Within the criminal framework knowledge 'implies that the defendant understood that he/she waived his/her rights ... [intelligence] implies that the waiver was the product of a rational reasoning process, and ... voluntariness implies that the situation was not so coercive that the defendant's will was overborne'.[133] In the decision-making context, knowledge would imply that the

---

[128]Ibid 218–219.
[129]Winick BJ (1997), p. 186.
[130]Winick BJ (1996–1997), p. 84.
[131]Winick BJ (1996c), pp. 160–161.
[132]Fulero SM and Everington C (2004), p. 56.
[133]Ibid.

person in question understood the importance of the will, enduring power of attorney and/or advance health directive that he or she was executing. Intelligence would mean that the document(s) were signed as a result of rational reasoning processes and voluntariness would imply the absence of undue influence. Therefore, the process would culminate in a 'totality of circumstances' being the legal capacity necessary to execute the particular document in question. Ensuring that a consistent and transparent competency assessment system exists is one way in which to attempt to redress problems produced by unsatisfactory legal processes which may heighten feelings such as anxiety, distress, anger or depression.

5.1 Testamentary Acts

Facing death and the associated preparation of a will can have both therapeutic and anti-therapeutic benefits. In examining the actual process of making a will, it can be an empowering process to make provision for the future—to determine what an individual wants to happen to his or her property on his or her death and to make provision for others. Alternatively, however, individuals can also become anxious about their own mortality which can impact the decisions made and thus make the experience somewhat anti-therapeutic.[134] Therefore, how this process is handled by the 'legal actors' involved (a notion extending to all those involved in capacity assessments, that is, the health professionals as well) can have a substantial impact on the individuals who are making significant life decisions.

To effectively apply therapeutic jurisprudence principles in this context, it is necessary to consider the therapeutic or anti-therapeutic impact of assessing testamentary capacity, the different approaches this can embody, as well as the impact upon the individuals affected.[135] Champine has noted that such contemplation will raise unanswered but, also, possibly unanswerable questions.[136] She reasons that any discussion of therapeutic jurisprudence in the context of testamentary capacity will not, and indeed should not, be the main, or even a central, consideration.[137] Further, the potential for paternalism that therapeutic jurisprudence provides is contrary to the autonomy that the very notion of executing a will provides.[138] The fundamental discord between paternalism and autonomy identified here is not, however, limited to issues of testamentary capacity. It is also apparent in areas such as mental health law and family law, particularly domestic violence.[139] Such challenges should not, however, prevent the application of the doctrine to this

---

[134]Glover M (2012), p. 437.
[135]Champine PR, (2003), p. 191.
[136]Ibid.
[137]Ibid 192.
[138]Ibid 192.
[139]Ibid 193.

context, especially when to do so could prove beneficial. Indeed, Champine postulated that such a discourse will prove to be invaluable.[140]

It has been suggested that human concern for autonomy throughout life is more important than protecting it after death and ensuring that an individual's wishes are respected.[141] However, it has been argued that property is increasingly being considered almost as valuable as autonomy, especially as the value of estates increase.[142] Ellis then takes this further arguing that 'in essence, it is our liberty and independence that are at stake when our voiceless wishes contained in a will are disregarded on the assumption of diminished capacity'.[143] This is principally talking to the contestation of wills, an area which is the epitome of the dichotomous balance between notions of testamentary freedom and the moral need to look after 'dependents' (however the term dependent is defined in the different jurisdictions). However, it can also extend to the lack of testamentary capacity which is another ground upon which the validity of a will can be contested, especially if, for example, the requirements for bringing a family provision claim to contest the will may not be met. Clearly the grounds to argue that testamentary capacity is lacking need to be satisfied but this is another example of the importance of ensuring rigorous assessment processes as not only can the determination of a lack of capacity have therapeutic or anti-therapeutic effects in life, but these can extend beyond death as well.

The therapeutic jurisprudence concepts of sanism and pretextuality are also raised in connection with undertaking and completing testamentary acts. It is argued that the goal is to combat these by setting higher standards to scrutinise the assessment of capacity, for example, of vulnerable groups such as the very old or persons with a disability.[144] Ellis has stated that this is necessary because sanism is rampant in will contests and that the manipulation of experts to challenge individual autonomy under the banner of 'paternalism' is common.[145] Paternalism, including the notion of 'practical paternalism', can be necessary when individuals are unable to protect themselves for example, because they may be isolated and/or suffer abuse, or be subject to the influence of a family member, carer or friend.[146] However, in examining the question of expert evidence in capacity matters, the 'manoeuvring' of experts, and indeed evidence, is undesirable and generally only possible because the expert in question has not been the testator's treating physician or is unfamiliar with the nature and standard of the requisite legal capacity. Further, often the 'expert' is making a retrospective competency assessment, as distinct from a contemporaneous determination, based upon medical records and evidence

---

[140]Ibid.
[141]Ellis HS (2003), p. 195.
[142]Ibid.
[143]Ibid.
[144]Ibid 195–196.
[145]Ibid 196.
[146]Ibid 198–199.

of potentially biased family and friends, thus championing pretextuality.[147] Balance between an objective capacity assessment and an individual's intent and well-being should ideally be sought. It is implementing this, however, which is the challenge. One way in which to accomplish this is to ensure that the assessment of capacity is undertaken by an independent third party which returns to the therapeutic jurisprudence notion of a neutral fact-finder.

The concept of the 'sanist will' has also been examined by Champine. In her opinion, the American test to determine testamentary capacity[148] is not sanist and therefore not offensive to therapeutic jurisprudence principles.[149] Ellis, however, argues that the test is not rigorous enough in its application to assess individual intent and thus to prevent sanism.[150] She cites the example of ageism to support her conclusion, stating that age can affect memory recall and that this can be confused with a lack of legal capacity which is clearly a falsity. Thus, ageism is another form of sanism perpetuated by the current test and one which is particularly relevant given ageing populations worldwide.[151] One solution which has been suggested in the American context is the concept of ante-mortem or living probate, a 'long-debated probate reform [which] allows the testator to personally defend his or her disbursement of property'.[152] This would enable a court to seek evidence from the best source, the testator, especially concerning any allegations of incapacity.[153] Such a system would also facilitate familial discussion of testamentary dispositions which could have therapeutic consequences such as preventing possible will contestations and encouraging conversations about any ill-feeling resulting from the testamentary decisions. Alternatively, instead of having the intended effect of facilitating discussion, a living probate may instead expose the testator to potential hostility, attempted influence, and perhaps even abuse. Consequently, it may create more problems than it solves. Obviously other problems with such a system also exist, not least being the ability to execute a will up until an individual either dies or loses capacity—a living probate could make this process more complicated and more expensive resulting in people being even less inclined to engage with estate planning than they already are. However, what is clear is that therapeutic jurisprudence offers a framework in which to examine testamentary capacity assessments as well as the role of legal and health professionals while recognising the need to preserve the balance between individual autonomy and protection.

---

[147] Ibid 196.

[148] The American test assesses whether the testator, '(a) know[s] the nature and extent of his property, (b) know[s] the natural objects of his bounty, (c) know[s] how the proposed will disposes of his property, and (d) [has] . . . the ability to make a rational plan to dispose of his property'. Ibid 197.

[149] Ibid; Champine PR (2003), p. 183.

[150] Ellis HS (2003), pp. 197–198.

[151] Ibid 198.

[152] Ibid 200.

[153] Ibid.

5.2   Supported and Substitute Decision-Making

It has been justifiably proposed that there is value, and consequently therapeutic benefits, in enabling individuals to make financial and lifestyle/health decisions for themselves, as long as is possible.[154] Thus, therapeutic jurisprudence principles appear to complement both substitute and supported decision-making. Substitute decision-making documents are not limited to naming a substitute decision-maker. They can also contain directions, for example, as to the exercise of the enduring power given under the document. The process whereby an individual (the principal) empowers another to make financial and/or lifestyle/health choices in anticipation of a time when the principal will be unable or incapable of making those decisions themselves exemplifies the principles of trust and autonomy promoted by therapeutic jurisprudence. The notion of retaining the ability to make one's own decisions for as long as possible through supportive mechanisms also exhibits the hallmarks of the principles of therapeutic jurisprudence, making the doctrine an ideal new lens through which to explore the assessment of decision-making capacity, especially in light of the paradigmatic shift occurring from substitute to supported decision-making.

6   Conclusion

It must be acknowledged that the law in practice does not always represent the original theoretical objective, no matter how idealistic, and it does not exist within a vacuum. Consequently, modern legal scholarship and the practical application of the law are becoming increasingly interdisciplinary in nature. This evolution is recognised by the adoption of empirical research methodologies to augment the traditional legal scholarship paradigm. Consequently, the appeal of therapeutic jurisprudence in this specific context is that it not only promotes interdisciplinary and empirical research but it also offers evaluative theoretical solutions.[155] Therapeutic jurisprudence cannot necessarily resolve specific debates or provide clear cut solutions to challenges which exist when assessing capacity, but it can be used to augment the quality of discussion and process, and to promote an ethic of care.[156] This is imperative when dealing with vulnerable individuals who may be on the verge of losing their legal capacity. Thus, the principles of therapeutic jurisprudence are particularly relevant to the capacity assessment context. The doctrine's discussion of the tension between individualism, autonomy and paternalism is especially pertinent.

---

[154]Winick BJ (1996c), p. 158.

[155]Winick BJ (1998), p. 919.

[156]McMahon M and Wexler D (2003), p. 3.

Admittedly, any hypotheses advanced through the lens of therapeutic jurisprudence needs to be tested by empirical research, which raises the empirical indeterminism dilemma, but this is not a problem which is unique to therapeutic jurisprudence. Further, this is part of the appeal of the doctrine—seeking new solutions to challenging issues which are only going to increase in magnitude, importance and frequency as society continues to age and issues of accurate, consistent and transparent capacity determinations continue to grow. Indeed, the application of therapeutic jurisprudence principles to the capacity assessment context and the promotion by therapeutic jurisprudence of interdisciplinary approaches only serves to highlight the practical impact of the law, rules, procedures and protagonists on society as a whole. Additionally, it also emphasises the importance of ensuring that an individual's interaction with the legal system, as well as legal and health actors, is as positive as possible when that individual's capacity is at risk.

References

Attorney General's Department of New South Wales (2008) Capacity Toolkit. http://www.justice. nsw.gov.au/diversityservices/Documents/capacity_toolkit0609.pdf. Accessed 1 Nov 2016

Australian Law Reform Commission (2014) Equality, Capacity and Disability in Commonwealth Laws, Summary Report 124

Carney T (1995) Judging the competence of older people: an alternative. Ageing Soc 15 (4):515–534

Champine PR (2003) Dealing with mental disability in trust & estate law practice: a sanist will? N Y Law School J Int Comp Law 22:177

Cockerill J, Collier B, Maxwell K (2005) Legal requirements and current practices. In: Collier B, Coyne C, Sullivan K (eds) Mental capacity, powers of attorney and advance health directives. Federation Press, Leichardt

Darzins P, Molloy DW, Strang D (eds) (2000) Who can decide? The six step capacity assessment process. Memory Australia Press, Adelaide

Ellis HS (2003) Dealing with mental disability in trust & estate law practice: "strengthen the things that remain:" the sanist will. N Y Law School J Int Comp Law 19:195

Finkelman D, Grisso T (1996) Therapeutic jurisprudence: from idea to application. In: Wexler DB, Winick BJ (eds) Law in a therapeutic key: developments in therapeutic jurisprudence. Carolina Academic Press, Durham

Freckelton I (2008) Therapeutic jurisprudence misunderstood and misrepresented: the price and risks of influence. Thomas Jefferson Law Rev 30:575–751

Freiberg A (2003) Therapeutic jurisprudence in Australia: paradigm shift or pragmatic incrementalism? In: McMahon M, Wexler D (eds) Therapeutic jurisprudence. Federation Press, Leichhardt

Fulero SM, Everington C (2004) Assessing the capacity of persons with mental retardation to waive Miranda rights: a jurisprudent therapy approach. Law Psychol Rev 28:53

Glover M (2012) A therapeutic jurisprudential framework of estate planning. Seattle Univ Law Rev 35:427

Hall MA (2002–2003) Law, medicine, and trust. Stanford Law Rev 55:463–527

Kapp MB (2003) The law and older persons is geriatric jurisprudence therapeutic? Carolina Academic Press, Durham

Magner E (1998) Therapeutic jurisprudence: its potential for Australia. Revista Juridica Universidad de Puerto Rica 67:121

McMahon M, Wexler D (2003) Therapeutic jurisprudence: developments and applications in Australia and New Zealand. In: McMahon M, Wexler D (eds) Therapeutic jurisprudence. Federation Press, Leichardt

Moye J, Marson DC (2007) Assessment of decision-making capacity on older adults: an emerging area of practice and research. J Gerontol B Psychol Sci Soc Sci 62(1):3–11

Moye J, Marson DC, Edelstein B (2013) Assessment of capacity in an aging society. Am Psychol 68(3):158–171

Parker M (2004) Judging capacity: paternalism and the risk-related standard. J Law Med 11 (4):482–491

Perlin ML (1992–1993) Pretexts and mental disability law: the case of competency. Miami Law Rev 47:625

Perlin ML (1996) The jurisprudence of the insanity defence. In: Wexler DB, Winick BJ (eds) Law in a therapeutic key. Carolina Academic Press, Durham

Perlin M (2000) "For the Misdemeanour Outlaw:" the impact of the ADA on the institutionalization of criminal defendants with mental disabilities. Alabama Law Rev 52:193

Perlin ML (2003) Dealing with mental disability in trust and estate law practice: "things have changed:" looking at non-institutional mental disability law through the sanism filter. N Y Law School J Int Comp Law 22:165

Schopp RF (1996) Therapeutic jurisprudence and conflicts among values in mental health law. In: Wexler DB, Winick BJ (eds) Law in a therapeutic key: developments in therapeutic jurisprudence. Carolina Academic Press, Durham

Schuck PH (1989) Why don't law professors do more empirical research. J Leg Educ 39:323

Slobogin C (1995) Therapeutic jurisprudence: five dilemmas to ponder. Psychol Public Policy Law 1(1):193–219

Small MA (1993) Legal psychology and therapeutic jurisprudence. St Louis Univ Law J 37:675

Tyler TR (1996) The psychological consequences of judicial procedures: implications for civil commitment hearings. In: Wexler DB, Winick BJ (eds) Law in a therapeutic key: developments in therapeutic jurisprudence. Carolina Academic Press, Durham

Wexler DB (1995) Reflections on the scope of therapeutic jurisprudence. Psychol Public Policy Law 1(1):220–236

Winick BJ (1991a) Competency to consent to treatment: the distinction between assent and objection. Houston Law Rev 28:15–61

Winick BJ (1996–1997) Advance directive instruments for those with mental illness' (1996–1997). Univ Miami Law Rev 51:57–94

Winick BJ (1996a) The side effects of incompetency labeling and the implications for mental health law. In: Wexler DB, Winick BJ (eds) Law in a therapeutic key: developments in therapeutic jurisprudence. Carolina Academic Press, Durham

Winick BJ (1996b) The jurisprudence of therapeutic jurisprudence. In: Wexler DB, Winick BJ (eds) Law in a therapeutic key: developments in therapeutic jurisprudence. Carolina Academic Press, Durham

Winick BJ (1996c) The MacArthur treatment competence study: legal and therapeutic implications. Psychol Public Policy Law 2(1): 137-166

Winick BJ (1997) The jurisprudence of therapeutic jurisprudence. Psychol Public Policy Law 3 (1):184–185

Winick BJ (1998) Client denial and resistance in the advance directive context reflections on how attorneys can identify and deal with a psycholegal soft spot. Psychol Public Policy Law 4 (3):901–923

Zimring FE (1983) Where do the new scholars learn new scholarship? J Leg Educ 33:453

Chapter 3
Legal Capacity

1 Introduction

The fact that no satisfactory assessment paradigm exists for individuals whose capacity is in doubt is concerning, especially when the outcome is the potential removal of individual autonomy. It is also perhaps somewhat surprising given that there is significant research on capacity assessment. However, this research has tended to focus on capacity to consent to or refuse medical treatment and the ability to participate in medical research rather than the assessment of capacity to execute a will or enduring documents. There is actually a dearth of research focussing on the assessment of testamentary and decision-making capacity, especially financial capacity. Given the challenges discussed in chapter one, the importance of an accurate and dependable approach to legal capacity assessment cannot be overemphasised.

This chapter will concentrate on capacity more generally within the overarching testamentary and decision-making context. Discussion will focus on the nature of capacity, including the types and varying standards, as well as the assessment of capacity. The principles underlying capacity assessment, particularly the concepts of autonomy, protection, beneficence and rationality, will then be considered together with the ethical concerns raised by the assessment process. Some of the main models of capacity assessment, including whether it is possible to attain the hallowed 'gold standard', will be explored. What will become evident is that the principles of therapeutic jurisprudence, principally the dualistic nature of autonomy and protection, are inherently interwoven into this discussion of capacity, thus cementing the importance of considering therapeutic jurisprudence as a new lens through which to examine the effectiveness of capacity assessment paradigms. The conduct, impact and repercussions of performing capacity assessments also highlights the importance of fortifying the increasingly interdependent relationship between the legal and health professionals involved in the actual determinations.

© Springer International Publishing AG 2017
K. Purser, *Capacity Assessment and the Law*, DOI 10.1007/978-3-319-54347-5_3

2   The Nature of Legal Capacity

Capacity is a highly variable construct. The lack of uniformity in the definitional requirements establishing legal capacity, or incapacity, has resulted in numerous and varied classifications of 'capacity' dependent upon the type of, as well as the jurisdiction in which, an individual's capacity is being assessed.[1] Generally, legal capacity refers to the ability of an individual to perform a particular task or make a specific, legally recognised decision. The level of legal capacity required depends upon the task at hand as capacity is jurisdiction, time and decision specific.[2] The particular decisions can range from simple to complex. The standard of capacity required is therefore determined by both the decision in question as well as the context in which that decision is to be made.[3] For instance, the capacity needed to marry differs from that necessary to make a will. Likewise, a person who is judged legally competent to make a decision about their medical treatment may not be deemed competent to make a financial decision.[4]

Historically there has been discussion about whether capacity is global, domain specific or decision specific.[5] Global competency was prevalent when capacity assessment first came to the fore as an issue which needed to be addressed. It is the premise that an individual is either universally competent or incompetent. That is, the particular individual could either make all or no decisions.[6] This is still a valid paradigm in the case of obvious incapacity cases such as comas although it clearly fails to adequately address any situation which does not fall into either extreme.[7] Global capacity was replaced by domain capacity—where individuals may be capable to make some decisions but incapable to make others depending upon the general domain in which the decision falls, for example, financial capacity or the capacity to consent to or refuse treatment.[8] However, as stated, it is now recognised that capacity is best determined with regard to the specific decision to be made.[9]

As noted above, a person's legal capacity may be prejudiced by mentally disabling conditions such as cognitive impairment, psychiatric illnesses or the effects of medication. Issues such as the complexity and manner of delivery of certain information, as well as a person's education level can also impede

---

[1]Berg JW et al. (1995–1996), p. 349; O'Neill N and Peisah C (2011), p. 1.2. See also *Gibbons v Wright* (1954) 91 CLR 423, 438.
[2]Attorney General's Department of New South Wales (2008), p. 27; Setterlund D et al. (2002), p. 28.
[3]Darzins P et al. (2000), pp. 4–6; Sullivan K (2004), p. 132.
[4]Grisso T (2003), p. 9.
[5]Darzins P et al. (2000), pp. 4–5.
[6]Ibid 4.
[7]Ibid.
[8]Ibid.
[9]Moye J et al. (2007), p. 592. See also Fitten LJ and Waite MS (1990), p. 1720.

capacity.[10] Assessments may vary depending upon a number of factors including the nature of the person's disability and/or illness, the information and support available, the jurisdiction in which the assessment is conducted, and the method of assessment employed by the legal and health professionals involved in the determination.

Capacity can be assessed contemporaneously when the decision is being made or retrospectively after a decision has been made.[11] A general common law definition of 'capacity' can be found in *Gibbons v Wright*.[12] In *Gibbons* Dixon CJ, Kitto and Taylor JJ stated the general principle as, 'the mental capacity required by the law in respect of any instrument is relative to the particular transaction which is being effected by means of the instrument, and may be described as the capacity to understand the nature of that transaction when it is explained'.[13] A similar definition was given in *Hoff v Atherton*[14] by Peter Gibson LJ stating that mental capacity: 'is a general requirement of the law that for a juristic act to be valid the person performing it should have the mental capacity (with the assistance of such explanation as he may be given) to understand the effect of that particular act . . .'.[15] That is, the individual needs to understand the nature of the instrument given the particular circumstances once it has been explained. There is a two pronged test to capacity generally: first, considering the individual in question; and second, the nature and complexity of the task being performed after it has been explained.[16] This includes the additional stipulation that it is the capacity demonstrated after the decision, transaction and/or document has been described which takes into account the complexities of modern life, as well as the complicated and intricate mechanisms being employed in modern estate planning. As Frost, Lawson and Jacoby note, however, explaining is far more than mere telling.[17]

It has been theorised that there are five fundamental components of all legal competencies, being functional, causal, interactive, judgmental and dispositional.[18] Functional competency refers to an individual's ability to accomplish tasks and the knowledge necessary to undertake that endeavour. It is within this general parameter that the specific contextual competency should become apparent.[19] The causal component seeks to explain an individual's functional competence, or lack thereof,

---

[10]Dunn LB et al. (2006), pp. 1323–1324.

[11]O'Neill N and Peisah C (2011).

[12](1954) 91 CLR 423, 438.

[13]*Gibbons v Wright* (1954) 91 CLR 423, 438. Applied in, for example, *Re Beaney deceased* [1978] 2 All ER 595 and *In the estate of Park deceased* [1954] P 89.

[14][2005] WTLR 99.

[15]*Hoff v Atherton* [2005] WTLR 99, [33] citing *Re K (Enduring Power of Attorney)* [1988] Ch 310, 313.

[16]Frost M et al. (2015), p. 6; *Masterman-Lister v Brutton* [2003] WTLR 259 CA.

[17]Frost M et al. (2015), p. 7.

[18]Grisso T (2003), p. 23.

[19]Ibid 23–24.

in relation to the context specific competency.[20] The interactive element is used to question whether an individual's ability is enough given the demands of the situation.[21] Judgmental and dispositional components entail a conclusion being made that the individual lacks sufficient abilities required and that the law prescribes consequences as a result of this determination.[22] What those consequences will be will, however, depend upon the type of capacity found to be lacking.

2.1 Financial and Testamentary Capacity

Financial capacity is a multifaceted and extremely complex concept.[23] It is a medico-legal construct focusing on an individual's ability to independently manage his or her own estate and financial affairs in accordance with his or her own self-interest and morals.[24] This includes understanding, as well as executing, testamentary documents and enduring powers of attorney. Consequently, it is of great significance in the environment in which people are living longer but often with diminished cognition and mental acumen.[25] It is presumed that financial capacity draws upon a multitude of 'brain networks and cortical hubs, semantic knowledge, reasoning, and judgment'.[26] Loss of a person's ability to complete basic calculations, and the associated impact on managing money, is one of the earliest indicators that financial capacity is in issue, and also one of the most confronting challenges for an individual.[27] It is important to note that testamentary capacity and the capacity to make an enduring power of attorney document and/or an advance health directive do differ. Although testamentary capacity can be defined as a category of financial capacity, the ability required to make a will is generally less than that necessary to make an enduring power of attorney. This is because the concept of a will is often more familiar and less complex than that of an enduring power of attorney.[28] In *Szozda v Szozda*,[29] Barrett J differentiated between the legal competency necessary to make a will and that required for an enduring power of attorney, especially when the attorney was given wide powers. However, although a lower standard of capacity is generally required for testamentary capacity, the

[20]Ibid 29.
[21]Ibid 32–33.
[22]Ibid 36.
[23]Marson DC and Hebert KR (2008).
[24]Marson DC (2013), p. 382.
[25]Marson DC and Hebert KR (2008). See also Pinsker DM et al. (2010), p. 333; Webber LS et al. (2002), p. 250.
[26]Marson D (2016), p. 13.
[27]Marson DC (2013), p. 383; Lock SL (2016), p. 18.
[28]O'Neill N and Peisah C (2011), p. 4.
[29][2010] NSWSC 804.

assessment of an individual's ability to make a testamentary instrument will be affected by the complexity of both the document and the testator's assets.[30]

To be able to live independently a person must demonstrate that he or she is able to perform activities of daily living (ADLs), which can be 'household' (such as cooking or completing household chores) or 'basic' (for instance getting dressed, showering), as well as instrumental activities of daily living (IADL) in a safe manner.[31] Financial capacity is generally thought to be an advanced or instrumental activity of daily living requiring higher cognitive functioning.[32] As such, it can be differentiated from household and basic ADLs.[33] It covers a wide range of complex abilities ranging from counting coins to making complicated investment decisions. As such, it can vary greatly depending not only on the decision to be made but also on the education, socio-economic position and experience of the individual in managing financial matters.[34] Financial capacity is generally considered to be one of eight identified domains of capacity requiring high levels of cognition.[35] Consequently, it is very susceptible to 'neurological, psychiatric, and medical conditions that affect cognition (such as dementia, stroke, traumatic brain injury, and schizophrenia)'.[36] Dementia is one of the most common conditions which can lead to the assessment of financial capacity and, although a diagnosis does not automatically evidence legal incompetency it should be carefully considered when assessing financial capacity.[37]

Key elements of financial capacity, including knowledge (both declarative and procedural) and judgment, generally help to conceptualise its cognitive and functional parameters.[38] Declarative knowledge being the ability to describe financial concepts, procedural knowledge the ability to implement decisions such as by signing documents, and judgment the capability to make sound financial choices.[39] Some commentators have suggested that these elements do not take into account the effect that social, cultural and familial factors can have on financial capacity, all of which can be important influences in whether an individual does or does not have capacity.[40] However, it should be clear that these factors, along with the person's longstanding values, must be taken into consideration. Similarly, regard should also be had for the fact that financial capacity has both a performance (that is, the individual should be able to perform the tasks necessary to live independently) and

---

[30]*Szozda v Szozda* [2010] NSWSC 804 [31]–[32] (Barrett J).

[31]Marson DC (2013), p. 383; Falk E and Hoffman N (2014), p. 860.

[32]Marson DC (2013), p. 383.

[33]Marson D and Zebley L (2001), pp. 31–32.

[34]Marson DC (2013), p. 384.

[35]The domains are also discussed in Pinsker DM et al. (2010), p. 333.

[36]Marson DC and Hebert KR (2008).

[37]Pinsker DM et al. (2010), pp. 334–335.

[38]Earnst KS et al. (2001), pp. 110–111; Pinsker DM et al. (2010), p. 333.

[39]Ibid.

[40]Pinsker DM et al. (2010), p. 333, 336, 338.

a judgment (making decisions to promote one's own financial self-interest) aspect to it.[41]

What is apparent is that both legal and health professionals lack the necessary awareness of the elements required to satisfactorily assess financial capacity.[42] This is exacerbated by the fact that there has been little consideration given to the intersection of satisfying the legal requirements with relevant clinical testing standards.[43] As can be seen, the medico-legal literature, including empirical studies, on financial capacity is scant.[44] Moye and Marson, writing in the context of the United States of America, have identified the 'few working conceptual models of financial competency'.[45] Financial capacity has only recently begun to receive the attention it deserves given its significance to individual functioning and autonomy. There is a desperate need for continued research including the development of appropriate clinical assessment instruments within the relevant legal framework.[46] In addition to this, research is also needed to determine the relationship between financial capacity and conditions such as depression or psychosis.[47] There is little direction about how to determine legal financial capacity other than ensuring that the donor understands the significance and extent of the power being given.[48] Such lack of guidance only complicates an area that already sees the intersection of complex legal, medical, psychological and ethical issues.

2.2   Capacity to Make Lifestyle/Health Decisions

There is no explicit authority to state that the capacity necessary to make advance health directives differs from that required for an enduring power of attorney. However, if the capacity required for an enduring power of attorney is greater than that for a will, arguably, it is possible that it is also greater than that required to make an advance health directive.[49] There are some diagnostic tools which have been developed in the United States of America which focus on the capacity to make an advance health directive. These include the Hopkins competency assessment test which does not assess potential clinical situations,[50] and criteria designed by Fazel, Hope and Jacoby which assesses capacity in a way that is analogous to

---

[41]Marson DC (2013), p. 384.
[42]Cockerill J et al. (2005), p. 49.
[43]See also Collier B et al. (2005a, b).
[44]Moye J and Marson DC (2007), p. 7; Marson DC et al. (2000a).
[45]Moye J and Marson DC (2007), p. 7.
[46]Ibid 8.
[47]Pinsker DM et al. (2010), p. 336.
[48]In re K, In re F [1988] 1 Ch 310, 316.
[49]Smith F (2010), p. 5.
[50]Fazel S et al. (1999), p. 494.

determining testamentary capacity.[51] The focus in both cases is on the individual's understanding of the nature and effect of the advance health directive.[52] Fazel, Hope and Jacoby argue that their model differs from the others because it does enable possible future situations to be taken into account. They argue that it is insufficient for an adult to merely understand what the document is.[53] Thus, similarly to financial capacity, there is a great need for more work to be done in determining cognitive standards to make health and lifestyle decisions within an appropriate overarching legal framework.

3 Assessing Capacity

The assessment of capacity is a dichotomous (yes/no) decision made initially by a legal and/or health professional, but ultimately by the court, regarding whether an individual can perform the specific task or make the specific decision in question.[54] Sometimes, however, legal professionals in particular fail to understand that it is the court who is the final arbiter.[55] This only serves to highlight one of the problems with defining the term 'legal capacity' and attempting to pinpoint the moment that it is lost, which is that it is essentially an artificial construct which is utilitarian in nature.[56] As Lord Cranworth LC stated in *Boyse v Rossborough*, 'between such an extreme [of 'a raving mad man'] and that of a man of perfectly sound and vigorous understanding, there is every shade of intellect, every degree of mental capacity. There is no possibility of mistaking midnight for noon; but at what precise moment twilight becomes darkness is hard to determine'.[57] Consequently, any assessment process is arguably a subjective tool of classification determined, in a large part, by the skills and experience of the assessor(s). The subjectivity of the assessment process inevitably raises the issue of what constitutes a 'good' or 'bad' decision, and who has the ability to sit in judgment about the quality of another's evaluation. This is especially important when considering the principles of autonomy and liberty.[58] The use of the word 'liberty' may appear sensationalist in this context but consider that legal capacity assessment is actually an invasive process whereby a third person, potentially relying on biased information received from individuals with an agenda, can reach a verdict that another individual is no longer capable of

---

[51]Ibid.

[52]Ibid.

[53]Ibid 496.

[54]Moye J and Marson DC (2007), p. 3.

[55]*Goddard Elliott (a firm) v Fritsch* [2012] VSC 87 (16 March 2012) [562]; Queensland Law Society, Allens Linklaters and Queensland Advocacy Incorporated (2014).

[56]Darzins P et al. (2000), p. 111.

[57](1857) 10 ER 1192, 1210.

[58]Darzins P et al. (2000), p. 113.

making his or her own decision. It can therefore deprive an individual of his or her freedom as he or she is potentially emotionally, intellectually, physically as well as environmentally beholden to another to make decisions on his or her behalf if determined to be legally incompetent.

What is clear is that both professions are increasingly recognising the growing importance and necessity of satisfactory capacity assessments. This includes the need to employ sound assessment methodologies, not only for the protection of the individual, but also for the protection of the professional conducting the assessment as concerns around professional responsibility and liability become more apparent. As Moye and Marson comment, 'assessment, previously a relatively peripheral aspect of clinical or legal practice, has over the past 20 years become a generic, everyday issue . . . [it] is a complex, cross-disciplinary endeavour involving knowledge of medical syndromes, clinical assessment, ethics, and the law . . .'.[59]

The question of whether a person is legally competent is indubitably a decision for a court to ultimately make. However, how many cases actually make it that far? As Justice Kirby has stated, 'there are thousands of decisions, made every day, which are never scrutinised by a lawyer, let alone a court . . .'.[60] The majority of determinations are, in fact, probably being made external to a courtroom.[61] This is because even before coming into contact with the law and associated 'actors', individuals, as well as family members and/or carers, may be making determinations about capacity, with an individual's lack of capacity sometimes being supported, hidden by, or taken advantage of in the familial setting. Thus, at first instance, 'assessments' are conducted within the familial unit with the 'assessors' having little to no training or knowledge of the legal (and medical) requirements. Even determining that there is a problem is a decision often being made by family members or carers. Whilst ideally family members would be acting in the best interests of the person whose capacity is in question, there is no doubting that individual agendas can, and do, exist—either innocent or more malevolent. Familial involvement, although generally positive, can also expose vulnerable individuals to abuse—abuse which will likely remain hidden, especially if the individual in question is relatively isolated.

The next 'level' is seeking the involvement of, or assessment by, legal and/or health professionals. However, here the skill level varies greatly with assessments being subject to the divergent training and knowledge of the respective assessor(s). Geographical impediments can also feature. For example, what of ageing rural communities who lack access to health and legal services and, if accessible, what is the quality of those services?[62] Whether an assessment is 'satisfactory' or not can also be subject to a number of other variables including whether the assessment is contemporaneous or retrospective, access to the individual and information about

---

[59]Moye J and Marson DC (2007), p. 4.

[60]Kirby M (2003).

[61]Moye J and Marson DC (2007), p. 3.

[62]See, for example, in the Scottish context: Farmer J et al. (2010).

the decision to be made as well as the assessment process, whether the assessor is an 'expert' or has a history of involvement with the individual, and whether, as well as who, is to pay for the assessment. The last question is a significant practical problem when assessments need to be paid for privately.

Court determinations do not guarantee a satisfactory assessment either however. Collier, Coyne and Sullivan note that 'there has been minimal consideration ... of legal requirements, in conjunction with meeting medical and psychological testing standards ... with courts either unprepared or unwilling to enter into the debate as to the adequacy of methods ...'.[63] Although this statement was made in 2005, it is still applicable. This fact alone is telling. Courts continue to be reluctant to elucidate clear assessment methodologies, instead making mercurial determinations on the unsystematic evidence presented before them. Courts are obviously restricted to making decisions about the facts of the matters being heard based on the evidence led. However, this does not prevent judicial comment being made which would assist in ensuring that the evidence is the best evidence available through a discussion of the ideal paradigm in which to both obtain, and present, evidence in court proceedings pertaining to capacity assessments. This obviously gives rise to concerns about the quality of the evidence currently being presented with questions being asked about the decision-making process employed by courts for instance, judicial reliance on legal and medical evidence with the former apparently being favoured over the latter. The issue of the nature and quality of evidence being obtained is a theme underpinning this entire area, however, before exploring this issue in more detail, some of the other issues relevant to any discussion about the best evidence available will first be examined.

3.1 The Presumption of Capacity

A general principle applicable across all jurisdictions, and a significant presumption central to the tenets of modern law, is the presumption of capacity.[64] That is, every adult over the age of 18 years is presumed to be legally capable until he or she has been found otherwise. This is a rebuttable presumption with the onus of proving incompetence falling on those claiming that an individual is no longer able to manage his or her own affairs to the relevant standard.[65] For example, a testator is presumed to have capacity and the burden falls to those alleging otherwise to prove the allegations. Different jurisdictions currently adopt divergent approaches to the question of whether, and how, the presumption should be legislatively enshrined. For example, in Australia although the principle applies in New South

---

[63]Collier B et al. (2005a, b), v.

[64]*Re Caldwell* [1999] QSC 182, 12 (Mackenzie J); Law Reform Committee, Parliament of Victoria (2010), pp. 109–110.

[65]Frost M et al. (2015), p. 120.

Wales, it is not expressly contained in legislation as is the case in Queensland.[66]
The presumption of capacity should be the commencement point for any capacity
assessment, although the primacy of the presumption should not alleviate govern-
mental responsibilities for individuals who lack capacity.[67] In determining if the
presumption has been rebutted, the courts are likely to place emphasis on the
evidence of independent third parties such as legal and/or health professionals, as
well as friends and/or family members who do not stand to gain from rebutting the
presumption.[68] This again demonstrates the need for a standardised methodology to
determine if capacity has been lost because it can underpin the provision of the best
evidence to a court with regard to rebutting the presumption.

3.2 Cognitive and Functional Capacity

Different decisions require different competencies which may be cognitive, functional or a combination of cognitive and functional.[69] Cognitive function is necessary for an individual to make competent decisions and there can be a disparity
between being cognitively capable and having capacity.[70] For instance, sufferers of
Alzheimer's disease who may be cognitively incapable may be capable of making
less complicated decisions, depending upon the context of the decision and the legal
competency required to make that decision.[71] The mixture of the cognitive and
functional capacity required will depend upon the specific decision to be made.[72]
For example, personal care decisions involve a relatively equal amount of cognitive
and functional competency whereas an advance care directive is almost exclusively
a cognitive exercise. The making of a will or enduring power of attorney, which
involves financial decision-making, predominantly requires cognitive ability but it
can also require functional tasks such as the signing of cheques.[73] The assessment
of capacity with respect to financial decisions can be confusing because, although
prima facie similar to personal and health care decisions which involve cognitive
and functional abilities, the functional tasks involved with financial decision-
making are more cognitive in nature.[74] Thus, functional tests, such as the Everyday

---

[66]*Powers of Attorney Act 1998* (Qld) schedule 1, part 1(1); *Guardianship and Administration Act 2000* (Qld) schedule 1, part 1(1). See also Standing Committee on Social Issues, Parliament of New South Wales (2010), p. 41.

[67]Standing Committee on Social Issues, Parliament of New South Wales (2010), xx, 3, 44.

[68]Cockerill J et al. (2005), p. 29.

[69]Ibid 8.

[70]Kerridge I et al. (2013), p. 371.

[71]Ibid 371–372.

[72]Darzins P et al. (2000), pp. 8–9.

[73]Ibid 72–73.

[74]Ibid 73.

Problem Test and the Independent Living Scales which test the ability of an individual to function with respect to everyday living tasks, are often inadequate to assess financial decision-making capacity.[75] These are issues which legal decision-makers need to be aware of when evaluating the evidence to determine if there has been a loss of capacity.

3.3 Decisional and Executional Capacity

There is discussion around drawing a distinction between decisional and executional capacity. Decisional capacity is fundamentally seen as the ability to make a decision while executional capacity is the ability to give effect to that decision.[76] Although the wording can vary, there are four abilities which are generally accepted as being necessary for a person to have decisional capacity. These are the ability to understand the situation, evaluate the consequences of making the decision, reason through the risks and benefits of the decision, and communicate the decision made.[77] A slightly different, but fundamentally similar, formulation can be found in literature from the United Kingdom, that decision-making comprises several abilities including, 'understanding relevant information; using the information to reach a decision, which may involve (1) appreciating its personal significance and (2) reasoning with it; and communicating a choice'.[78] Common elements underpinning decisional capacity therefore incorporate understanding, evaluating, reasoning and communication. The ability to reach a conclusion which is based on an individual's own experiences and morals has also been termed 'rational manipulation' wherein a 'reasonable process' is differentiated from a 'reasonable conclusion'.[79] That is, if the process was a reasoned one then the individual has the right to make a decision which may seem eccentric to others.

Within the context of mental health law in the United States of America, Grisso has also identified four similar elements: first, individuals have the right to make their own decisions; second, some individuals may not have the ability to make their own decisions which may jeopardise either themselves or other individuals; third, legal competence provides a vehicle to identify legal *in*competency; and finally, where legal incompetence is determined, it justifies third party intervention to ensure the welfare and safety of the individual in question.[80] Despite the

---

[75]Sullivan K (2004), p. 136; Darzins P et al. (2000), p. 9.

[76]Falk E and Hoffman N (2014).

[77]O'Neill N and Peisah C (2011), p. 955; Berg JW et al. (1995–1996), p. 351; Karlawish JHT et al. (2005), p. 1514. See also Cairns R et al. (2005), p. 373; MacArthur Research Network on Mental Health and the Law (2004); Gurrera RJ et al. (2006), p. 1367; Kitamura T and Takahashi N (2007), p. 579; Sturman ED (2005), p. 955; Lai JM and Karlawish J (2007), p. 105.

[78]Suto WMI et al. (2005), p. 200.

[79]Arias JJ (2013), p. 144.

[80]Grisso T (2003), p. 2.

American mental health law contextualisation, these abilities are also applicable within the capacity assessment environment. The issue is whether legal and health professionals know how to identify and correctly assess the relevant legal capacity. Further, can each profession communicate effectively with both the other profession, as well as the individual whose capacity is being assessed? This again echoes therapeutic jurisprudence concerns around building a positive interaction between the individual, the legal system, and the 'legal' actors including health professionals. The absence of a standard method for legal testamentary and decision-making capacity assessment, particularly with respect to financial capacity, hinders both the legal and health professions.[81] This is somewhat extraordinary given that capacity, and especially financial capacity, is fundamental for individuals to be able to function independently in their communities.[82]

3.4   The Functional, Status and Outcome Approaches

The functional approach, the status approach and the outcome approach are three models to determine capacity.[83] Under the status approach whether an individual is capable at law is determined by her or his status, for example, the individual's age (a minor generally not having legal capacity), or any recognised disability or condition. It is a person's 'status' which indicates her or his capacity, or lack thereof. This could be extended to include particular diseases or medical conditions such as advanced dementia.[84] It is more an all or nothing premise that does not take into account the particular decision or time the decision is made as the functional approach does. Consequently, the status approach can be needlessly restrictive, running contrary to therapeutic jurisprudence principles.[85]

Some jurisdictions, for example New South Wales in Australia and the United Kingdom through the *Mental Capacity Act*,[86] adopt an amalgamation of the status and functional tests.[87] This hybrid approach usually first determines if a condition or disability exists (the diagnostic or status approach) before assessing the individual's ability to make a specific decision at a particular point in time (the functional approach). The use of the status approach as a diagnostic threshold is intended to

---

[81]Marson DC et al. (2006), p. 81.

[82]Ibid.

[83]Queensland Law Reform Commission (2008), p. 106; Queensland Law Reform Commission (2010), p. 243.

[84]Queensland Law Reform Commission (2008), p. 106; Queensland Law Reform Commission (2010), p. 266.

[85]Queensland Law Reform Commission (2010), pp. 266–267.

[86]2005. The Act is recently been the subject of review, for example: House of Lords Select Committee on the Mental Capacity Act 2005 (2014); HM Government (2014); Tingle J (2014), p. 864.

[87]Queensland Law Reform Commission (2008), p. 110; Boyle G (2011), p. 1.

ensure that before an individual's legal capacity can be questioned there needs to be a reason validating such an enquiry.[88] However, a relatively recent New South Wales inquiry recommended that the status approach should be expressly rejected, noting that an individual should not be considered incapable merely because of a condition or disability.[89] The status approach also gives rise to concerns about incompetency labelling and the role it can have as a self-fulfilling prophecy, hazards identified by therapeutic jurisprudence.

The functional approach examines an individual's ability to make a decision within a given context. Applying the functional approach, an individual has impaired legal capacity if he or she cannot understand the nature and effect of a decision at the time the decision is made.[90] This approach views capacity as a continuum rather than an endpoint. Therefore, capacity is neither present nor absent but is instead dependent upon the decision that is to be made, at the specific time it is to be made, in the particular context in which it is to be made.[91] The functional approach is supported by research conducted into capacity to make financial decisions by people with mild intellectual disabilities in the United Kingdom where it 'has received the most informed empirical, clinical and legal support'.[92] There is a general movement towards the functional approach and jurisdictions in which there has been relatively recent reform for example, Queensland, have primarily adopted a statutory test of decision-making capacity based on the functional approach.[93]

The functional approach considers the reasoning process employed, particularly 'the abilities to understand, retain and evaluate the information relevant to the decision (including its likely consequences)', as well as the individual's ability to evaluate information to make the decision.[94] The functional approach is consistent with the principles enunciated in article 12 of the Convention on the Rights of People with Disabilities and respects that capacity is decision specific.[95] Unlike the status model, the functional approach is not dependent upon the existence of a particular disability or condition. Consequently, it avoids the negative effects that labelling individuals by reference to a disease or condition can cause and which therapeutic jurisprudence warns against. These effects can manifest themselves as paternalism, stigmatisation, infringement upon individual autonomy in favour of

---

[88]Queensland Law Reform Commission (2010), p. 267.

[89]Recommendation 1 in the Standing Committee on Social Issues, Parliament of New South Wales (2010), p. xx.

[90]Queensland Law Reform Commission (2008), p. 106; Queensland Law Reform Commission (2010), p. 243.

[91]Queensland Law Reform Commission (2008), p. 265.

[92]See also Suto WMI et al. (2005), p. 200.

[93]Queensland Law Reform Commission (2010), pp. xv, 243, 266; Queensland Law Reform Commission (2008), pp. 107, 306.

[94]Queensland Law Reform Commission (2010), p. 265.

[95]*United Nations Convention on the Rights of Persons with Disabilities*, opened for signature 30 March 2007, (entered into force 3 May 2008).

protection and facilitating the self-fulfilling prophecy.[96] However, appropriate safeguards for the assessment of legal capacity nevertheless need to be established. This is because if taken literally the functional approach would require that capacity should be assessed for every decision, an absurdity if legal capacity has been irretrievably lost.[97]

The third approach, the outcome approach, considers the decision from an objective standard and whether the decision is in the individual's best interests.[98] A person will be legally incompetent when his or her decision does not reflect the decision that other individuals think is correct.[99] The outcome approach basically assesses capacity according to the morals and values of the assessor(s).[100] Thus, if an individual's decision is deemed capricious or improvident he or she can be deemed to lack legal competency. This approach is widely rejected in modern capacity assessment. In some jurisdictions it has even been recommended that the ability of people to make capricious decisions without such decisions being determinative of a lack of capacity should be enshrined in legislation.[101]

3.5 A Fixed or Sliding Threshold

Capacity is able to be assessed by applying either a fixed or sliding scale. Problematic with a fixed level of legal competency is ensuring that it is not so high as to assess competent people as incompetent but also not so low as to be meaningless.[102] However, a fixed scale would ensure a measure of consistency as well as giving health practitioners a guide from which to work. Alternatively, a sliding scale would address the issue of setting too rigorous a standard. Further, if the elements are consistently applied this would still enable some measure of uniformity in application.

What is apparent is that there are (at least) three components that need to be taken into consideration. First, the elements of the type and standard for assessing the particular legal capacity need to be identified; second, the application of the standards to the requisite capacity (cognitive and/or functional) has to be determined including which approach is to be adopted (for example, the functional approach) and identifying what the trigger was for assessing the individual's

---

[96]Queensland Law Reform Commission (2008), p. 265.

[97]Queensland Law Reform Commission (2010), p. 266.

[98]Queensland Law Reform Commission (2008), p. 106; Queensland Law Reform Commission (2010), p. 243.

[99]Ibid.

[100]Queensland Law Reform Commission (2010), p. 268.

[101]See, for example, the Standing Committee on Social Issues, Parliament of New South Wales (2010). This was also supported by Law Reform Committee, Parliament of Victoria (2010), p. 117.

[102]Berg JW et al. (1995–1996), p. 388. See also Gunn MJ et al. (1999), p. 278.

capacity to make a specific decision; and finally, what information and/or behaviour (abilities) the standards are to be applied to should be identified.[103] Ideally, any set of criteria should acknowledge the decision and time specific nature of capacity, focusing on the primacy of the presumption of capacity, thus avoiding automatically associating capacity with a disability or condition. The four abilities should be recognised.[104] Ideally, there should also be more than one assessment unless there is an emergency, which can incorporate elements of education for the individual involved to heighten his or her chances of a positive assessment.[105] The environment in which the assessment is to take place is likewise a key concern. Underpinning all of this is one very important factor which has little to do with the actual assessment and that is the question of cost—a major impediment to the satisfactory assessment of legal capacity. Consideration will similarly need to be given to the intersection of the legal standards with medical notions of clinical capacity, especially if a health professional either is, or should be, involved in the assessment process. This intersection itself will demand that thought be given to the medico-legal relationship, especially taking into account the historic problems of miscommunication and misunderstanding that can exist between legal and health professionals when assessing capacity.

3.6   The Legal and Medical Intersection

The issue of the medico-legal relationship is at the core of ensuring that satisfactory assessments occur. Questions arise not just about the nature of the evidence given in capacity determinations, but also over who is best placed to provide it. Questions such as, what should occur in the event of conflicting legal and medical evidence? These types of concerns, as was seen in chapter one, can serve to heighten the tension existing between the professions so it is very important that clear communication exists around the answers that are given. The legal system's concern to correctly determine legal capacity has undoubtedly led to increasing requests for members of the medical community to be involved with assessments, often being asked to provide an 'expert opinion'.[106] This raises the issue of what is an 'expert' in capacity assessment, especially as it is arguable that the methodology employed by 'experts' is inconsistent.[107] Further, should, for example, the evidence of 'experts' such as geriatricians, psychologists or neuropsychologists be favoured

---

[103]Berg JW et al. (1995–1996), p. 388.

[104]O'Neill N and Peisah C (2011), p. 1.2; Berg JW et al. (1995–1996), p. 351; Karlawish JHT et al. (2005), p. 1514. See also The MacArthur Research Network on Mental Health and the Law (2004); Gurrera RJ et al. (2006), p. 1367.

[105]Appelbaum PS and Roth LH (1981), p. 1465.

[106]Parker M (2008), p. 25.

[107]Ibid 30.

over that of general medical practitioners? What qualifications constitute an 'expert' in capacity assessment?

It has been suggested that there should be two elements for an expert opinion, first, adequate qualifications and second, expertise in conducting legal capacity assessments.[108] Whilst useful, consideration must likewise be given to the reliability of those determinations given that there is no accepted assessment methodology. Further, there is a need for training as there is little opportunity for practitioners to conduct a comparison between assessment paradigms and their utility within a legal framework to assess a specific capacity.[109] Compounding this problem is the divergent overabundance of potential sources of guidelines developed by different industry, professional and government bodies, amongst others, any of which can be used to call into question the validity of any assessment undertaken in accordance with another assessment model. Attention needs to be focused on the development of clinical assessment tools and how these can be effectively utilised in the assessment of capacity within a legal framework. Absent clear guidelines, what are courts to base critical evaluations of the assessment methodology employed by those giving evidence against? These are all questions demanding further research, especially as it becomes increasingly necessary to ensure a satisfactory assessment process through the adoption of transparent and consistent assessment methodologies.

The nature of this discussion also gives rise to questions of responsibility. The health profession generally states that it is a legal question, a statement with which the legal profession agrees. Although, this agreement is with the rider that it may be necessary to consult with health professionals, again raising issues as to consistency and transparency of process, as well as clarity of communication.[110] Ideally, health professionals will be provided with instructions regarding what they are to assess, including to what standard, what information is expected from them, and in what format. However, no two legal professionals will provide identical instructions. Consequently, the methodology and standard applied for making capacity determinations is unpredictable, being dependent upon the individual legal and/or health professionals involved in the assessment.[111] This is only compounded by the terminological inconsistencies and the miscommunication that are inherent in this area.

What is generally agreed upon is that answers are needed, especially when society worldwide is facing ageing populations and increasing rates of mentally disabling conditions as a result of which both the demand for, and the frequency of, legal competency assessments will increase.[112] Although empirical evidence is limited, there was shown to be a 50% documented increase in the number of

---

[108]Kim SYH (2006), p. 94.

[109]Ibid 95.

[110]Carney T and Keyzer P (2007).

[111]Marson DC et al. (2000b), p. 912.

[112]Sullivan K (2004), pp. 132–133.

referrals for capacity assessments in North America for people aged 65 years and over between the first and second half of the 1980s.[113] This is clearly dated research. Nevertheless, it does demonstrate the rise in people seeking capacity assessments, and that was approximately three decades ago before the full impact of the ageing population and increasing mentally disabling conditions were beginning to be realised. Therefore, further research is required measuring the number of capacity assessments worldwide and establishing if these figures are indeed increasing and, if so, the underlying causes for the upsurge in assessments. Ascertaining the experiences and perceptions of those people who are having their capacity assessed, as well as the family and carers of people who have been through an assessment, is paramount to not only improving the assessment methodology, but to also ensuring that the interaction between the law and individuals is as therapeutic as possible in what is an incredibly challenging environment. This will help inform the dialogue about how to satisfactorily determine decision-making capacity taking into account the presenting mentally disabling condition(s), any comorbidities, the cognitive and functional abilities of the individual in question, the relevant legal standard of capacity, any overarching policy considerations, and the individual's values and culture. Similarly, such an approach also demonstrates respect for an individual's fundamental human rights.[114]

4 Principles of Capacity Assessment

Inherent in any discussion about the assessment of capacity are the general principles applying to the assessment paradigm, as well as recognition for the human rights of those who are being assessed. In fact, both meeting and defending the needs of people with impaired capacity is a human rights issue as the notions of autonomy, inherent worth, and dignity of each and every individual form the very heart of the principles of international human rights.[115] As capacity issues are undeniably a matter of ever increasing international importance, it is imperative that individuals with impaired capacity, as well as their families and carers, should be able to access inexpensive, reliable and well-informed services, including the actual capacity assessment process itself.[116] This currently is not happening. Given the ad hoc implementation of capacity determinations which are dependent on assessor skill and experience, individuals are not guaranteed a consistent, transparent or accurate assessment. This will impact their ability to function independently in society, and potentially how they, as well as others, perceive themselves. The idea that someone can no longer make their own legally recognised decisions may

---

[113]Ibid 134.

[114]Sullivan K (2004), p. 134; Marson DC and Moye J (2007), p. 19.

[115]Kirby M (2003), pp. 1–2.

[116]Carney T and Keyzer P (2007), pp. 255–256.

then have a cumulative effect meaning that a lack of autonomy to make one decision then flows onto the ability, or perceived lack of, to make other decisions, thus creating the self-fulfilling prophecy recognised in therapeutic jurisprudence.

General principles do exist which are intended to help support and protect capacity and decision-making autonomy as a basic human right. They are generally framed around notions of dignity, equality, autonomy, inclusion, participation and accountability.[117] More specifically, they include first, the least restrictive alternative, which postulates that any intervention in an individual's life should be as minimal as possible.[118] Second, the normalisation principle, which promotes the ideal that people with a disability should, as far as practicable, be treated like 'ordinary' individuals.[119] That is, their right to, for example, medical treatment, education and employment should be the same as for individuals not living with a disability.[120] Third is the promotion of self-management, which encourages an incompetent individual to make their own decisions, as far as possible, and promotes self-reliance and maximum participation in the evaluation process.[121] One other fundamental principle is the importance of respect for individual autonomy. Other relevant principles include ensuring that procedural fairness in any assessment process is observed, as well as avoiding conflicts of interest both in the evaluation process and in the management of someone else's personal and, especially, financial affairs.[122] As was foreshadowed in the previous chapter exploring therapeutic jurisprudence, the tenets of the doctrine already run through the existing general principles thus reaffirming the jurisprudence's viability as an innovative lens through which to view capacity assessments.

However, it is arguable that although these general principles are an important commencement point, they are not adequately utilised when assessing testamentary and decision-making capacity. For example, one concern is that the principles have not been consistently adopted within different jurisdictions, thus calling into question their effectiveness as general principles when they are not 'generally' adopted.[123] Further, where the principles have been adopted, their application is not uniform throughout each jurisdiction, both within and between countries, which can create confusion about the role and, ultimately, the effectiveness of the principles.[124] Despite the difficulties in adoption and application, general principles nevertheless provide invaluable guidance in the development and implementation

---

[117]Australian Law Reform Commission (2013), p. 7; Australian Law Reform Commission (2014), pp. 12–14.
[118]Creyke R (1995), p. xxxi.
[119]Ibid xxxii.
[120]Ibid.
[121]Ibid xxxii. See also Howard M and Dare K (2007), p. 4.
[122]Creyke R (1995), pp. 103–104.
[123]Howard M (2006), p. 167.
[124]Creyke R (1995), p. 39.

of a satisfactory testamentary and decision-making assessment process and should
be uniformly adopted.

4.1 Autonomy, Protection and Beneficence

The dualistic nature of autonomy and protection was explored in chapter two through
a therapeutic jurisprudence lens, including whether it is possible to successfully
balance the two concepts.[125] The legal concept of protection is reflected in the medical
notion of beneficence. Beneficence is the belief that medical professionals should act
in the patient's best interests while attempting to facilitate the individual's participation in the decision-making process where possible.[126] Autonomy is not just a key
legal concept but is also a significant component of contemporary bioethics.[127] In
order to be 'truly autonomous', the choice made must be done so voluntarily and by
someone capable of making the decision. Consequently, accurate assessments of
decision-making ability are fundamental to ensuring not only the protection of
individual rights, but in also guarding against potential undue influence and abuse of
vulnerable people.[128] Given the lack of a 'gold standard' for capacity assessment
processes, autonomy can be useful as a marker for determining capacity because it is
synonymous with free will. Capacity should therefore be assessed with consideration
for a holistic approach to an individual's values, emotions, requirements and ideals
rather than focussing solely on what they specifically want at the particular point in
time.[129] Consequently, both legal and medical evaluations of capacity are increasingly
complex and crucial to promoting and preserving individual autonomy.[130]

4.2 Rationality

Rationality is difficult to define and includes individuals, their actions and
beliefs.[131] It is context and person specific, and decisions need only be rational in
the given circumstances with respect to the belief system of the particular individual.[132] However, rationality also takes into consideration societal norms, whether

---

[125]On this point, see further: Appelbaum PS (2007), p. 1834; Buchanan A (2004), p. 416; Moye J
and Marson DC (2007), p. 3.
[126]O'Neill N and Peisah C (2011), p. 1.1.
[127]Kapp MB (2007), p. 12.
[128]Ibid 12.
[129]Kitamura T and Takahashi N (2007), p. 579.
[130]Moye J et al., (2007), p. 592. See also Lai JM and Karlawish J (2007), p. 101.
[131]See also Kerridge I et al. (2013), p. 372.
[132]Ibid.

the decision is in the person's best interests and whether the individual's beliefs are lucid.[133] Rationality can be viewed as containing three categories: substantive, formal and procedural. Substantive decisions are realistic.[134] Formal rationality is conferred by the decision reflecting the morals and values of the individual.[135] Procedural rationality occurs when a decision is based upon a careful and considered reasoning process.[136] The label of rationality poses some unavoidable problems. For instance, removing an individual's decision-making ability, and therefore his or her autonomy, may not always be in his or her best interests.[137] Further, an individual's beliefs and morals will inevitably influence their opinion about someone else's decision, especially if those beliefs and morals conflict or diverge.[138] Who is to say that they are right and someone else is wrong with the decision that they have made? This is especially the case when what is rational to one person may appear irrational to someone else.

Decisions are rarely made based solely upon objective decision-making as a result of a critical analysis of all the relevant facts. There is an inherent element of instinct and morality which responds to the complexities of the modern world when making a decision.[139] Often individuals will make decisions based upon what they 'feel' to be right depending upon their own experiences, knowledge, fears and hopes. As such, there is no definitive definition for what is 'rational' and one is unlikely to be developed given the inherent problems facing any attempted characterisation.

4.3   Ethical Considerations

There are obvious significant ethical considerations concerning both the declaration of an individual as incapable and the process through which that declaration is made.[140] Further, ethical obligations also arise in the context of the legal professional-client relationship which is fiduciary in nature. Surprisingly, bioethicists have given little attention to ethical issues arising in capacity assessments, but especially financial capacity and the effects that it can have not only on the individual in question, but also on his or her family, caregivers and health professionals.[141] Marson notes that this is particularly concerning as 'financial capacity

---

[133]Ibid 372–373.
[134]Ibid.
[135]Ibid.
[136]Ibid.
[137]Darzins P et al. (2000).
[138]See also Kerridge I et al. (2013), pp. 372–373.
[139]Ibid.
[140]Marson DC et al. (2009), p. 807.
[141]Marson DC (2013), p. 383.

is critical to, and possibly the single best litmus for, a person's ability to function independently in the community'.[142]

Ethics officers are available to legal professionals and biomedical ethics committees exist for health professionals. The interesting point that Marson and Moye raise is whether a similar body could exist within the community.[143] They note the Quebecois example wherein a guardianship tribunal can appoint a plenary guardian or curator, limited guardian or tutor, or an advisor. An advisor, although legally appointed, cannot make decisions on behalf of an individual. The advisor does however receive guidance from a 'tutorship counsel' which is constituted of three members and involves the general public.[144] The importance of access to accurate information for members of the general community cannot be underestimated and any idea resulting in this should be given careful consideration, which is also representative of the ideals of therapeutic jurisprudence. However, as with capacity assessment generally, the practicalities of cost and staffing such bodies could prove prohibitive. Having said this, innovative solutions are needed which will require communication and lateral thinking by, and between, all stakeholders to ensure that individual autonomy, values and preferences are respected.[145]

The ethical obligations and duties of legal professionals must also be considered in any discussion of the ethics of capacity assessment. There is generally a duty to follow competent instructions—although whether the legal professional is able to adequately determine if a client is capable of providing instructions can sometimes be questionable. The other ethical duties relevant to this context include the paramount duty to the court and the administration of justice, as well as the duty to act in the client's best interests including respecting client autonomy. This latter duty is, however, contingent upon clearly identifying who the client is, an issue which is not always as simple as it seems when individuals with impaired capacity are being supported by a third party who may, or may not, have an agenda. Legal professionals, despite populist opinion, also have an ethical obligation to be honest and courteous in dealings, and cannot exhibit conduct which is discriminatory in nature.[146]

Especially significant within the context of capacity assessment is the duty of confidentiality owed to a client, thus making the acquisition of appropriate authorities to assess, refer and share information between those involved in the assessment critical and sometimes difficult.[147] Explaining that a refusal to participate in an assessment when preparing, for example, a will can potentially lead to arguments at a later stage about the validity of the will causing familial upset and financial

---

[142]Ibid.

[143]Marson DC and Moye J (2007), p. 18.

[144]Ibid.

[145]Ibid.

[146]Queensland Law Society, Allens Linklaters and Queensland Advocacy Incorporated (2014), p. 7.

[147]British Medical Association and the Law Society (2015), p. 16.

consequences can often help if a client is refusing to consent.[148] Arguably, it is feasible that failing to outline the impact of refusing to participate in an assessment could amount to a failure of the legal professional's duty to the client. For example, in *Badenach v Calvert*[149] it was held by the Tasmanian Full Court that a legal practitioner should not only have advised a client about the risk of a family provision application but also of the possible actions which could be taken in order to avoid such a claim, even if the testator chose not to pursue any of the courses of action outlined. Although this was ultimately overturned by the High Court of Australia, and whilst capacity assessment is clearly different, that is not to prevent a similar argument being run in this context, especially given the growth of both the ageing population and the size of estates. That is, by not explaining the consequences of the failure to agree to be assessed to a client, a legal professional could be opening him or her-self up to a professional misconduct claim.

Failure to comply with the ethical duties can result in professional misconduct and legal sanctions. It can also lead to practical problems of increased cost and, especially interesting when applying a therapeutic jurisprudence lens, increased stress to the client resulting from the client's interaction with both the law and the legal actor(s) in question. This differs to the position in the United States of America where specific provisions exist directing how a legal professional should act when his or her client either has questionable capacity or impaired capacity has been established.[150]

5 Select Models of Capacity Assessment

Legal and health scholars acknowledge that there are no universally accepted, standardised and objective criteria for assessing capacity.[151] That is, there is no 'gold standard'.[152] Consequently, a number of different approaches may be employed to assess capacity, for instance, non-structured and structured interviews, theoretical vignettes, standardised tests such as general cognitive ability tests, specialised neuropsychological tests, and purpose built tests. One of the problems with an (ever growing) number of assessment instruments is that the sheer multitude of instruments interferes with the validation process—how can they all adequately assess capacity? Which ones are reliable? Which ones are suitable for which legal capacity? How do practitioners know which ones they should use and

---

[148]Ibid 18.

[149][2016] HCA 18.

[150]See, for example, American Bar Association (2013), r 1.14. See also The Bar Council (UK) (2015).

[151]Sullivan K (2004), p. 135.

[152]Cairns R et al. (2005), p. 377; Kitamura T, Takahashi N (2007), p. 579; Ganzini L et al. (2003), p. 237.

whether they can rely on them? It must also be noted that these tests focus on clinical capacity distinct from legal capacity which presents its own complexities including: how do the clinical tests match up to the legal standards, indeed if they do at all? Does, for example, the legal notion of insane delusions match the clinical notion of fluctuating capacity? Indeed, rather than assisting, the assortment of assessment instruments appears instead to augment the confusion surrounding any attempt to standardise the methodology for the assessment of legal capacity. This therefore reinforces the miscommunication and consequently the misunderstandings that can exist between the two professions. This is concerning not least because of the (potential) resultant negative practical impact.

The variety of tests creates the potential for inconsistency in the assessment process and outcome, making both dependent upon individual preferences for, and skill in utilising, the various capacity assessment tools. In addition to identifying the number and variety of tests available, it is also important to determine whether legal and health professionals recognise, and are able to correctly evaluate, the nuances of mentally disabling conditions and the impact these can have on the decision-specific capacity in question throughout the assessment process. Consequently, further research is needed into capacity, especially financial capacity, which expands upon existing knowledge, assessment paradigms and training.[153] In fact, a unifying conceptual model is needed to assess capacity across all domains.[154] However, despite the fact that the need for a unifying model has been agreed upon and the increasing attention this area is garnering, the actual development of such a model is proving elusive.

In response to the dilemmas posed by attempting to assess capacity, clinical assessment models have increasingly been developed since the 1990s.[155] Each model has its own ideology, mechanisms and procedures, which can include a number of assessment mechanisms ranging from formal tests and semi-structured interviews to observing the individual in question. Proposed legal criteria for determining capacity are as varied as the clinical models being utilised to assess it. As has been seen, basing the criteria for capacity on rationality or reasonableness, which faces similar definitional challenges, is problematic given the subjective notion of both rationality and reasonableness. Evidence of choice is not necessarily any clearer given that no doubt questions will arise with respect to what evidence is suitable and the standard such evidence would need to meet. While understanding or appreciation of an individual's situation is important, it is merely one factor which needs to feature in the assessment of legal capacity. Errors can occur in the assessment process, often at a critical time. In some instances tests are utilised which have not been accepted as adequate for establishing the specific capacity in question, or where the overall utility of the test has not yet been accepted by the

---

[153]Kershaw MM and Webber LS (2004), p. 338.

[154]Wadley VG et al. (2003), p. 1621. See also Pinsker DM et al. (2010), p. 333. See also Suto WMI et al. (2005), p. 202; Kershaw MM and Webber LS (2008), p. 40.

[155]Sullivan K (2004), p. 137. See also Berg JW et al. (1995–1996), pp. 349–351.

relevant field thus calling into question its use as an evaluative measure.[156] Conse-quently, this can cause confusion and uncertainty both within, and between, the legal and health professions when assessing legal capacity.[157]

As it stands, the clinical tests can be divided into two main categories, general ability tests which test cognitive skills, and purpose-built assessment tools.[158] The advent of task specific assessment models was a response to the pre-eminence of the concept of decision-specific capacities.[159] These models, however, are plagued by problems such as how to measure capacity, as well as how to apply the assessment in different contexts which require different levels of decision-making competence.[160] This is without taking into account the added difficulty of then situating the cognitive assessment within the applicable legal framework. The prolonged use of capacity assessment methods that are not standardised are of questionable veracity, and the lack of well-defined, universally accepted criteria suggests that individual autonomy is not being protected as well as it could be.[161] A selection of legal and clinical models commonly referred to in the testamentary and substitute decision-making context will be examined in this section. It should be noted that this is not meant to be exhaustive, and indeed, it cannot be given the number of models in existence. It is instead discussing some of the more commonly mentioned assessment methods.

5.1   The Capacity Assessment Toolkit

The Attorney General's Department of New South Wales, Australia has produced a 'Capacity Toolkit'[162] ('the Toolkit') which 'aims to assist people in correctly identifying whether an individual has the competency to make their own deci-sions'.[163] The Toolkit defines capacity as the ability to understand facts, appreciate the main choices, evaluate the consequences of a decision, comprehend the effect of the consequences and effectively communicate a decision.[164] It reiterates that capacity is decision specific and can be regained, increased or lost.[165] Capacity can be affected by the type of decision being made, the timing of the decision, as well as the nature of the decision and how complicated it is.[166] How much

---

[156]Drogin EY (2004), p. 50.

[157]Lai JM and Karlawish J (2007), p. 103.

[158]Sullivan K (2004), p. 135.

[159]Ibid 137.

[160]Darzins P et al. (2000), p. 7.

[161]Ibid 139.

[162]Attorney General's Department of New South Wales (2008).

[163]Ibid 6.

[164]Ibid 18.

[165]Ibid 19, 23.

[166]Ibid 21–22.

information the individual has to make the decision is also relevant, as is the level and effectiveness of communication between the decision-maker and the person assessing whether the decision-maker is capable.[167] Consideration also has to be had for the circumstances in which the decision is being made, the individual's experience, the individual's health, and whether any additional factors are causing stress to the individual.[168]

The Toolkit outlines six assessment principles: first, the presumption of capacity; second, the decision and time specific nature of capacity; third, that capacity is not affected by appearances; fourth, the assessment should focus on an individual's ability to make a decision, not the decision itself; fifth, respect for an individual's privacy; and finally, substitute decision-making should be an avenue of last resort.[169] The Toolkit also outlines triggers which would indicate when capacity should be assessed. These have been categorised as conduct and circumstantial triggers. The identified conduct triggers include making decisions which place the individual at serious risk of harm or mistreatment; making decisions which are out of character and may result in harm or mistreatment; no longer understanding issues that have been understood previously; being confused about dates, times and places; noticeably forgetting things; losing the ability to communicate, interact socially and/or express emotions; sudden changes in personality; and deteriorating ability to read and write and/or determine distance or direction.[170] The recognised circumstantial triggers are: changes in the way an individual maintains himself/ herself or his/her home which places him/her or his/her health at substantial risk; not meeting financial obligations such as paying bills; making extravagant purchases or sudden and excessive displays of generosity when this is unusual for the individual; being diagnosed with a mentally disabling condition which can affect their capacity; or they have previously lacked the capacity required to make decisions.[171]

The Toolkit is very thorough in outlining and explaining the key capacity assessment principles and some triggers. Notably, however, the triggers identified here differ to the other assessment paradigms looked at adding to the potential confusion in an already complex area. Additionally, the Toolkit is arguably too simplistic. It was not intended to establish a definitive capacity assessment process, nor be a diagnostic tool, but there is instead a danger that it potentially over-simplifies legal capacity assessment. This could be especially problematic if used by inexperienced practitioners in assessments.

---

[167]Ibid. Kitamura T and Takahashi N (2007), p. 580.

[168]Attorney General's Department of New South Wales (2008), pp. 21–22.

[169]Ibid 27.

[170]Ibid 50–51.

[171]Ibid 51–52.

5.2   The Six Step Capacity Assessment Process

An alternative assessment method developed by Dārziņš, Molloy and Strang is the six step capacity assessment process.[172] It was originally utilised when assessing capacity to prepare advance health directives, and subsequently to assess financial and personal decision-making capacity.[173] Dārziņš, Molloy and Strang note that the six step capacity assessment process should not be treated as the veritable 'gold standard' but rather should be used with other tests to reach a reliable and satisfactory determination.[174] This again raises too many issues of potential inconsistency—which tests should be used? How many are needed to achieve a satisfactory assessment? To what extent should each of these tests be applied? Who should be applying them? How do they navigate the challenging intersection of the legal requirements with clinical assessments?

As the name implies, the capacity assessment process has six steps: step one ensures that a valid trigger must be present before the assessment of decision-making capacity will occur; step two seeks to engage the person who is having his or her capacity assessed in the process; step three requires the gathering of information to explain the context, as well as the individual's choices and any resultant consequences; step four advocates that the person who is having his or her capacity assessed then be educated about the context, choices available to them as well as the consequences of those choices; step five sees the assessment taking place; and finally, step six sets out any actions that should be taken as a result of the assessment.[175] The triggers identified here are not dissimilar to those in the Toolkit, although the descriptions vary and are fewer in number. The triggers noted by Dārziņš, Molloy and Strang, although similar to the triggers contained in the Toolkit, do not correlate. The triggers in the Toolkit are much more detailed. Dārziņš, Molloy and Strang have also not made the distinction between conduct and circumstantial triggers. This raises the question whether the fewer triggers identified by Dārziņš, Molloy and Strang are more effective for a streamlined, but consistent, assessment process. Alternatively, the detailed Toolkit triggers may be seen to offer more certainty. The Toolkit contains further criteria indicating when capacity may need to be assessed. Although these would appear to be 'triggers', the Toolkit manages these separately from the identified conduct and circumstantial triggers. For example, one element in the further criteria is that there is a trigger, which seems to be unnecessarily confusing, especially as Dārziņš Molloy and Strang have included these further elements as actual triggers.

Interestingly, the six step assessment process has therapeutic jurisprudence overtones. For example, steps two and four, that it is necessary to engage the individual in the process and to educate them about it, promote avoidance of incompetency labelling and the removal of individual autonomy without the

---

[172]Darzins P et al. (2000).
[173]Ibid 10.
[174]Ibid 7.
[175]Ibid 12.

individual having a full understanding of what is occurring. The concept of information gathering, which is step three, introduces the 'assessor' whose role is to 'explore the triggers, establish the relevant choices for dealing with triggers and determine the reasonably foreseeable consequences of each specific choice'.[176] The notion of an assessor reflects the therapeutic jurisprudence concept of a neutral fact finder. Further on the notion of an 'assessor', Dārziņš, Molloy and Strang state that any assessor 'should have adequate training, content knowledge and experience in the areas being assessed to help establish the available choices, or be able to access the relevant content knowledge and expertise if they themselves lack it'.[177] However, this does little to address the issues of who and how. Who should the assessors be? Who will train them in the applicable legal and medical standards? How will they be trained? Finally, what measures are necessary, and how will they be implemented, to guarantee a satisfactory training model and assessment process?

Additionally, the existence of certain diseases, such as Alzheimer's disease, are problematic in the assessment process. Nevertheless, these are not specifically noted which could be challenging for more inexperienced practitioners who may be unaware of the impact of the nuances of illnesses such as Alzheimer's disease on legal capacity. For instance, sufferers of Alzheimer's disease can commonly suffer from delusions, particularly the belief that someone is stealing from or abusing them.[178] While this may not necessarily mean that they are legally incompetent or will not have moments of lucidity, this will influence the information gathering stage.[179] It will likewise impact the assessment process unless the assessor is adequately trained, and can recognise the symptoms. Specific decisional aids for property and financial decisions as well as health care directives are used.[180] The decisional aids are designed to help ensure that the assessments are comprehensive. However, they do not provide standard questions or approaches that the assessors should use. This again raises the issue of consistency, transparency and accuracy of process.

Dārziņš, Molloy and Strang discuss examples of how the process would work when applied to specific decision-making competencies for example, financial capacity.[181] Although undeniably valuable, theoretical illustrations lack the credibility of practical testing—of which there is a notable gap in this area generally. Further, evidence that has been collected suggests that although the six step capacity assessment process is relatively well-known amongst health professionals, it is not being applied by legal professionals.[182] The lack of recognition and adoption by both professions is a significant issue confronting not just this paradigm, but all of them.

---

[176]Ibid 15.

[177]Ibid.

[178]Ibid 121, 123.

[179]Ibid 132.

[180]Ibid 29.

[181]Ibid 75.

[182]See, for example Purser K and Rosenfeld T (2014).

5.3   Standardised Tests

Standardised tests such as the Mini-Mental State Examination ('MMSE') and the Montreal Cognitive Assessment (MoCA), as well as more specialised neuropsychological tests are generally used to assess cognitive function. They use norms to compare the individual in question to a large sample of people representing the population of people who took the test.[183] Functional abilities can also be assessed. Falk and Hoffman note that functional abilities can be assessed by asking a friend, family member or caregiver to complete the Katz Index of Independence in Activities of Daily Living and the Lawton Instrumental Activities of Daily Living Scale.[184] The problem is that there are so many standardised tests that the benefits of standardisation can become lost. It also becomes a question of knowing which test to use in what circumstance, which can be very difficult, especially if the assessors are not familiar with the role of having to assess capacity. Further, how these tests align, if indeed they do at all, with the requisite legal capacity is not settled. So, again, the assessment of capacity in a clinical context remains independent of the legal framework within which capacity will ultimately be determined.

Turning to, for example, the MMSE, which is often referenced in connection with capacity assessments, especially by those who are inexperienced in the area. This is a 30-item questionnaire which takes a relatively short period of time to administer, and which is designed to test mental status.[185] A range of cognitive abilities are incorporated. For instance, memory is assessed through, for example, a delayed recall of three objects. Language ability is tested by individuals being asked to name common items, repeat a difficult phrase, follow a three-step directive and compose a sentence. Spatial ability is assessed through the request to copy a figure; and, set-shifting is assessed by requesting the individual to count backwards from 100 by sevens.[186] Scores are out of 30 and anything under 24 is considered concerning although age, cultural differences and education are recognised as being able to negatively influence the result.[187] Education in particular is an important factor in administering the MMSE.[188] Low education levels can increase the possibility of a cognitively capable person being classified as incapable whereas high education levels can assist those who may be cognitively incapable to appear capable.[189] Individuals should be given every opportunity to be educated about the decision(s) to be made, including the process of assessment, thus increasing their chances of a positive finding of capacity.[190] It is uncertain whether the drawbacks of

---

[183]Falk E and Hoffman N (2014), p. 860.
[184]Ibid.
[185]Molloy DW and Standish TIM (1997), p. 87.
[186]Sabatino CP (2001), p. 5.
[187]Ibid. Sullivan K (2004), p. 136.
[188]See also Crum RM et al. (1993), p. 2386.
[189]Darzins P et al. (2000), p. 8.
[190]Ibid.

the MMSE are well-known, especially in the legal profession, in the conduct of capacity assessments. This can (obviously) have a negative impact on the assessment of capacity leading to a label of a lack of capacity, as well as a loss of autonomy and personal sovereignty. The drawbacks are particularly notable when comparisons are made between, for example, the MMSE and the MoCA, with such comparisons tending to suggest that the latter may be the stronger of the two for capacity assessment purposes.[191]

However capacity is tested, the instrument used should take into account an individual's mood, for example whether they are tired, anxious or stressed, as well as whether they are taking any medication and if so, the nature and effect(s) of such medication.[192] The environment in which the test is being conducted is also important to the assessment process. An individual may perform better in the comfort of familiar surroundings such as their own home. After a capacity assessment has been made, it needs to be determined whether the cause of the disorder can be treated to enhance cognitive performance and lead to the individual being found to be competent. It is also necessary to note that neuropsychological screening tests, such as the MMSE and the MoCA, while potentially indicating the need for further evaluation, are not, in and of themselves sufficient to establish the legal requirements of capacity or incapacity as the case may be.[193] For example, the particular elements required for testamentary capacity play no role in the MMSE. Consequently, it is important to note that general cognitive tests cannot be used as the sole basis upon which to assess legal capacity.[194]

5.4   The Two Stage Capacity Assessment Model

Sullivan suggests the use of a two stage capacity assessment process which would incorporate assessing general cognitive status through the use of neuropsychological testing and ascertaining the individual's knowledge in connection to the capacity being assessed and the decision being made.[195] There are some general cognitive abilities which are required for capacity, including 'orientation, reasoning/judgment, general knowledge, memory, [and] calculation ability'.[196] Consequently, purpose built tests, question sets and vignettes can be used to test specific capacities, while neuropsychological assessment, which is more comprehensive than tests such as the MMSE, can be used to evaluate fundamental cognitive

---

[191]Frost M et al. (2015), p. 273.

[192]Kerridge I et al. (2013), p. 371.

[193]Darzins P et al. (2000), p. 7; Falk E and Hoffman N (2014), p. 856; Frost M et al. (2015), p. 271.

[194]Kerridge I et al. (2013), p. 372.

[195]Sullivan K (2004), p. 131.

[196]Ibid 139.

abilities.[197] Indeed, a reasonably short and structured interview may be the most practical approach given issues of cost.[198]

5.5   A Conceptual Model of Capacity Assessment

Despite the lack of research on financial and decision-making capacity, a conceptual model of assessment has been developed which assesses the independent-living ability of individuals. It should be noted, however, that this was in the context of guardianship proceedings.[199] Nevertheless, it may be feasible to extend this model to augment those discussed above to form a more comprehensive base paradigm from which to assess capacity in the testamentary and decision-making context. The unpredictability and inadequacy of medical capacity assessments and consequently legal capacity determinations in guardianship proceedings is a cause for concern in the United States of America, a concern which is echoed internationally.[200] Although this criticism is outside the specific scope of the testamentary and decision-making capacity context, it is relevant to the financial capacity context generally because similar issues exist with a lack of clearly defined assessment models which are leading to similarly inconsistent and imprecise results.

This conceptual model was developed through a process 'in which legal provisions for guardianship and prevailing clinical practices for capacity assessment were integrated, through expert group consensus and external review by legal and health care professionals …'.[201] As stated, the model is intended to be used for assessment in the guardianship context and concentrates on six assessment domains being '(a) medical condition, (b) cognition, (c) functional abilities, (d) values, (e) risk of harm and level of supervision needed, and (f) means to enhance capacity. The template also addresses the participation of the person … confidentiality and privilege issues, and certification by the examiner'.[202] Interestingly, domain (a) 'medical condition' makes reference to the terms mental disability and advanced age as being 'amorphous and discriminatory labels'[203] and domain (e) 'risk of harm and level of supervision needed' highlights the promotion of the least restrictive alternative.[204] These concerns again highlight therapeutic jurisprudence principles and the doctrine's concerns about the impact of labelling.[205]

---

[197]Ibid.
[198]Parker M (2008), pp. 33–34.
[199]Moye J et al. (2007), p. 591.
[200]Ibid 591–592.
[201]Ibid 591.
[202]Ibid.
[203]Ibid 594.
[204]Ibid 596.
[205]Berg JW et al. (1995–1996), p. 377.

5.6 The Financial Capacity Assessment Model

Financial capacity itself comprises both theoretical and practical abilities and, as stated, is incredibly difficult to assess.[206] The lack of adequate attention financial capacity has received from scholars and researchers, legal and health alike, has resulted in few, if any, reliable models of financial capacity assessment.[207] Marson and Zebley are attempting to redress this situation. They have developed a conceptual model focusing on financial capacity which can be used in different 'patient populations' such as sufferers of Alzheimer's disease.[208] Financial capacities can be categorised as separate domains, within which are specific financial tasks or abilities.[209] This model comprises three levels. First are the specific financial abilities, each of which falls within an identified domain of financial competency. The second level comprises the general domains and finally, there is the overall concept of financial capacity.[210] The criteria for developing the domains include '(1) theoretical relevance to the independent functioning of community-dwelling older adults, (2) clinical relevance to legal and healthcare professionals who treat older adults ... and (3) general relevance to extant and prior state statutory criteria for financial competency'.[211] Six domains were initially identified, but this was subsequently modified to include two additional domains. The domains include basic monetary skills, financial conceptual knowledge, cash transactions, cheque book management, bank statement management, financial judgment, bill payment, and knowledge of personal assets and estate arrangements.[212]

Based upon the identified domains, four approaches to assessing financial capacity were subsequently developed which include observational, psychometric, interview based and neuropsychological testing.[213] It is also possible to evaluate financial capacity reasonably reliably with a semi-structured clinical interview.[214] It has been suggested that individuals should engage in legal and financial planning when at risk of an accelerated loss of financial capacity, for example, where there has been a diagnosis of Alzheimer's disease.[215] The difficulty, however, is in getting individuals to engage with estate planning and execute documents such as wills, enduring powers of attorney and advance health directives. Take up rates

---

[206]Ibid 806.
[207]Marson D and Zebley L (2001), p. 32; Marson DC et al. (2000a), p. 879; Marson DC et al. (2009), p. 807.
[208]Marson DC et al. (2009), p. 33.
[209]Marson D and Zebley L (2001), p. 33.
[210]Ibid.
[211]Ibid.
[212]Ibid 33–34.
[213]Ibid 34–35.
[214]Marson DC et al. (2009), p. 806, 812.
[215]Ibid.

have historically proven that this is not happening despite attempts to promote the benefits of having such mechanisms in place.

Overall, two models being Marson's financial capacity instrument ('FCI') and the six step capacity assessment process both evaluate eight dimensions of capacity. Yet, as can be seen with all capacity assessment models, there is little agreement on the parameters of those dimensions and how to satisfactorily assess them, especially when placed within the legal framework necessary to assess legal capacity.[216] Research supporting the Toolkit, the six step capacity assessment model and the other models mentioned above is scarce, while the evidence available in support of the FCI focuses on older adults with dementia—a particular group with a particular mentally disabling condition. It is untested with other adults whose financial capacity may need to be assessed.[217] Further, none of these models has been universally adopted.[218] As a result, even more models are being developed and yet they are all facing the same problems with regards to the lack of rigorous testing and veracity. For example, Kershaw and Webber proposed their own model, the financial competence assessment inventory ('FCAI'), which has 'four main dimensions: everyday financial abilities, debt management, estate management, and financial judgement'.[219] Kershaw and Webber's model is generally consistent with other models, such as the six step capacity assessment process and the FCI, demonstrating that although it is, at least theoretically, possible to develop general criteria to satisfactorily assess financial capacity, practical acceptance and implementation of a consistent and transparent paradigm remains elusive.[220] Consistency, transparency and accuracy of process require consolidation of current knowledge, utilising both legal and medical skills. This is because clear legal standards are needed to develop satisfactory assessment paradigms, which does not always happen with each profession developing intra-disciplinary models which may not be known to the other.[221]

5.7   The MacArthur Treatment Competence Study

The MacArthur Competence Assessment Tools for Treatment and Clinical Research are considered to be the most widely used, validated and therefore reliable assessment techniques.[222] The tools include the MacArthur Treatment Competence Study which was designed to standardise tools to assess capacity to consent to treatment; the

---

[216]Kershaw MM and Webber LS (2004), p. 339.

[217]Ibid.

[218]Ibid 41.

[219]Ibid 339.

[220]Ibid 347.

[221]Ibid 53.

[222]Berg JW et al. (1995–1996), p. 73.

MacArthur Competence Assessment Tool—Treatment ('MacCAT-T')[223] which streamlines the MacArthur Treatment Competence Research Instruments in clinical settings; and the MacArthur Competence Assessment Tool—Clinical Research ('MacCAT-CR') which was devised from the MacCAT-T to assess competency in clinical research.[224] It is important to note that the focus of these tools is the decision-making ability of people with mental illness who are hospitalised, not testamentary and decision-making capacity.[225] What they do prove in this context is that it is possible to achieve some level of standardised assessment for decision specific capacity.

6 Conclusion

It is accepted that assessing capacity is a contentious issue, not least because it is individual autonomy which is at stake. The development of a satisfactory testamentary and decision-making capacity assessment paradigm facilitating the involvement of cognitively impaired individuals (where possible) will require an understanding of not only the relevant legal principles and the mentally disabling conditions that can impact capacity, but also the effect of any medications.[226] From the above discussion it is apparent that a 'gold-standard' assessment model does not currently exist. A standardised, valid and rigorous model assessing clinical capacity within the parameters of the relevant legal framework is, in fact, far from being developed. The evaluation and comparison of existing capacity assessment models is a difficult task because of the multitude of models (as demonstrated by the small selection of them included here), differences in the specific capacity to be assessed, the paradigm chosen, and its contextual application. What such an analysis does demonstrate is that imposing an unyielding capacity assessment tool is undesirable if not impossible.[227]

A satisfactory model and guiding principles, especially absent a standardised assessment measure, are needed. This will provide a base from which to conduct assessments which will ensure a level of uniformity and transparency but which is malleable enough to adapt to specific circumstances. The process will need to incorporate both legal and health standards and knowledge. This is because to satisfactorily assess legal competence in this context it is also necessary to evaluate elements of clinical capacity, particularly given the increasing prevalence of mentally disabling conditions such as dementia. A dialogue is needed between legal and health professionals to accomplish this because law practitioners alone generally do

---

[223]MacArthur Research Network on Mental Health and the Law (2004), p. 3.

[224]Sturman ED (2005), pp. 957–962.

[225]MacArthur Research Network on Mental Health and the Law (2004), p. 1.

[226]O'Neill N and Peisah C (2011), 1.1.

[227]Darzins P et al. (2000), p. 138.

not have the ability to assess capacity in the context of the differing mentally disabling conditions, and health professionals lack guidance and training to assess capacity in a legal setting.[228] Ideologically, the model will attempt to achieve a balance between the dualistic notions of autonomy and protection, whilst recognising the importance of including the assessed person in the assessment process as well as the impact that incompetency labelling can have—exemplifying therapeutic jurisprudence principles. The paradigm should maximise findings of legal capacity and thus protect autonomy, acknowledging the importance of human rights issues in this area. However, any such model should similarly ensure that incapable people are not found capable. To do so would be counterproductive to maintaining a balance between autonomy and protection as it could place vulnerable individuals at risk. It is important now, before considering the content of such proposed guidelines, to examine capacity and its assessment within the specific testamentary and decision-making contexts.

References

American Bar Association (2013) Model rules of professional conduct. http://www.americanbar. org/groups/professional_responsibility/publications/model_rules_of_professional_conduct/ model_rules_of_professional_conduct_table_of_contents.html
Appelbaum PS (2007) Assessment of patient's competence to consent to treatment. N Engl J Med 357(18):1834–1840
Appelbaum PS, Roth LH (1981) Clinical issues in the assessment of competency. Am J Psychiatr 138(11):1462–1467
Arias JJ (2013) A time to step in: legal mechanisms for protecting those with declining capacity. Am J Law Med 39(1):134–159
Attorney General's Department of New South Wales (2008) Capacity Toolkit. http://www.justice. nsw.gov.au/diversityservices/Documents/capacity_toolkit0609.pdf. Accessed 1 Nov 2016
Australian Law Reform Commission (2013) Equality, Capacity and Disability in Commonwealth Laws, Issues Paper 44
Australian Law Reform Commission (2014) Equality, Capacity and Disability in Commonwealth Laws, Summary Report 124
Berg JW, Appelbaum PS, Grisso T (1996) Constructing competence: formulating standards of legal competence to make medical decisions. Rutgers Law Rev 48(2):345–396
Boyle G (2011) Early implementation of the mental capacity act 2005 in health and social care. Crit Soc Policy 31(3):365–387
British Medical Association and the Law Society (2015) Assessment of mental capacity: guidance for doctors and lawyers, 4th edn. Law Society Publishing, London
Buchanan A (2004) Mental capacity, legal competence and consent to treatment. J R Soc Med 97 (9):415–420
Cairns R et al (2005) Reliability of mental capacity assessments in psychiatric in-Patients. Br J Psychiatry 187(4):372–378
Carney T, Keyzer P (2007) Planning for the future, arrangements for the assistance of people planning for the future of people with impaired competency. Queensl Univ Technol Law Justice J 7(2):255–278

---

[228]Moye J et al. (2007), p. 592.

Cockerill J, Collier B, Maxwell K (2005) Legal requirements and current practices. In: Collier B, Coyne C, Sullivan K (eds) Mental capacity, powers of attorney and advance health directives. Federation Press, Leichhardt

Collier B, Coyne C, Sullivan K (2005a) Preface. In: Collier B, Coyne C, Sullivan K (eds) Mental capacity, powers of attorney and advance health directives. Federation Press, Leichhardt

Collier B, Coyne C, Sullivan K (eds) (2005b) Mental capacity, powers of attorney and advance health directives. Federation Press, Leichhardt

Creyke R (1995) Who can decide? Legal decision-making for others. Australian Government Publishing Service, Canberra

Crum RM et al (1993) Population-based norms for the mini-mental state examination by age and education level. J Am Med Assoc 269(18):2386–2391

Darzins P, Molloy DW, Strang D (eds) (2000) Who can decide? The six step capacity assessment process. Memory Australia Press, Adelaide

Drogin EY (2004) Jurisprudent therapy and competency. Law Psychol Rev 28:41–51

Dunn LB et al (2006) Assessing decisional capacity for clinical research or treatment: a review of instruments. Am J Psychiatr 163(8):1323–1334

Earnst KS et al (2001) Loss of financial capacity in Alzheimer's disease: the role of working memory. Aging Neuropsychol Cogn 8(2):109–119

Falk E, Hoffman N (2014) The role of capacity assessments in elder abuse investigations and guardianships. Clin Geriatr Med 30(4):851–868

Farmer J et al (2010) Territorial tensions: misaligned management and community perspectives on health services for older people in remote rural areas. Health Place 16(2):275–283

Fazel S, Hope T, Jacoby R (1999) Assessment of competence to complete advance directives: validation of a patient Centred approach. Br Med J 318(7182):493–497

Fitten LJ, Waite MS (1990) Impact of medical hospitalization on treatment decision-making capacity in the elderly. Arch Intern Med 150(8):1717–1721

Frost M, Lawson S, Jacoby R (2015) Testamentary capacity law, practice, and medicine. Oxford University Press, Oxford

Ganzini L et al (2003) Pitfalls in assessment of decision-making capacity. Psychosomatics 44 (3):237–243

Grisso T (2003) Evaluating competencies: forensic assessments and instruments. Perspectives in law and psychology, 2nd edn. Kluwer Academic/Plenum Publishers, New York

Gunn MJ et al (1999) Decision-making capacity. Med Law Rev 7(3):269–306

Gurrera RJ et al (2006) Cognitive performance predicts treatment decisional abilities in mild to moderate dementia. Neurology 66(9):1367–1372

HM Government (2014) Valuing every voice, respecting every right: Making the case for the Mental Capacity Act The Government's response to the House of Lords Select Committee Report on the Mental Capacity Act 2005. https://www.gov.uk/government/uploads/system/uploads/attachment_data/file/318730/cm8884-valuing-every-voice.pdf. Accessed 1 Nov 2016

House of Lords Select Committee on the Mental Capacity Act 2005 (2014) Mental Capacity Act 2005: post-legislative scrutiny. Report of Session 2013–14, HL Paper 139. http://www.publications.parliament.uk/pa/ld201314/ldselect/ldmentalcap/139/139.pdf. Accessed 1 Nov 2016

Howard M (2006) Principles for substituted decision-making about withdrawing or withholding life-sustaining measures in Queensland: a case for legislative reform. Queensl Univ Technol Law Justice J 6(2):166

Howard M, Dare K (2007) Elder Abuse and Elder Law – A Critical Examination. In: Queensland Law Society Elder Law Conference, Brisbane, 14 June 2007

Kapp MB (2007) Assessing assessments of decision-making capacity: a few legal queries and Commentary on "assessment of decision-making capacity on older adults". J Gerontol B Psychol Sci Soc Sci 62(1):12–13

Karlawish JHT et al (2005) The ability of Persons with Alzheimer disease (AD) to make a decision about taking an AD treatment. Neurology 64(9):1514–1519

Kerridge I, Lowe M, Stewart C (2013) Ethics and law for the health professions, 4th edn. Federation Press, Leichardt

Kershaw MM, Webber LS (2004) Dimensions of financial competence. Psychiatry Psychol Law 11(2):338–349

Kershaw MM, Webber LS (2008) Assessment of financial competence. Psychiatry Psychol Law 15(1):40–55

Kim SYH (2006) When does decisional impairment become decisional incompetence? Ethical and methodological issues in capacity research in schizophrenia. Schizophr Bull 32(1):92–97

Kirby M (2003) Book review: who can Decide? The Six Step Capacity Assessment Process Elder Law Review 7

Kitamura T, Takahashi N (2007) Ethical and conceptual aspects of capacity assessments in psychiatry. Curr Opin Psychiatry 20(6):578–581

Lai JM, Karlawish J (2007) Assessing the capacity to make everyday decisions: a guide for clinicians and an agenda for future research. Am J Geriatr Psychiatr 15(2):101–111

Law Reform Committee, Parliament of Victoria (2010) Inquiry into Powers of Attorney Final Report of the Victorian Law Reform Committee. http://www.parliament.vic.gov.au/images/stories/committees/lawrefrom/powers_of_attorney/Report_24-08-2010.pdf. Accessed 1 Nov 2016

Lock SL (2016) Age-friendly banking: how we can help get it right before things go wrong. Public Policy Aging Rep 26(1):18–22

MacArthur Research Network on Mental Health and the Law (2004) The MacArthur Treatment Competence Study Executive. http://www.macarthur.virginia.edu/treatment.html. Accessed 1 Nov 2016

Marson D (2016) Commentary: a role for neuroscience in preventing financial Elder abuse. Public Policy Aging Rep 26(1):12–14

Marson D, Zebley L (2001) The other side of the retirement years: cognitive decline, dementia, and loss of financial capacity. J Retirement Plann 4:30

Marson DC (2013) Clinical and ethical aspects of financial capacity in dementia: a commentary. Am J Geriatr Psychiatry 21(4):382–390

Marson DC et al (2000a) Assessing financial capacity in patients with Alzheimer disease a conceptual model and prototype instrument. Arch Neurol 57(6):877–884

Marson DC et al (2000b) Consistency of physicians' legal standards and personal judgments of competency in patients with Alzheimer's disease. J Am Geriatr Soc 48(8):911–918

Marson DC et al (2009) Clinical interview assessment of financial capacity in older adults with mild cognitive impairment and Alzheimer's disease. J Am Geriatr Soc 57(5):806–814

Marson DC, Hebert KR (2008) Financial capacity. In: Cutler BL (ed) Encyclopedia of psychology and law. Sage Publications, Thousand Oaks, pp 314–316

Marson DC, Moye J (2007) Empirical studies of capacity in older adults: finding clarity amidst complexity. J Gerontol B Psychol Sci Soc Sci 62(1):18–19

Marson DC, Savage R, Phillips J (2006) Financial capacity in persons with schizophrenia and serious mental illness: clinical and research ethics aspects. Schizophr Bull 32(1):81–91

Molloy DW, Standish TIM (1997) Mental status and neuropsychological assessment a guide to the standardized mini-mental state examination. Int Psychogeriatr 9(1):87–94

Moye J et al (2007) A conceptual model and assessment template for capacity evaluation in adult guardianship. The Gerontologist 47(5):591–603

Moye J, Marson DC (2007) Assessment of decision-making capacity on older adults: an emerging area of practice and research. J Gerontol B Psychol Sci Soc Sci 62(1):3–11

O'Neill N, Peisah C (2011) Capacity and the law. Sydney University Press, Sydney

Parker M (2008) Patient competence and professional incompetence: disagreements in capacity assessments in one Australian jurisdiction, and their educational implications. J Law Med 16(1):25–35

Pinsker DM et al (2010) Financial capacity in older adults: a review of clinical assessment approaches and considerations. Clin Gerontol 33(4):332–346

Purser K, Rosenfeld T (2014) Evaluation of legal capacity by doctors and lawyers: the need for collaborative assessment. Med J Aust 201(8):483–485

Queensland Law Reform Commission (2008) Shaping Queensland's Guardianship Legislation: Principles and Capacity Discussion Paper, Working Paper No 64

Queensland Law Reform Commission (2010) A Review of Queensland's Guardianship Laws, Report No 67, Volume 1

Queensland Law Society, Allens Linklaters, Queensland Advocacy Incorporated (2014) Queensland Handbook for Practitioners on Legal Capacity

Sabatino CP (2001) Assessing clients with diminished capacity. Bar Assoc Focus Aging Law 22 (4):1–12

Setterlund D, Tilse C, Wilson J (2002) Older people and substitute decision making legislation: limits to informed choice. Australas J Ageing 21(3):128–134

Smith F (2010) Succession Law Focus. In: Gold Coast Local Symposium, Gold Coast, 21–22 May 2010

Standing Committee on Social Issues, Parliament of New South Wales (2010) Substitute Decision-Making for People Lacking Capacity. https://www.parliament.nsw.gov.au/committees/DBAssets/InquiryReport/ReportAcrobat/5892/100225%20SDM%20Final%20Report.pdf. Accessed 1 Nov 2016

Sturman ED (2005) The capacity to consent to treatment and research: a review of standardized assessment tools. Clin Psychol Rev 25(7):954–974

Sullivan K (2004) Neuropsychological assessment of mental capacity. Neuropsychol Rev 14 (3):131–142

Suto WMI et al (2005) Capacity to make financial decisions among people with mild intellectual disabilities. J Intellect Disabil Res 49(3):199–209

The Bar Council (UK) (2015) Client Incapacity. http://www.barcouncil.org.uk/practice-ethics/professional-practice-and-ethics/client-incapacity/. Accessed 1 Nov 2016

Tingle J (2014) The mental capacity act 2005: riding the storm of criticism. Br J Nurs 23 (15):864–865

United Nations Convention on the Rights of Persons with Disabilities, opened for signature 30 March 2007, (entered into force 3 May 2008)

Wadley VG, Harrell LE, Marson DC (2003) Self- and informant Report of financial abilities in patients with Alzheimer's disease: reliable and valid? J Am Geriatr Soc 51(11):1621–1626

Webber LS et al (2002) Assessing financial competence. Psychiatry Psychol Law 9(2):248–256

Cases and Legislation

Badenach v Calvert [2016] HCA 18
Boyse v Rossborough (1857) 10 ER 1192
Gibbons v Wright (1954) 91 CLR 423
Goddard Elliott (a firm) v Fritsch [2012] VSC 87 (16 March 2012)
Guardianship and Administration Act 2000 (Qld)
Hoff v Atherton [2005] WTLR 99
In re K, In re F [1988] 1 Ch 310
In the estate of Park deceased [1954] [1954] P 89
Masterman-Lister v Brutton [2003] WTLR 259 CA
Powers of Attorney Act 1998 (Qld)
Re Beaney deceased [1978] 2 All ER 595
Re Caldwell [1999] QSC 182
Re K (Enduring Power of Attorney) [1988] Ch 310
Szozda v Szozda [2010] NSWSC 804

Chapter 4
Testamentary Capacity

1 Introduction

In the context of the execution of testamentary documents, capacity assessment is growing in complexity and increasingly demands an interdisciplinary approach which utilises the skills of legal and health professionals. The degree of complexity of a testator's affairs and testamentary wishes directly impacts the level of cognitive function required to make the testamentary instrument. That is, the more complex the action, the more cognitive function is required.[1] There are no discreet tests which can be used to assess testamentary capacity.[2] The unpredictability of the outcomes of testamentary capacity assessment, which results from ambiguous assessment standards and processes, is a problem.[3]

Consideration of the seminal case, the 1870 decision of *Banks v Goodfellow*[4] (*'Banks'*), is essential in any testamentary capacity discourse. By way of brief introduction, *Banks* states that to have testamentary capacity a testator must be able to understand the nature and extent of his or her property, the potential beneficiaries who have a moral claim upon the testator, the effect of making a will, and that 'no disorder of the mind' has affected the contents of the will.[5] The American approach seems similar in that the focus is on knowledge that the testator is making a will, knowing the extent and nature of the property, the natural objects of the testator's bounty, and the manner in which the property will be distributed according to the will.[6]

---

[1]Shulman KI et al. (2009), p. 435.

[2]Sousa LB et al. (2014), p. 218.

[3]Champine P (2006), pp. 31, 75; See also Shulman KI et al. (2007), p. 724; Spar JE and Garb AS (1992), p. 169.

[4](1870) LR 5 QB 549. See also Peisah C (2005), p. 709.

[5]Posener HD and Jacoby R (2008), p. 754. See also *Boughton v Knight* (1873) LR 3 P & D 64, 65 (Sir James Hannen).

[6]Regan WM and Gordon SM (1997), p. 13.

© Springer International Publishing AG 2017
K. Purser, *Capacity Assessment and the Law*, DOI 10.1007/978-3-319-54347-5_4

The test itself is well settled and not in dispute. What is of concern is whether the test needs to be updated for the challenges posed by modern society.

It has recently been suggested, predominantly in the medical literature, that there is now a need to go beyond this criteria to adequately assess capacity.[7] Indeed, it is remarkable that the test for testamentary capacity has undergone so little refinement since its establishment.[8] The applicability of the test in modern society has been questioned, partly because of the age of the foundational elements.[9] Arguably more relevant, however, is the point that the facts giving rise to the test for testamentary capacity focus on psychosis which has different markers to dementia, a significant issue when considering that dementia is one of the main mentally disabling conditions confronting modern society.[10] Dementia cases significantly outweigh cases in which psychosis is the basis for challenging a will on the grounds of the alleged legal incompetency of the testator.[11] This is especially noteworthy given the ageing population and increasing appetite for litigating the validity of an individual's will.[12] It also raises issues around the efficacy of contemporaneous and retrospective assessments. Reservation has likewise been expressed about whether the test for testamentary capacity adequately takes into account the complexity of modern estate planning and testamentary structures. Additionally, as with capacity generally, there are also misunderstandings and miscommunication between the legal and health professions as to the nature and application of the actual test.

Accordingly, this chapter will explore the current testamentary capacity assessment paradigm with a view to determining whether a more satisfactory assessment model could be developed, and what this should include. This will include discussion of the 'golden rule' from the United Kingdom. This chapter will also consider the test for capacity adopted in the context of statutory or court ordered wills. The use of such wills is a relatively new phenomenon arising over approximately the last decade. Statutory wills are designed, in part, to counteract legal incompetency again raising issues regarding consistency, transparency and accuracy of the assessment process adopted.

Although the general validity of a will is not the focus here, it should be noted that for a will to be valid, a testator must be of sound mind, memory and understanding,[13] and the will must meet the formalities as required in each jurisdiction. It is accepted that arbitrariness, capriciousness, eccentricity, perceived injustice and

---

[7]See also Peisah C (2005); Shulman KI et al. (2005), p. 67. See also Hamilton B and Cockburn T (2008), p. 14.

[8]Spaulding WJ (1985), p. 114.

[9]Champine P (2003), p. 181.

[10]See also Peisah C (2005), p. 709.

[11]O'Neill N and Peisah C (2011).

[12]Shulman KI et al. (2009), p. 433; Sprehe DJ and Kerr AL (1996), p. 263. This also appears to be the case in the United Kingdom. Jacoby R and Steer P (2007), p. 155; Roked F and Patel A (2008), p. 552.

[13]*In the Will of Edward Victor Macfarlane Deceased* [2012] QSC 20, [9] (McMeekin J); *Tippet v Moore* (1911) 13 CLR 248; Posener HD and Jacoby R (2008), p. 754.

maliciousness are not grounds for alleging testamentary incapacity.[14] Furthermore, the testator must intend the will to operate as such while knowing and freely approving of its contents, absent any suspicious circumstances. The testator's actions must also be free from undue influence and fraud.[15] The significance of undue influence cannot be underestimated—either on the testator or on the assessment process. This is because it appears that some professionals conflate the legal requirement of capacity with that of a lack of undue influence being exerted over the testator. While factually similar, and closely connected, they are separate at law. This further serves to emphasise the need for an interdisciplinary approach to assessing testamentary capacity, especially when clinical evaluations are to be conducted within a legal framework foreign to the health professionals conducting those assessments.

2 Testamentary Capacity

In order to make a valid will, a testator must have the requisite testamentary capacity. Capacity is likewise required for an individual to be able to revoke his or her will unless the revocation occurs by operation of the law if the testator has, for example, married or divorced (which can affect all or parts of the will in accordance with the relevant legal provisions). If a revocation clause has been included in a later will then the relevant capacity is generally the capacity necessary to make a new will.[16] The testamentary capacity necessary to make a will is both task specific and a question of fact.[17] So, for example, the existence of an order under guardianship legislation is not conclusive evidence that an individual lacks testamentary capacity at that particular point in time.[18] In fact, the relevant time at which the testator must be shown to have had legal capacity is usually when the will is executed. However, if the instructions were given on a day antecedent to the execution of the document, or the testator loses legal capacity between the giving of the instructions and the execution of the document, then the relevant time is when the instructions were given.[19] Practitioners must be alive to whether the potential for cognitive and physical (where relevant) deterioration exists with their clients.

The general rule is that any declarations made by a testator are admissible to demonstrate his or her state of mind and the existence of testamentary intention at the time of making a will. However, if a testator suffered from Alzheimer's disease,

---

[14]*Bird v Luckie* (1850) 68 ER 375, 378 (Knight Bruce V-C); *Public Trustee v Clarke* (1895) 16 NSWR B & P 20, 27 (Owen CJ).

[15]*Astridge v Pepper* [1970] 1 NSWLR 542.

[16]See British Medical Association and the Law Society (2015), pp. 93–94.

[17]Jacoby R and Steer P (2007), p. 155; Shulman KI et al. (2009), p. 434; Marson DC et al. (2004), p. 82.

[18]*Fuggle v Sochacki* [1999] NSWSC 1214, [37] (Austin J).

[19]*Parker v Felgate* (1883) 8 PD 171; *Bailey v Bailey* (1924) 34 CLR 558, 567, 572.

the court will need to be satisfied that the mental degeneration caused by the disease did not affect legal capacity at the requisite time. When testamentary capacity is called into question, the onus is on the propounder of the will to prove that legal incompetency did not influence the contents of the will.[20] The party alleging the legal incompetency must then give particulars evidencing the alleged incapacity, with incompetency to be determined based upon the whole of the evidence and on a case by case basis.[21] The propounder's duty is discharged by the establishment of a prima facie case in which the court is satisfied that the will before it is the last will and testament of the testator. It is the integrity of the mind not the body that affects legal capacity and thus age, once over 18, is irrelevant. The question of whether the will is rational or irrational needs to be considered, as does the exclusion of potential beneficiaries who would normally be included in the will. Finally, the risk of undue influence must be taken into account. Evidence of legal incapacity or undue influence will cause the court to displace a prima facie valid will.

Importantly, a solicitor has a duty to act on any coherent instructions.[22] This is a significant point seemingly not widely understood by health professionals. Unless a client clearly lacks capacity, a legal practitioner will generally be required to make a will—not only because it is their duty to do so, but also because it is ultimately the court's decision as to whether the individual in question has capacity or not.[23] Prior to *Banks* any question about the soundness of an individual's mind could result in a determination of incompetency.[24] In *Banks* however, Lord Chief Justice Cockburn reconsidered testamentary capacity.

In the case of *Banks* the testator, John Banks, was a bachelor in his 50s who resided with his niece, Margaret Goodfellow. Banks suffered from paranoid schizophrenia. He believed that spirits were chasing him and that a grocer was going to molest him. The grocer in question was deceased. Banks prepared a will in 1863 which left his estate, comprising 15 houses, to his niece. He died in 1865. Margaret was underage and unmarried. She died shortly after receiving the inheritance which subsequently passed to her half-brother. The fact that the half-brother was not related to Banks apparently led the members of Banks' family to contest the will. The ground cited for doing so was that Banks lacked testamentary capacity when he made the will because he suffered from paranoid delusions. It was held that partial unsoundness of mind which does not affect the disposal of property in a testamentary instrument is insufficient to establish testamentary incapacity.[25]

---

[20]*Bull v Fulton* (1942) 66 CLR 295, 299 (Latham CJ); 341 (Williams J). *Shaw v Crichton* [1995] NSWCA BC 9505228 (23 August 1995) 2–4 (Handley, Cole & Powell JJ).

[21]*Bailey v Bailey* (1924) 34 CLR 558.

[22]Jacoby R and Steer P (2007), p. 156.

[23]*In the Will of Edward Victor Macfarlane Deceased* [2012] QSC 20, [3] (McMeekin J).

[24]*Waring v Waring* (1848) 6 Moo PC 341; *Smith v Tebbitt* (1867) LR 1 P & D 398; See Frost M et al. (2015), pp. 27–29 for a concise discussion of the formulation of the test for testamentary capacity prior to *Banks*.

[25]This was reaffirmed in, for example, the Australian case of *Tippet v Moore* (1911) 13 CLR 248.

Lord Chief Justice Cockburn observed in *Banks* (in the oft-repeated statement) that it was 'essential' that a testator should

> understand the extent of the property of which he is disposing; shall be able to comprehend and appreciate the claims to which he ought to give effect; and, with a view to the latter object, that no disorder of the mind shall poison his affections, pervert his sense of right, or prevent the exercise of his natural faculties – that no insane delusion shall influence his will in disposing of his property and bring about a disposal of it which, if his mind had been sound, would not have been made. ... If the human instincts and affections, or the moral sense, become perverted by mental disease; if insane suspicion, or aversion, take the place of natural affection; if reason and judgment are lost, and the mind becomes a prey to insane delusions calculated to interfere with and disturb its functions and to lead to a testamentary disposition, due only to their baneful influence – in such a case it is obvious that the condition of the testamentary power fails, and that a will made under such circumstances ought not to stand.[26]

That is, a testator must be able to understand the nature and extent of his or her property, the potential beneficiaries who have a moral claim upon them, as well as the effect of making a will.[27] The testator must also not be suffering from any cognitive impairment which influences the will-making.[28] There is some discussion as to whether the test to establish capacity for a codicil is lower as codicils, ideally, should be being used for only small changes to the will.[29] This would mean that if only a minor alteration was required then the best way to approach it would be through the use of a codicil rather than a will. Further, the greater the alteration to be made the higher the standard of capacity required. This makes sense as a proposition when considering that more complex wills require a higher standard of capacity.[30] In *Banks*, Lord Chief Justice Cockburn queried why the existence of a mental disease should result in the inability to make a will if the disease does not exist in such a degree and form so as to interfere with testamentary capacity.[31] This is an early example of the functional model in practise emphasising the decision and time specific nature of capacity. In this approach Lord Chief Justice Cockburn has, in effect, rejected the status model of assessment based upon the existence of a mentally disabling condition.

In *Sharp v Adam*,[32] ('*Sharp*') an English decision, the trial judge indicated that there may be a requirement that the testator have a 'rational, fair, and just' will. The Court of Appeal, however, held that this did not alter the elements contained in the

---

[26]*Banks v Goodfellow* (1870) LR 5 QB 549, 565–6 (Cockburn CJ). *Banks* has been applied in, for example, *Read v Carmody* [1998] NSWCA 182 (23 July 1998).

[27]*Boughton v Knight* (1873) LR 3 P & D 64, 65 (Sir James Hannen). Posener HD and Jacoby R (2008), p. 754.

[28]See Frost M et al. (2015), pp. 40–48 for a detailed discussion of what each limb requires.

[29]Frost M et al. (2015), p. 33; *Hay v Simpson* (1898) 11 LR (NSW) Eq 109; *D'Apice v Gutkovich—Estate of Abraham (No 2)* [2010] NSWSC 1333.

[30]Frost M et al. (2015), p. 33.

[31]*Banks v Goodfellow* (1870) LR 5 QB 549, 565–566 (Cockburn CJ).

[32]*Sharp v Adam* [2006] EWCA Civ 449.

Banks test.[33] In *Sharp* it was alleged that that testator, who died shortly after executing his last will in 2001, did not have testamentary capacity. The testator had executed a previous will in 1997 in which his two daughters were the principal beneficiaries. They were disinherited in the 2001 will. The testator had suffered from secondary progressive multiple sclerosis. At the time of his death in 2001 the testator could not speak or read, instead communicating through hand, head and eye gestures. The Court held that the testator lacked testamentary capacity because it could not be demonstrated that the will was made by a legally competent person, or that his feelings for his daughters were not affected by a mentally disabling condition. *Sharp* highlights the importance of the fourth limb of *Banks*.

The position in the United Kingdom is complicated by the interplay between *Banks* and the *Mental Capacity Act 2005*.[34] After the decision in *Walker v Badmin*[35] it does seem, however, that the common law test continues to prevail, at least for the time being, outside the Court of Protection. That is, the statutory test for capacity would apply to statutory wills.[36] *Perrins v Holland*[37] summarises the modern approach to the test, stating that: because it is a common law test, it is therefore able to be reflective of current attitudes; that the general understanding of capacity has increased remarkably since the decision in *Banks*; the decision-making paradigm shift has meant the recognition of individuals who are able to make decisions with some assistance; consequently, the test should focus on the task at hand and not an all-embracing notion of capacity; there is greater recognition for individual autonomy in modern society; and even a pure application of the *Banks* test must be done within the parameters of the particular testator and estate in question.[38] A review of the adequacy of the test for testamentary capacity is being undertaken by the Law Commission and final recommendations are expected in 2018.

The position in the United States of America is generally similar, where testamentary capacity is the 'ability of the testator to mentally understand in a general way the nature and extent of the property to be disposed of, and the testator's relation to those who would naturally claim a substantial benefit from the will, as well as a general understanding of the practical effect of the will as executed'.[39] A specific and detailed knowledge by the testator of his or her assets is not necessary, provided that the testator understands the general proportions in which he or she wishes to leave his or her estate and the reasons for this distribution are rational.[40]

---

[33]Jacoby R and Steer P (2007), p. 155.
[34]See for discussion on this British Medical Association and the Law Society (2015), pp. 85–86; Myers P (2014), p. 44; Frost M et al. (2015), pp. 55–63.
[35][2014] All ER (D) 258.
[36]McBride C (2015), p. 50.
[37][2009] EWHC 1945 (Ch); [2009] WTLR 1387.
[38]*Perrins v Holland* [2009] EWHC 1945 (Ch); [2009] WTLR 1387 [40].
[39]Newman v Smith 77 Fla. 633, 673–674, 82 So. 236, 247–248 (1918); Kapp M (2015), p. 165.
[40]*Kerr v Badran* [2004] NSWSC 735 (17 August 2004) [49] (Windeyer J); Shulman KI et al. (2009), p. 435.

As mentioned above however, the more complex the will, the more cognitive function is required. For example, the cognitive function necessary to prepare a will establishing a discretionary trust would be higher than that required for a 'straightforward' will. This increasing complexity of assessment arguably supports contemporaneous assessment in preference to a retrospective attempt to determine if a testator had legal capacity at an earlier point of time.[41]

Banks has consistently been applied since 1870, although it has been done so in light of modern approaches. For example, in, *In the Will of Edward Victor Macfarlane Deceased*[42] the testator had two wills dated 11 May 2000 and 16 April 2008. The testator's testamentary capacity at the time of making the second will was in issue because the death certificate listed 'multi-infarct dementia' as a cause of death. The executors initially sought to administer the estate in accordance with the second will. After legal advice as to the problems presented with seeking probate of the second will, the executors sought and were granted probate for the first will. This case is of particular interest because of the reference to evidence from two health professionals. The testator's general practitioner was not prepared to express an opinion as to the testator's testamentary capacity. This could be for a number of reasons, including the fear of being involved in litigation. The possibility of becoming involved in litigation is a very real motivator for a number of health, as well as legal, practitioners.[43] The solicitors acting for the executors therefore sought a report from a second general practitioner, Dr. Easton, regarding the testator's capacity. Dr. Easton provided two reports. In the first, he indicated that the testator would have had testamentary capacity, whereas in the second, he expressed the opinion that the testator did not have the requisite capacity. It was unclear what Dr. Easton's involvement was with the testator and little weight was given to either of the two reports.

This case highlights the importance of first, obtaining useful medical evidence that aids the court in determining the existence, or otherwise, of testamentary capacity; and secondly, of clearly characterising the relationship between the legal and health professionals, as well as of establishing processes to facilitate the gathering of relevant evidence in the face of potential litigation. It also demonstrates that just because medical evidence has been obtained, it does not mean that this evidence will be useful or given significant weight by a court. Once determined to be of relevance, and therefore admissible, it is the issue of the weight accorded to the evidence which is important, especially when considering that such reports cost money to obtain. Thus, ensuring the efficacy of the report is in everyone's interests when establishing whether a testator has capacity or not.

Medical evidence was also featured in the case of *Jones and Jones v Jones and Lindsay as executors of the Estate of TG Jones deceased*.[44] In this matter the

---

[41]Shulman KI et al. (2009), p. 436.
[42][2012] QSC 20.
[43]See further on this point: Purser K (2015).
[44][2012] QSC 113.

testator had two wills dated 22 October 2008 and 23 October 2008 respectively. The will dated 22 October 2008 was handwritten. The wills were identical. The testator died on 28 October 2008. He was suffering from 'widely disseminated non-small-cell lung cancer'.[45] The deceased's parents contested both wills on the ground that the testator was not of sound mind and lacked testamentary capacity. The plaintiffs further alleged that the will was executed in suspicious circumstances and, although the subject of cross-examination, this allegation was not part of the final submissions.

No specific assessment of testamentary capacity had been undertaken.[46] This was identified by the presiding judge as contributing to making it a difficult matter to determine.[47] Evidence was given by Dr. Tucker, the testator's treating physician, and Ms. Roberts, the solicitor who prepared the will.[48] Of note, the court recorded that the evidence given by Ms. Roberts 'was not of great assistance' because the testator was previously unknown to her. This had the effect of limiting her ability to determine his state of mind because she had no knowledge against which to test how he presented to sign the will.[49] This is a significant observation given that arguably a large majority of wills are prepared by solicitors for clients who are not known to them outside the will-making process, thus calling into question the evidence of the legal professional given in this setting.

It was further noted in the evidence given by Dr. Tucker that 'an impairment of cognitive capacity may not be obvious to a lay observer and that the type of questioning used by Ms. Roberts would not necessarily demonstrate any disordered thought processes'.[50] This highlights the importance of the questions being asked and needing to design them to assess capacity in light of both the relevant legal standard but also the specific mentally disabling condition. In this matter both the legal and health professionals had acted appropriately in the circumstances. Nevertheless, the result was still the 'difficult' assessment of testamentary capacity which could have been less problematic if the assessment process itself was more rigorous and dependable. What this implies is that, at the very least, there can be a breakdown in the application of the test for testamentary capacity which means that the process, the actual determination, or the evidence given about the assessment can be called into question. This again highlights the need for an interdisciplinary approach to ensure satisfactory and worthwhile assessments are being conducted, not to mention the necessity of establishing guidelines and principles which can both supplement and support the implementation of the legal test to assess testamentary capacity.

---

[45]Ibid [1] (Martin J).
[46]Ibid [31].
[47]Ibid.
[48]Ibid [14] - [21].
[49]Ibid.
[50]Ibid [22].

A more modern interpretation of the test for testamentary capacity was contained in the case of *Re Loxston, Abbott v Richardson*[51] in the United Kingdom and in *Read v Carmody ('Read')*[52] in Australia. It is suggested that the *Read* formulation contains 'a more complex definition of capacity [which] has been modified for clinicians' than that contained in *Banks*.[53] In *Read*[54] the appellant sought to have the grant of probate in common form of a will dated 5 February 1993 revoked on the grounds that the testator lacked testamentary capacity when the will was made. The appellant instead sought probate in solemn form of one of three earlier wills dated 3 February 1993, 11 December 1992 and 14 July 1988 respectively. Powell JA noted that seeking a grant of probate with respect to the will dated 2 days previously to the one in question was 'to say the least incongruous'.[55]

Read reinforces that the testator needs to appreciate, or at least be aware of: the significance of making a will; the nature, value and extent of the estate, at least in general terms; the potential beneficiaries who may have a claim upon the estate; and finally, must have the ability to evaluate and determine each claim.[56] Powell JA noted that it is necessary to determine if the testator, at the relevant time, suffers from a mental illness such as psychosis, or a mental disorder which includes higher cognitive function and dementia which 'detrimentally affects ... consciousness or sense of orientation, or has brought about disturbances to ... intelligence, cognition, thought content and thought processes, judgment and the like'.[57] Powell JA further noted that although the conditions may be transient, manageable or reversible, it is 'more probable than not' that if they exist then the testator will be held to lack testamentary capacity.[58] *Read* does offer some guidance on mentally disabling conditions and their effects on testamentary capacity. However, adequate direction as to the actual assessment process and guiding principles in light of meeting the legal criteria for establishing testamentary capacity are still lacking.

The traditional legal formulation of the test for testamentary capacity has obviously withstood the passage of time having been consistently applied in subsequent cases. It is a sound, general formulation of the legal elements which need to be examined. There is no need to discard or replace it in its entirety.[59] However, it is only a general statement which does not acknowledge the nuances that exist, or the developments that have occurred in capacity assessment generally. It should be noted that the *Banks* formulation was never intended to take on the importance of a statutory provision. Whether Cockburn CJ's comments have, in

---

[51][2006] WTLR 1567.
[52][1998] NSWCA 182 (23 July 1998).
[53]Peisah C (2005), p. 710; O'Neill N and Peisah C (2011), 4.9.5.2.
[54][1998] NSWCA 182 (23 July 1998).
[55]Ibid 20 (Powell JA).
[56]Ibid 2–3. See also See also Peisah C (2005), p. 710.
[57]*Read v Carmody* [1998] NSWCA 182 (23 July 1998) 3 (Powell JA).
[58]Ibid.
[59]See, on this point, Purser K (2015).

effect, been elevated to legislative authority is arguable. Nevertheless, whilst there are legal and health professionals who use the *Banks* criteria as the guideline it was intended to be, there are those from both professions who mechanically assess capacity in line with the four elements. Little regard, and perhaps questionable understanding, exists concerning the gradations that can impact testamentary capacity which have to be taken into consideration in any determination. What is apparent is that the continued use of the test for testamentary capacity in the twenty-first century requires recognition of modern techniques, data and information.[60] The existence of mentally disabling conditions which were unheard of in the nineteenth century reinforce the need to develop unambiguous assessment paradigms for both the legal and health professions which supplement the legal test. That is, they will help inform the cognitive assessment taking place within the parameters of the overarching legal framework. This will assist with the consistent, transparent and accurate determination of testamentary capacity but also in increasing the quality of evidence available for courts when deciding testamentary capacity matters. This is especially important given the individual, ad hoc basis on which assessments are currently being conducted by legal and health professionals with varying degrees of experience and training.

3   Insane Delusions and Lucid Intervals

A testator may be either completely legally incompetent or suffer from periods of legal incompetency, delusions and/or lucid intervals. A delusion has been defined as 'a fixed and incorrigible false belief which the victim could not be reasoned out of'.[61] An insane delusion 'is a belief that has absolutely no foundation in fact; even slight evidence that provides a basis for the belief negates the conclusion that it constitutes an insane delusion'.[62] Thus, it is necessary to distinguish 'delusional' from merely 'over-valued'.[63] It also seems that these terms mean different things to legal professionals, including judges, and health professionals once again demonstrating the impact that different language, training and approaches can have.[64] The delusion is 'insane' if it remains in the face of a reasoned and truthful challenge. A delusional belief must be distinguished from a paranoid ideation which is a suspicion usually acquiescent to reason.[65] The existence of a delusion however does not automatically deprive a testator of legal capacity.[66] The validity of the will is not

---

[60]Peisah C et al. (2009), p. 7.

[61]*Bull v Fulton* (1942) 66 CLR 295, 337 (Williams J). See also Frost M, Lawson S, Jacoby R (2015), pp. 250–252 for a discussion on delirium.

[62]Perlin ML et al. (2008), p. 225.

[63]Frost M et al. (2015), p. 251.

[64]Ibid 252.

[65]Mullins D (2006), p. 4.

[66]*Bull v Fulton* (1942) 66 CLR 295, 342 (Williams J).

impinged upon if the delusion has no influence on the disposition and whether it does have such influence is a question of fact.[67] If the court decides that the testator suffers from an insane delusion which is unchanging, persistent and which they cannot be reasoned out of,[68] as well as finding that the delusion affected the testamentary disposition, then a determination of legal incompetence will most likely follow.[69] Insanity is distinguished from insane delusions. This is because it is recognised that personality disorders can have just as significant an effect on a testator's capacity as an 'insane delusion'.[70] Mental illness does not preclude a testator from having the requisite testamentary capacity if the will was executed during a lucid interval.[71]

The phrases testamentary capacity, lucid interval, undue influence and insane delusion have all been criticised as exemplifying legalese and are legal 'terms of art', often from other eras.[72] A testator may demonstrate legal incompetency centring on a particular individual or property and thus delusions are only relevant to the issue of testamentary capacity when they affect distributions contained in a will.[73] Thus, one question is whether testamentary capacity is dependent upon sanity. If it is not, but delusions affect legal competency, the issue is whether the disposition arising from that delusion is severable from the will. In the English decision of *Estate of Bohrmann*,[74] it was held that the part of the will that was affected by the testator's delusions could be severed. In the more recent Australian decision of *Woodhead v Perpetual Trustee*,[75] Needham J took the view that delusions must either invalidate all or none of the will, but never a part of it. The position appears to be that delusions do not automatically invalidate a will unless they specifically impact the testator and influence a particular disposition.[76]

Further, a testator who is generally incompetent at law may experience lucid intervals in which they are able to make a will.[77] It should be noted that the medical literature suggests that lucid intervals are actually legal fictions, which enable legal professionals and the courts to resolve complex matters, rather than a medical reality.[78] The link between the legal concept of lucid intervals and the medical notion of fluctuating cognition has recently been the subject of exploration by Shulman et al.[79] They take the notion of lucid intervals as being merely a legal

---

[67]*Woodhead v Perpetual Trustee* (1987) 11 NSWLR 267, 272 (Needham J).

[68]*Re Estate of Griffith (dec'd); Easter v Griffith* (1995) 217 ALR 284, 290–292 (Gleeson CJ).

[69]*Woodhead v Perpetual Trustee* (1987) 11 NSWLR 267, 273 (Needham J).

[70]O'Neill N and Peisah C (2011), 4.9.3.7.

[71]Perlin ML et al. (2008), p. 224.

[72]Moye J et al. (2013), p. 163.

[73]*Tippet v Moore* (1911) 13 CLR 248, 250 (Griffith CJ).

[74][1938] 1 All ER 271.

[75](1987) 11 NSWLR 267, 274–245 (Needham J).

[76]Jacoby R and Steer P (2007), p. 155.

[77]*Timbury v Coffee* (1941) 66 CLR 277 applied in *Challen v Pitt* [2004] QSC 365.

[78]Marson DC et al. (2004), p. 78.

[79]Shulman KI et al. (2015), p. 287.

fiction further, noting that the findings from their research 'cast doubt on the validity of the lucid interval and invite a critical rethinking of this legal concept as applied to will challenges involving testators with dementia'.[80] They propose that the legal concept of a lucid interval is best matched by the medical notion of fluctuating capacity or 'spontaneous alterations in cognition, attention, and arousal'.[81]

A review of American cases in light of medical understanding of cognitive fluctuations was undertaken. The authors determined that it may be necessary to revise the legal interpretation and application of the notion of 'lucid interval' in light of scientific findings which do not support the current legal approach. In fact, they further note that 'the current application of a lucid interval may not be valid, because the traditional notion of good and bad days in individuals with dementia may not extend to testamentary capacity in the manner that courts have traditionally applied it'.[82] Unfortunately, the methodology employed to undertake the case review was not discussed. In examining the legal notion of lucid interval, the authors, rightly, note that courts often use the notion of a lucid interval as a means to an end—a way in which to justify the finding of testamentary capacity to reach an equitable conclusion.[83] Criticism of the interpretation of the term is founded in the age of the concept, noted as originating in 1902.[84] Age alone, however, does not indicate that the legal approach is outdated, especially given the flexibility inherent in the law in this area which is required to recognise the exigencies of modern society.

What is more important is the increasing use of cognitive assessments and whether these are occurring within an appropriate legal framework. To this end the authors note that, 'cognitive fluctuations do not occur to a significant degree in cognitive domains that are essential to achieving testamentary capacity, such as episodic memory and higher-level executive brain functions. Thus cognitive fluctuations may not be an appropriate justification for the legal determination of a lucid interval'.[85] This does not necessarily impugn the appropriateness of the legal test, rather, it is about the clarity of communication—what is being assessed, how and to what standard—between the legal and health professionals involved in the capacity assessment. What is clear is that this is a fascinating and potentially significant issue with the capability to fundamentally influence the approach that courts take to the assessment of lucid intervals in testamentary capacity—and certainly to the evidence forthcoming from health professionals about the existence of lucid intervals, including how the legal concept may be measured in a clinical context. Further research is needed, especially as this study is American specific, and it is imperative

---

[80]Ibid.
[81]Ibid.
[82]Ibid 288.
[83]Ibid 288.
[84]Ibid 289.
[85]Ibid 289.

that any such research adopt a transdisciplinary approach informed by both legal and medical knowledge.

4 Statutory Wills

A brief note on statutory wills is required. Statutory wills enable an individual, after obtaining the leave of the court, to apply to ask the court to make, alter or revoke a will for a testator who lacks the requisite testamentary capacity to make, alter or revoke his or her own will.[86] In each case a draft will or alternate provisions must be approved by the court. Statutory wills require an assurance that the assessment of testamentary capacity is beyond reproach. The intricacies of statutory wills are beyond the scope of this work. What is important is the actual assessment of testamentary capacity that occurs when applying for a statutory will. The test, as stated, is whether the individual lacks testamentary capacity. This assessment should be no different to what has been discussed with the exception that it has to be, by the very nature of a statutory will, contemporaneous. The standard to which a lack of capacity needs to be proven may vary depending upon the stage of the application, that is when seeking leave or in the substantive material. For example, the case of *Application of J. R. Fenwick and Re Charles*[87] was a decision dealing with two cases. The first, *Fenwick*, is an application about a 60 year old man who had previously made a will about 10 years previously but had since suffered from a disabling accident. The application was designed to avoid a potential intestacy. In the second proceeding, *Re Charles*, the individual was an 11 year old child who had suffered a severe and irreversible brain injury aged 4 months. His parents were suspected of causing the injuries. The application in this case was made to avoid the possibility of the estate passing to the parents on intestacy. In his decision Palmer J, unsurprisingly, applied the established test for testamentary capacity. However, he did note that the threshold to establish testamentary capacity in a leave application, at its lowest, would merely require that 'the applicant demonstrate that there is reason to believe that the subject person is reasonably likely to lack testamentary capacity'.[88] Potential applicants would, however, only be able to provide the minimum information in situations of 'real urgency'.[89]

Palmer J discussed the evidence necessary to establish testamentary capacity, categorising it as the 'best evidence', 'next best evidence' and the 'least satisfactory evidence'.[90] His Honour stated that the best evidence will always be expert evidence from a specialist, for example, a psychiatrist or consultant physician, who has

---

[86]Croucher RF (2009), p. 728; O'Neill N and Peisah C (2011), 4.10.
[87][2009] NSWSC 530.
[88]Ibid [126].
[89]Ibid [126].
[90]Ibid [126]–[130].

undertaken a contemporaneous assessment of the testator and who provides a report to the court abiding by the rules of evidence.[91] The report should specify the testing conducted and how the results equate to each element necessary to establish testamentary capacity.[92] This is to be the position except if it is a clear case of legal incompetency, such as a coma, in which case it is not necessary to describe the testing procedures. If such a report is unavailable the next best evidence is that of the testator's treating physician or general practitioner. A report should again be obtained in accordance with the requirements discussed for the best evidence.[93] If this is unavailable then the least satisfactory evidence may be accepted. The least satisfactory evidence is that provided by lay people demonstrating the testator's apparent erratic and/or demented behaviour and showing who stands to benefit under the statutory will or codicil.[94] This type of evidence, alone, will be treated with the 'utmost suspicion'.[95] Despite Palmer J's comments, the lack of legislative and judicial guidance given defining what would amount to 'satisfactory evidence' as to when an individual is incapable of making a will, or detailing what assessment should occur to determine that an individual lacks testamentary capacity or is unlikely to regain it remains concerning. Thus, the problem remains the same. The test used for assessing testamentary capacity will be that based upon the traditional formulation. This does not address the underlying complexities involved in the assessment process, such as the terminological confusion surrounding capacity, the legal and medical construct in which it is considered, or the lack of adequate and accepted testing method(s). The tension that can exist between the legal and health professions is likewise not addressed.

5   The Golden Rule

The development of the golden rule is one avenue through which to attempt to manage the relationship between legal and health professionals. The golden rule is an English notion recognising the desirability of the involvement of both legal and health professionals when capacity is questionable. It was first established in *Kenward v Adams*,[96] and was encouraged in the recent decision of *Burns v Burns*.[97] It basically states that where a will has been prepared for an elderly or seriously ill person, or where legal capacity may be questionable, the will should be witnessed by a health practitioner who can formally assess the testator's capacity.[98] However, it is less a rule and

---

[91]Ibid.
[92]Ibid.
[93]Ibid.
[94]Ibid.
[95]Ibid.
[96][1975] CLY 3591.
[97][2016] EWCA Civ 37.
[98]*Re Key* [2010] EWHC 408; [2010] 1 WLR 2020.

more a statement of good practice.[99] The golden rule was upheld in *Re Simpson*[100] and again more recently in *Buckenham v Dickinson*.[101] In *Buckenham* the solicitor in question was criticised for failing to follow the golden rule and procure the involvement of a health professional. In *Re Key*,[102] one of the more relatively recent endorsements of the golden rule, Briggs J described the failure to comply with this rule, noting that although it does not affect the validity of the will, the purpose of the rule is to help avoid, or at least minimise, disputes. Sagaciously, it was further noted that,

> persons with failing or impaired mental faculties may, for perfectly understandable reasons, seek to conceal what they regard as their embarrassing shortcomings from persons with whom they deal, so that a friend or professional person such as a solicitor may fail to detect defects in mental capacity which would be or become apparent to a trained and experienced medical examiner, to whom a proper description of the legal test for testamentary capacity had first been provided.[103]

The impact of the negative connotations which can attach to an 'incompetency' label can be pervasive, having a deep effect on the individual as well as on those that the individual interacts with. Thus, the perceptions of the individual are fundamental in attempting to ensure that their interaction with the law and capacity assessments are beneficial in order to help protect not only individual autonomy but to also ensure that the individual does not become vulnerable to abuse.

Although indicative of best practice, the practical application of the golden rule can however prove problematic.[104] It assumes that legal and health professionals will be willing to cooperate in the assessment process. Unfortunately, this is not always the case.[105] As discussed, health professionals can be reluctant to participate in legal capacity determinations, especially with the possibility of either being a witness in, or the subject of, litigation. Conversely, legal professionals do not necessarily provide adequate guidance to health professionals as to the nature and standard of the legal capacity being assessed, nor of the type of report required. Confronting both professions is the challenge of identifying what is actually being assessed, and the impact the specific mentally disabling condition has on the legal capacity in question to make the specific decision being contemplated. This is then further compounded by both the uncertainty of the assessment process, and by a lack of knowledge and skills necessary to satisfactorily assess testamentary capacity.[106]

---

[99]*Hoff v Atherton* [2004] EWCA Civ 1554; [2005] WTLR 99; *Re Key* [2010] EWHC 408 (Ch); [2010] WLR 2020.

[100]*Re Simpson* (1977) 121 Sol Jo 224.

[101]*Buckenham v Dickinson* [1997] CLY 661.

[102]*Re Key* [2010] EWHC 408; [2010] 1 WLR 2020.

[103]Ibid [8].

[104]See Frost M et al. (2015), pp. 51–52 for what the authors call a 'much clearer articulation of the duty of the draftsman' as set out in a series of Canadian cases.

[105]See, for example, Purser K (2015).

[106]Shulman KI et al. (2009), p. 434.

Critically important for practitioners is the need to be aware of circumstances which can give rise to the necessity of assessing capacity, the 'triggers'. *Legal Services Commissioner v Ford*[107] examines the role of a legal professional in assessing capacity in the Australian context. It was noted in that case that the legal professional's conduct 'fell short of the standard of competence and diligence that a member of the public was entitled to expect of a reasonably competent Australian legal practitioner'.[108] Fryberg J commented that the solicitor should have been alert to capacity issues given that the client was in her late 80s, lived in a nursing home, was cutting her family out of her will and leaving everything to the person who was facilitating the process.[109] Of relevance was also the fact that a nursing home employee commented specifically in relation to the client's memory loss. Although Fryberg J did emphasise that this was not necessarily a precedent because it was an unusual case, it does serve as a warning that legal professionals must be aware of the circumstances which give rise to questions about capacity.[110]

Adherence to the golden rule is a step towards not only strengthening the potential validity of a will, but also helping to implement best practice. However, until a satisfactory assessment paradigm, including guiding principles, is developed practitioners will continue to take an individualistic approach representative of their own knowledge and skills, exposing them to increasing questions of professional liability. This is one example of the limitations of the current assessment process. Some of the other questions being raised about the adequacy of the existing assessment paradigm will be discussed in the next section.

6 The Adequacy of the Existing Assessment Paradigm

The adequacy of current methods to assess testamentary capacity has been questioned.[111] The absence of judicial guidance regarding what amounts to satisfactory assessment processes to demonstrate the absence of testamentary capacity is only serving to compound the problem of the ad hoc assessments which are occurring. Writing in the American context, Champine maintained that the testamentary capacity doctrine is currently inadequate, calling, at the very least, for its reformulation, arguing that 'the sole certainty in testamentary capacity case law is unpredictability'.[112] Further, the lack of a set standard for the proof required to establish either capacity or incapacity only exacerbates this problem.[113] In fact,

---

[107][2008] LPT 12.
[108]Ibid 23 (Fryberg J).
[109]Ibid 21 (Fryberg J).
[110]Ibid 25 (Fryberg J).
[111]O'Neill N and Peisah C (2011), 4.9.5.2; Peisah C and Brodaty H (1994), p. 381.
[112]Champine P (2006), pp. 29–30.
[113]Ibid 39.

Champine has queried what purpose the testamentary competency doctrine serves given its inconsistent results.[114] Although these comments were made within an overarching focus on the contrasting issues of testator autonomy and familial protection they, nevertheless, are just as relevant in the present context. Champine's statement that the testamentary capacity doctrine stagnated in the twentieth century and should not be allowed to do so for the 21st cannot be ignored.[115]

6.1 'Practical' Concerns

Practical concerns have been raised regarding a modern testator's ability to understand the nature and extent of his or her financial assets and resources.[116] It is estimated that a massive transfer of wealth will be gifted to the baby boomer generation by today's older generation, with it eventually to be transferred to younger generations.[117] The increase in personal wealth means that it is not uncommon for estate planning schemes to utilise a potentially complicated series of, for example, trusts and companies to ensure wealth growth, management, protection, and transition. Consequently, whether an individual can actually understand the nature and extent of his or her property is increasingly arguable, especially in light of the intricate estate planning mechanisms being used. One of the growing challenges here is, if a capable person without legal training (and even on occasion with) struggles to understand what a trust is, how then are individuals going to understand the use of such a vehicle in their personal estate planning? Further, what impact does, and should, if indeed at all, that have on the elements necessary to establish testamentary capacity? The potential lack of understanding due to the complexity of the estate planning mechanisms employed is only going to be exacerbated if an individual does have a mentally disabling condition.

Another 'practical' concern is that of 'deathbed wills'—those made when an individual's death is imminent. The exact timing of what makes a will a 'deathbed will' is not defined, nor in fact definable.[118] Physical and psychological comorbidities can exist alongside the primary condition which makes assessing testamentary capacity in these circumstances extremely difficult.[119] Further exacerbating the challenges presented by assessing capacity at the end of life are the effects of any medications as well as the intense feelings brought about by death—not only for the individual but also for the friends and family members of that person. Lawyers can miss issues pertinent to testamentary capacity presenting from

---

[114]Ibid 48–49.

[115]Ibid 93.

[116]As referred to in *Kerr v Badran* [2004] NSWSC 735, [49] (Windeyer J).

[117]Moye J and Marson DC (2007), p. 3; Finkel SI (2003), p. 65.

[118]Peisah C et al. (2014), p. 210.

[119]Purser K and Rosenfeld T (2016), p. 334; Peisah C et al. (2014), p. 209.

delirium.[120] This is concerning given that, generally, delirious people are unable to balance competing claims of potential beneficiaries, and, for the most part, do not possess the capacity necessary to be able to make a will.[121] The problem is that legal professionals often do not consult with health professionals, or do consult and the health professionals themselves can miss these issues given the difficulty of engaging in cognitive assessment within a legal framework.[122]

Undue influence is an ever present concern when an individual has lost, or has limited, capacity to make his or her own legally recognised decisions. It can be a complicating factor when assessing testamentary capacity, especially as the circumstances giving rise to undue influence can also often involve capacity concerns. Health professionals are being increasingly asked whether the loss of capacity could make the individual more or less susceptible to undue influence.[123] This is problematic if the health professionals do not understand the legal notion of undue influence and if the legal practitioners do not clearly explain it—not to mention that probate and equitable undue influence differ. Fundamentally, undue influence requires the will of the person to be overborne. This necessarily implies that the person must be capable, at law, of exercising their will in order for it to be 'overborne'. Therefore, if the person is incapable then arguably they are not able to exercise their will and whilst incapable will not be able to be subject to undue influence. This obviously places vulnerable people at risk of abuse, especially if the loss or lack of capacity is not known outside of the abuser(s) and thus the abuser (s) is able to take further and continued advantage of the vulnerable person.

Capacity issues and undue influence present in factually similar circumstances and even though viewed as capable at law, a person can be vulnerable because of, for example, loneliness, isolation, as well as emotional and physical dependence.[124] Of note, Peisah et al. state that 'nursing and medical staff, who are often the gatekeepers of access to terminally ill testators may unwittingly facilitate or collude with the exploitation of an impaired testator merely by virtue of their failure to identify delirium'.[125] This is an important statement, not least because it is true. The reliance on health professionals is increasing and as a result of this, especially in light of the ageing population and the increasing mentally disabling conditions, it is vital that if medical assessments are being undertaken within a legal framework then all parts of the assessment process are working well. What this also demonstrates is the different medical and legal approaches. Even though deemed capable by the dichotomous yes/no approach of the law, on the continuum favoured by the

---

[120]Peisah C et al. (2014). For a discussion on delirium and testamentary capacity see Frost M et al. (2015), pp. 247–248.

[121]Frost M et al. (2015), p. 260.

[122]Peisah C et al. (2014), p. 211.

[123]Falk E and Hoffman N (2014), pp. 854–855.

[124]Ibid 855.

[125]Peisah C et al. (2014), p. 212.

clinical approach the existence of capacity is not so clear cut. It is reconciling these approaches to best protect vulnerable individuals which is the key.

Situations have also occurred wherein health care professionals become aware of legal professionals preparing wills where, in the health professional's opinion, the individual has lost capacity.[126] A legal professional has a duty to make a will unless it is abundantly clear that the individual lacks capacity, remembering that it is ultimately the decision of the court as to whether an individual does or does not have the requisite ability at law. This highlights the underlying medical and legal tension—does the individual lack capacity in the clinical or the legal sense? Arguably, from the legal perspective, it is even more imperative in these circumstances that the legal professional prepare the will promptly and, at the very least, ensure that a handwritten document is prepared at the time of taking instructions.[127] A typed document can then be executed if the individual is able. Collection of appropriate evidence—file notes, and assessments if necessary - should also take place to ensure that the best evidence is able to be presented to the court in the event that there is a dispute about capacity.

Suicide also gives rise to questions of capacity. Whilst not automatically displacing the presumption of capacity, clinical factors which can be in issue with suicidal ideations such as depression and psychosis can also have an impact on testamentary capacity.[128] Little research has been undertaken in this area as well so there is further scope for a detailed examination into how these mentally disabling conditions coupled with suicidal propensities impact capacity.

Interestingly, the relationship between marriage and will-making also gives rise to practical concerns, or at least incongruities. Marriage, generally, revokes a will unless it is made in contemplation of the marriage. However, the standard of capacity required to marry is lower than that required to make, and revoke, a will. Therefore, through marriage a person can achieve what they may not have the capacity to do otherwise—a probably unintentional, but somewhat absurd result.[129]

6.2 Mentally Disabling Conditions and Testamentary Capacity

Medical advances and recognition of diseases such as dementia have added to the growing complexity involved in testamentary capacity assessments which means that medical, including psychological and neuropsychological, opinion is increasingly being utilised by the courts in order to accurately assess capacity.[130] The

---

[126]Ibid 213.

[127]For a recent decision see *Feltham v Freer Bouskell* [2013] ECH 1952.

[128]Sinyor M et al. (2015), p. 72.

[129]Frost M et al. (2015), pp. 16–17.

[130]Shulman KI et al. (2009), p. 434; Shulman KI et al. (2007), p. 722.

necessary involvement of health professionals recognises that legal professionals are not trained to detect neurodegenerative diseases or the effects of these diseases on an individual's testamentary capacity. Consequently, the legal test is open to scrutiny by the health professionals who have critically engaged with it, and its utility in the modern health setting.[131] What is being questioned is the capability of the current test to take into account the nuances of all the potentially mentally disabling conditions as well as the transitory nature of legal capacity. As Shulman et al. have noted, 'while there is some evidence that the courts have developed principles relevant to Alzheimer's and other dementias, a deeper and wider knowledge base among jurists surely will enhance the law's ability to adjudicate will contests'.[132] It is time for the legal and health professions to develop novel and innovative approaches to address the important and increasingly frequent challenge presented to modern society by the assessment of capacity.[133]

In therefore considering the test for testamentary capacity, it has been observed that the legal formulation focuses on cognition or knowingness, whereas conation and affect can be just as relevant to a health professional, a distinction which a legal professional would not necessarily make. Already complex clinical evaluations of testamentary capacity are made even more challenging when, for example, the individual in question suffers from severe aphasia, and/or where familial circumstances are complicated by multiple marriages which may result in natural, adopted and/or step children.[134] It is possible that an individual may have a mentally disabling condition and be unsure as to the date and location, and yet meet the elements necessary to establish testamentary capacity.[135] There is currently no method of assessment to correlate the diagnosis of a mentally disabling condition with the specific element relevant to establishing testamentary capacity, especially in the context of dementia.

Identifying the form of dementia can assist in the assessment process because education or treatment plans may be implemented which would facilitate legal competency.[136] It is assumed that testamentary capacity is retained in early dementia but lost in late dementia. However, in the absence of a defined testamentary capacity threshold, this assumption cannot be tested.[137] The concept of a 'testamentary competency threshold' was suggested as early as 1994 by Peisah and Brodaty.[138] However, they noted, even then, that a definitive test is unlikely to be developed stating that it would always depend on the particular situation and the assessor's judgment.[139] It has also been suggested that there should be a higher

---

[131]Shulman KI et al. (2005), p. 63.

[132]Shulman KI et al. (2007), p. 725.

[133]Shulman KI et al. (2005), p. 68.

[134]Falk E and Hoffman N (2014), p. 854.

[135]Posener HD and Jacoby R (2008), p. 755.

[136]O'Neill N and Peisah C (2011), p. 3.

[137]Peisah C and Brodaty H (1994), p. 382.

[138]Ibid.

[139]Ibid 384.

standard in environments characterised by conflict to ensure that the testator understands what he or she is doing and the effects of the decision.[140] In a similar vein, methods exist for assessing capacity to give informed consent as well as some screening mechanisms relating to comprehension, judgment, long term memory, immediate memory and registration, as well as expressive and receptive language which may be able to be modified to assess testamentary capacity. However, they have not yet been validated in the testamentary context.[141] Heinik, Werner and Lin have also discussed the use of a clinically based (as opposed to legally supported) testament definition scale ('TDS'), comprising six items designed to measure an individual's testamentary capacity.[142] No application outside the Israeli context in which the TDS was developed through which to authenticate the model seems to have occurred.

Legal professionals may not be aware of issues arising from the existence of presenting mentally disabling conditions, any comorbidities, and/or the effects of medications. Consequently, they may not realise that the instructions they have received may be tainted by the person's mentally disabling condition, especially if the legal professional is not conversant with the intricacies of a client's particular illness. For example, it is estimated that about a third of people with dementia will, at some time during their illness, suffer from delusions which could affect testamentary dispositions. Further, it is expected that approximately 30% of people will have depressive illnesses which may present as delusions of poverty.[143] Failing to detect issues underlying testamentary intentions is a real possibility, especially given that health practitioners and nursing staff often miss the existence of, for example, dementia.[144] An incorrect label will place individual autonomy at risk so the determination of capacity, or a lack thereof, is vitally important and must be beyond reproach.

6.3 Evidence about Testamentary Capacity

A challenging relationship exists between the evidence of legal and health professionals. Medical evidence is not necessarily conclusive in courts of the existence, or otherwise, of testamentary capacity.[145] Distrust of the expertise of health care professions can exist, which means that reliance is generally placed upon the contents of the will unless the health professional was the treating physician.[146] In

---

[140]Shulman KI et al. (2005), p. 68.

[141]Peisah C and Brodaty H (1994), pp. 382, 384.

[142]Heinik J et al. (1999), pp. 23–24.

[143]Peisah C and Brodaty H (1994), p. 382.

[144]O'Neill N and Peisah C (2011).

[145]Burns FR (2005), p. 161.

[146]Champine P (2006).

fact, it has been noted that courts should be very careful about accepting evidence
from health care professionals where the practitioner involved did not actually meet
the testator.[147] In *Kerr v Badran*[148] Windeyer J commented on the failure of the
parties to call the testator's treating physician, noting that 'evidence would have
been of great value in determining this case and certainly of far more assistance
than the evidence of expert psychiatrists who did not see or treat the deceased'.[149]
Windeyer J also commented on the differences in society, especially the management of assets, from the time of *Banks* to modern society and that the test has to be
applied in light of these societal changes.[150] Another example is provided by the
case of *Bertoldo v Cordenos*.[151] Here the inquiries made by the legal professional
into the testator's capacity to make a will and ability to communicate in English
were criticised as being 'shallow, to say the least'.[152] It was noted that the records of
the solicitor, Mr. Anthony, fell 'far short of the standard required of solicitors
dealing with the preparation of wills for aged, enfeebled or ill clients'.[153] The
solicitor was relying upon the health care professional's assessment as to the
testator's capacity but, as noted by Jones J, this does not relieve the legal professional from the responsibility of making his own inquiries and keeping a suitable
record of the investigations made.[154] This was highlighted by the fact that the legal
professional, by his own admission, was unaware that the testator suffered from
both depression and dementia for some time prior to giving instructions.[155]

    Growing reliance on the opinions of health professionals does not, however,
guarantee that the medical evidence regarding legal capacity will be accepted.[156]
That legal professionals will increasingly be expected by the courts to not only
obtain expert advice on the issue of an individual's testamentary capacity but to also
rely on it, often above their own assessment, is an ideal as to what the position
perhaps should be.[157] The concern, however, is who that expert will and should be,
what training they will have undertaken and what process they will be applying to
satisfactorily assess legal capacity. The health professions appear to hold the view
that legal professionals are unable to satisfactorily assess capacity and overcome
the legally competent façade which dementia sufferers, for example, can erect. This
is a fair suspicion when legal professionals are trained in the intricacies of the legal
system, not the differences between a deluded mind and one which simply

---

[147]*Hawes v Burgess* [2013] WTLR 453 CA; EWCA Civ 74.
[148][2004] NSWSC 735 (17 August 2004).
[149]Ibid [39].
[150]Ibid [49].
[151][2010] QSC 79.
[152]Ibid 21.
[153]Ibid 10.
[154]Ibid.
[155]Ibid.
[156]Sprehe DJ and Kerr AL (1996), p. 255.
[157]O'Neill N and Peisah C (2011), 4.4.

overvalues an idea because of a mentally disabling condition. However, the evidence of health care professionals can also be problematic, in a large degree, because a clinical assessment is conducted often without adequate reference to the legal framework. In *Woodhead v Perpetual Trustee*,[158] for example, three medical professionals gave evidence. Dr. Norris was a general practitioner who had known the testator. In Dr. Norris' opinion the testator was capable. The remaining two medical practitioners, both psychiatrists who had never met the testator, disagreed about the testator's testamentary capacity. Dr. Roberts diagnosed the testator with paranoia vera. Dr. Smith's diagnosis was that the testator suffered paranoid schizophrenia. Dr. Roberts testified that it was his opinion that none 'of the delusions or hallucinations from which the testatrix suffered would have affected her capacity to assess the moral claims on her of potential beneficiaries'.[159] Whereas Dr. Smith testified that 'if the testatrix, at the time of making the will, had delusions concerning her relations, that would seriously affect her capacity to sum up her moral obligations to her family'.[160] In this instance, the Court preferred the evidence of Dr. Roberts.

The evidence of the treating physician may be preferred to expert evidence because the treating physician will often have interacted with the testator over a period of time, possibly years, which enables them to assess any unusual or changing cognitive, behavioural or emotional characteristics. It is also contemporaneous evidence of testamentary capacity whereas expert opinions are often not sought until after the testator's death. However, the issue here is whether the treating physician has made an (accurate) assessment as to the existence, or otherwise, of testamentary capacity at the requisite time, being the time the will is made, or whether they are being asked to make a decision about a period in time which is long past. The question is whether this is any better than a retrospective assessment conducted after the death of the individual in question. Additionally, it can create intense pressure on a health professional to reach a certain outcome, especially if that professional has a relationship with the individual and/or his or her family. However, it is clear that a court does not always prefer the evidence of the treating physician when determining if a testator was legally competent. Further to this, criticism has been levelled both at legal professionals, for not obtaining an appropriately qualified health professional to witness a will where the testator's capacity was in question, as well as at health professionals for avoiding legal professionals because the health professional did not want to be involved.[161]

Fuggle v Sochacki[162] presents another example of the tension which can exist between legal and health professionals in this context. In this case the New South Wales Supreme Court discounted the evidence of a specialist geriatrician with

---

[158](1987) 11 NSWLR 267.

[159]Ibid 269–271 (Needham J).

[160]Ibid.

[161]*O'Connor v Shortland* (1989) 51 SASR 337, 348.

[162][1999] NSWSC 1214.

13 years' experience assessing individuals with dementia to reach a finding that the testator had testamentary capacity. This was despite the fact that the Court was impressed with the evidence of Dr. Fairfull-Smith, the specialist geriatrician in question.[163] The Court explained this decision stating that the antagonism that the testator felt towards the English relatives that led to them being disinherited had an objective basis which was not irrational.[164] The concern here is that medical opinion is being erroneously discounted in situations where differing legal and medical conclusions are reached. This is despite Dixon CJ stating in *Middlebrook v Middlebrook*[165] that 'ultimately the comparison must be between conflicting judgements formed on different material and involving no necessary conflict of veracity',[166] and Sir James Hannen in *Boughton v Knight*[167] noting that it is a question to be guided by common-sense, 'and that it does not depend solely on scientific or legal definition'.[168] With respect, this last statement seems too ambiguous to provide any useful guidance to either the legal or the health professions.

The relationship between medical and lay evidence is also important. This was discussed in *Zorbas v Sidiropoulous*,[169] where it was noted that the criteria to establish testamentary capacity

> are not matters that are directly medical questions, in the way that a question whether a person is suffering from cancer is a medical question. They are matters for common sense judicial judgment on the basis of the whole of the evidence. Medical evidence as to the medical condition of a deceased may of course be highly relevant and may sometimes directly support or deny a capacity in the deceased to have understanding of the matters in the *Banks v Goodfellow* criteria. However, evidence of such understanding may come from non-expert witnesses. Indeed, perhaps the most compelling evidence of understanding would be reliable evidence (for example, a tape recording) of a detailed conversation with the deceased at this time of the will displaying understanding of the deceased's assets, the deceased's family and the effect of the will. It is extremely unlikely that medical evidence that the deceased did not understand these things would overcome the effect of evidence of such a conversation.[170]

While evidence from non-experts can be central with respect to the testator's wishes, behaviour and morals, it is obviously of a different category to expert legal and medical evidence, hence the different requirements for it to be admissible. There is also the issue of whether the lay individual in question is attempting to further his or her own private agenda. Consequently, lay evidence needs to be treated with the utmost care.

---

[163]Ibid [43].

[164]Ibid [66].

[165](1962) 36 ALJR 216.

[166]Ibid 172 (Dixon CJ).

[167](1873) LR 3 P & D 64.

[168]Ibid 67.

[169][2009] NSWCA 197.

[170]Ibid [65] (Hodgson JA with whom Young JA and Bergin CJ in Eq agreed).

6.4   The Role of 'Expert' Evidence

The assessment of testamentary capacity is a specialised area which should be conducted by an assessor(s) who has the necessary credentials to support making such a determination.[171] Given the increasing complexity of cases coming before the courts, the need for expert assessors who are versed in both the legal and medical concepts is rising.[172] However, to date, the role of the 'expert' in this context has been somewhat 'uncertain and not so much controversial as inconsequential'.[173] Health care practitioners, people giving 'expert' evidence and expert assessors are not necessarily one in the same.[174] The notion of 'expert evidence' in capacity assessment cases requires further investigation – who is an expert, how this is to be established, and what happens when, for example, the evidence of the legal and the health professional are in conflict?

When it is a health care professional providing evidence, there is uncertainty over whether the 'expert' should be the general practitioner who has interacted with the individual or a specialist such as a neuropsychologist or perhaps a neurologist or geriatrician.[175] The selection of the 'expert' will depend upon numerous factors including the individual's circumstances as well as the cost involved. If a specialist is involved then this can obviously increase the costs quite substantially as each side will arguably want to present their own 'expert' evidence. Even determining whether a health practitioner is an expert can be problematic, requiring discussion of various factors which can include, for example, whether the field is recognised as a field of specialised knowledge, if the witness is an expert in that field, the evidence given must be within that field, the factual foundation for the evidence must be established, and expert reasoning must be demonstrated.[176] The answers to such questions are questions of judgment, so again, potentially muddying the already confused and confusing process of capacity assessment. The variability of the assessor further highlights the importance of ensuring that the assessment *process* is satisfactory.

In any assessment paradigm, it is ideal that the health 'expert' has the necessary expertise in medico-legal issues to assess the relevant capacity. Clear guidelines and principles regarding the legal capacity to be assessed should be provided by the legal professional to the health care practitioner.[177] It is also vital for the method of communicating the assessment findings to be established. Health professionals who are asked to provide an opinion should determine whether it is the legal professional or the testator who is requesting the assessment and for what purpose. If it is the

---

[171]Shulman KI et al. (2009), p. 434.

[172]Perlin ML et al. (2008), pp. 244–245.

[173]Spaulding WJ (1985), p. 121.

[174]Shulman KI et al. (2005), p. 63.

[175]O'Neill N and Peisah C (2011), 4.9.4.1.

[176]*Makita (Australia) Pty Ltd. v Sprowles* (2001) 52 NSWLR 705 at [85].

[177]Perlin ML et al. (2008), pp. 244–245.

legal professional, it must then be determined whether the testator has agreed to undertake such an assessment. That the testator should understand the nature and purpose of the assessment and consent to participate is closely tied to obtaining an individual's authority to assess their capacity (if the individual in question is able to give such an authority). This recognises the individual's autonomy but also provides him or her with the knowledge to ideally augment their participation in and comprehension of the process thus presenting him or her with the optimal environment in which to have his or her capacity assessed.[178] That the individual being assessed should understand and participate in the assessment process resonates with therapeutic jurisprudence principles. The consensual participation of the individual whose capacity is in question goes someway to addressing the question of whether the request for an assessment arises from the legal professional's determination or from the concerns of a third party. Obviously, if the request is emanating from a third party this can give rise to questions of hidden agendas and/or undue influence which assessors must be aware of.

It is suggested that when assessing testamentary capacity, a health professional should be familiar with any prior testamentary instruments, both will(s) and codicil (s), the current will, the testator's assets and liabilities, as well as relevant medical records including any reports from nursing homes and/or community care agencies.[179] Knowledge of the familial and personal environment is also important. This is to provide contextual information about the testator which can assist with the assessment process. Ideally, it can, on occasion, be best practice to interview third parties to resolve any ambiguity regarding assets or outstanding concerns that require independent corroboration, as well as minimising potential bias from relying on one source of information. However, one significant and practical problem with best practice is cost—who is to pay for all of this and who is best situated to conduct such an assessment?

6.5   Contemporaneous and Retrospective Assessment

An increase in will contests is one expected consequence of our ageing society.[180] People are living longer and accumulating more wealth, thus making their estates potentially more litigable. Litigation can occur for a variety of reasons, including when beneficiaries either do not receive what they think they are 'entitled' to, or, if they think that others who have been included in estate planning mechanisms have been so because of either a lack of capacity on behalf of the testator or because of undue influence. Obviously whether someone can contest the will depends on the relevant law and the facts at hand but there are a variety of mechanisms through

---

[178]Ibid.
[179]Shulman KI et al. (2009), p. 436.
[180]Ibid 433.

which to attempt to achieve this—based both in probate but also increasingly in the equitable jurisdiction, for example, inter vivos undue influence and unconscionable conduct, estoppel, and breach of fiduciary obligations in relation to both enduring powers of attorney and trusts. A lack of testamentary capacity, therefore, is just one avenue through which to attempt to invalidate estate planning mechanisms.

In addition to this, and as discussed, capacity assessments are becoming ever more complex especially when taking into consideration the wide variety of mentally disabling conditions that can impact a testator's testamentary capacity and the complex nature of the actual assessment process. The assessment process itself is then even further complicated by the medico-legal relationship and the increasingly significant questions of liability for both legal and health practitioners if they get the assessment wrong. Consequently, it is realistic to expect that legal professionals seeking medical input in testamentary capacity assessments will intensify in number as well as (potentially) complexity.[181] This is because understanding is growing that legal practitioners alone do not always have the complete skill-set to assess testamentary capacity, but also because a medical assessment can add a needed objective clinical perspective to judicial determinations of capacity.[182]

These assessments can then be conducted either contemporaneously or retrospectively. Marson and Champine have both argued for contemporaneous assessment instruments, although Shulman et al. have noted that there are 'methodological challenges' with such an approach, primarily because of the task specific nature of legal competency.[183] Retrospective assessment involves assessing the testamentary capacity of a deceased testator relying on evidence such as the deceased's medical records and testimony from third parties.[184] They are often referred to as a 'neuropsychological autopsy'.[185] It is the most common form of assessment because people are either not aware of the risks of a challenge based on a lack of capacity or do not wish to go to the trouble and expense of obtaining a contemporaneous assessment. A common thought being that the testator will not be around to see the consequences, so why should they care? They should care because the fact that retrospective assessments are frequently undertaken by 'experts' who have never met the testator and thus are basing their assessments often on documentary evidence and third party statements can also be a threat to the decision-making autonomy, as well as the testamentary freedom, exercised by the testator when making the will. That retrospective assessments occur after the death of the testator can likewise be evidentially problematic, making contemporaneous determinations attractive but not without their own difficulties.

---

[181]Ibid 434.

[182]Perlin ML et al. (2008), p. 244.

[183]Shulman KI et al. (2009), p. 438.

[184]Ibid 434; Marson DC et al. (2004), p. 82.

[185]Marson DC et al. (2004), p. 85.

Contemporaneous assessment is generally ideal because it enables the assessment of a living testator at the time of, or as near as possible to, the execution of the will. This can be contrasted to the need to rely upon documents and evidence from parties other than the testator as is the case when capacity is assessed retrospectively.[186] Contemporaneous assessment can also heighten a testator's chances of being assessed as legally competent.[187] This is because the testator may be able to gain an understanding of the process, enabling them to not only increase their ability to be found capable but also ideally making for a more positive interaction with the legal system, and the health and legal actors involved in the assessment. Contemporaneous assessment can help improve the testator's understanding of any conflict in their environment as well as the effect of their decision to include or exclude particular individuals who may expect to be beneficiaries. Subsequently, any allegations of impaired capacity, including any behavioural, cognitive or psychiatric symptoms, can be addressed while the testator is still alive.[188]

If contemporaneous assessment occurs, however, it can highlight that legal capacity may be an issue, which can be tactically problematic if litigation is a possibility.[189] The question of cost and who is going to pay for the assessment again arises as a very real obstacle. Other practical problems also exist. How does a practitioner broach the very difficult conversation with an individual, and/or their family, that: the individual may not actually have the capacity necessary to make a will; or that the practitioner thinks that the individual needs to have their capacity assessed, and thus the practitioner needs an authority from the individual to speak to a health professional. What of the situation where the client may not possess the capacity necessary to instruct the legal professional? Consequently, although contemporaneous assessment is generally thought to be the superior assessment method there can be difficulties that need to be taken into account when considering the utility of such a determination. For assessments, whether contemporaneous or retrospective, to be as reliable as possible it is necessary to provide health professionals with the information pertinent to the requisite legal framework that will enable them to conduct assessments leading to the best evidence possible which can then be relied upon by the courts.[190]

6.6   Cost

As can be seen from the preceding discussion, the issue of cost is significant. It is important to identify who is to pay for capacity assessments (be they

---

[186]Shulman KI et al. (2009), p. 436.

[187]Ibid. See also Perlin ML et al. (2008), p. 244.

[188]Shulman KI et al. (2009), p. 436.

[189]Ibid 433.

[190]Ibid.

contemporaneous or retrospective) and how this payment is to be calculated, that is, whether pursuant to an hourly rate or fixed fee.[191] The question arises as to whether assessments should be specifically covered by a government or user pays system. Arguably, there are more pressing concerns for government monies than providing contemporaneous assessments in will contests based on the alleged incapacity of a particular testator. However, any such 'contest' will be indicative of larger concerns confronting society as a whole, including the increase in cognitively degenerative diseases such as dementia and the impact this has on society, services and systems, including the legal system. Similarly, a user pays scheme raises public policy considerations such as how many testators are actually going to seek legal capacity assessments when they are not going to be alive to deal with the consequences of failing to do so—'who cares, I'll be dead'. Further the issue of losing legal capacity may simply be too confronting for people to contemplate, let alone accept and act upon. Funding, as ever, is a crucial concern with no easy answer. However, it is a very real possibility that people will increasingly contest wills based upon allegations of testamentary incapacity and to ignore this would be ill-considered and short sighted.

7 What to Assess

What is apparent is the complexity involved in assessing testamentary capacity and that the area has been neglected. There are no cognitive assessment models or designated neuropsychological instruments designed to assess it.[192] There is no uniformity in the application of capacity assessment paradigms, or in the tests themselves generally, leading to a proliferation of suggested models.[193] Literature in this area, especially the health literature, calls for more research into developing consistent models for assessing capacity, especially financial and testamentary capacity. It is clear that a clinical assessment ideally includes taking a detailed medical, psychiatric and family history, as well as determining mental status using appropriate cognitive and functional tests.[194] The challenge is identifying which cognitive and functional tests should be applied and how they fit into the legal assessment framework.

A study conducted by Green demonstrated that there is a far greater chance that testators who treat family members 'fairly' will be deemed legally competent.[195] That is, it is in actuality the morality of the will which is being evaluated.[196] In

---

[191] Ibid.

[192] Marson DC et al. (2004), p. 87.

[193] Ibid 88; Perlin ML et al. (2008), p. 221.

[194] Shulman KI et al. (2009), p. 437.

[195] Green MD (1943–1944), pp. 278–279; Champine P (2006), p. 28.

[196] Champine P (2006), p. 33; Posener HD and Jacoby R (2008), p. 753; Jovanovic AA et al. (2008), pp. 487, 492.

effect, a 'moral' sanist approach. Green's paper is dated and empirical research is needed exploring whether the notion that morality is a framework within which testamentary capacity, freedom and intention should be evaluated still persists. What this does, however, is demonstrate an ideological clash between notions of 'fairness' determined by external arbiters on the one hand, with the doctrines of testamentary freedom and testamentary capacity on the other. It also raises numerous questions. What is 'fairness'? Fairness to whom? Who determines what is fair? Fair in accordance with what standard? Notions of 'fairness' and morality should be irrelevant to issues of legal capacity given that an 'eccentric' and capricious will is a testator's legal right. Evaluating the perceived fair-mindedness and overall 'decency' of a will, including whether it is in accordance with vague and arbitrarily imposed collective attitudes, as opposed to actually assessing the task-specific legal capacity of the testator in question at the relevant time, is erroneous and hypercritical.[197] Both testamentary capacity and testamentary freedom are facilitated by a focus on the cognitive ability to make a decision rather than the outcome of the decision made.[198] This is in keeping with the ideals of personal sovereignty and individual autonomy. In fact, an outcome based approach to capacity assessment has generally been rejected in favour of a functional or hybrid methodology.

Champine has proposed adopting a single cognitive standard for testamentary capacity which requires a testator to know and understand the factors relevant to his or her wishes, and which would include the traditional four limb formulation from *Banks*.[199] She notes that such a single cognitive standard would include two presumptions being: first, a rebuttable presumption of capacity when wills reflect intestacy provisions; and second, an irrebuttable presumption of capacity when testators validate their capacity inter vivos by undergoing an assessment which tests cognition against the requirements for legal testamentary capacity.[200] Whether there should be a rebuttable presumption in favour of wills that reflect relevant intestacy provisions is contentious. This is because it raises the question of morality in wills and who has the right to decide whether what a testator chooses to do is correct (or fair) or not. It also presupposes that familial relationships will reflect those in the intestacy provisions, which is obviously not always the case. That a presumption of capacity exists generally would also seem to make establishing a separate rebuttable presumption where testamentary provisions reflect those on intestacy unnecessary.

The proposed adoption of the irrebutable presumption clearly promotes the use of contemporaneous assessment to evaluate testamentary capacity. While benefits to having such an irrebutable presumption exist, for example, the reduction of will contests based on a lack of capacity, and questions of undue influence or elder abuse more broadly because the individual in question has been certified as capable,

---

[197]Champine P (2006), p. 28.
[198]Perlin ML et al. (2008), p. 224.
[199]Champine P (2006), p. 73.
[200]Ibid.

problems do exist. Practically, such a presumption would mean that every time a testator wanted to make a new will or codicil they would need to undertake testing to avail him or her-self of the irrebutable presumption. This process could prove costly given the discussion above regarding funding for capacity assessments. Further, at what stage is a testator expected to engage in such conduct? At what point does his or her capacity become an issue such that he or she feels the need to engage in this process? It also raises the issue of autonomy—why should a testator have to engage in a potentially costly exercise to obtain a contemporaneous capacity assessment to circumvent potential allegations of testamentary incapacity because someone else calls into question their mental acumen, and thus freedom, to leave their assets as they choose.

What is interesting is this notion of trying to champion testamentary capacity through the use of rebuttable and irrebutable presumptions in addition to the general presumption of capacity. Is this because the presumption of capacity is not being respected? Is it no longer sufficient with the advent of modern mentally disabling conditions? In which case, what utility is there in developing additional presumptions, certainly rebuttable presumptions, which will not carry the gravitas that the presumption of capacity carries in modern law? Or, alternatively, is the advent of further presumptions actually trying to augment testamentary capacity and testamentary freedom by enabling the living and capable testator to implement measures which will ensure that their wishes are respected on the (potential) loss of capacity and/or death? That a presumption would exist premised upon the perceived 'fairness' of a will is erroneous, but that a presumption or presumptions may exist based upon the attainment of a contemporaneous capacity assessment may have some utility, at the very least as evidence of the testator's cognitive ability to make his or her will at the relevant time. The problem with this, as discussed, being the need to re-engage with this process every time a new will is made, as well as the need for such a presumption to exist in the first place, especially given the primacy of autonomy in modern society.

Champine discussed the use of a 'forensic assessment instrument' ('FAI') which would provide guidelines for both procedural and substantive assessment of testamentary capacity.[201] She notes that procedurally, the methodology for assessment should be consistent and well-developed. The medical evidence should be reviewed in light of the prevailing legal tests, which need to be streamlined, and the individual in question should be able to fully participate in the process which necessarily includes understanding what is happening and why. Testamentary capacity cannot be solely dependent upon the diagnosis of any mentally disabling condition because to make it so subverts therapeutic jurisprudence as well as natural justice principles.[202] Further, making it dependent on a diagnosis is also representative of the status approach, which is not the preferred approach to capacity assessment. Any assessment paradigm should therefore consider the cognitive

---

[201]Champine P (2006), p. 80.
[202]Ibid 79–80.

and functional abilities of the individual and not just the mentally disabling condition, unless the cause is a coma or other clear determinant of incapacity. The cognitive components for the legal elements need to be addressed, including the ability to assess the cognitive functions related to understanding the nature of a will; knowing the nature and extent of property; knowing the objects of one's bounty; and planning for the distribution of assets.[203] Attempts have been made to develop such instruments, for example that by Marson, Huthwaite and Hebert which they suggest can be conducted as a standalone evaluation or one preferably with a neuropsychological assessment.[204]

Characteristics of a satisfactory assessment model have also been proposed by Shulman et al. These include the rationale for any serious changes in dispositions; an appreciation of the consequences of any disposition, especially if there has been a change in the beneficiary and an explanation as to why beneficiaries may have been excluded from the will or bequeathed a lower amount than might be expected, although this is a very objective criteria.[205] In their research, Shulman et al. note that the mental status examination should assess six things: 'appearance, speech, behaviour, mood, thought process, thought content (including evidence of delusions or hallucinations with specific reference to any paranoid ideation) as well as insight into any identified mental or cognitive disorder'.[206] It is also necessary to take into account the education, age, intelligence and language of the individual being assessed. Consideration should be had for the specific contextual environment in which a decision is being made, including why an individual may decide to change the terms of his or her will. Effective communication with the individual whose capacity is being assessed is crucial.[207] When conducting the assessment, more than one interview may be desirable to counterbalance any disruptive environmental concerns or to give the testator the information necessary to enable him or her to be able to understand the assessment process.[208]

It is necessary to recognise four factors when assessing testamentary capacity: first, the identification of the legal competency to be determined and the requisite standard; second, that limited capacity can exist, that is, legal competency is not necessarily a yes/no proposition but fluctuates as it is time and decision specific; third, a diagnosis of a particular disease or disability does not automatically denote legal incompetency, in fact a diagnosis can assist to retain or regain legal competency if an appropriate treatment plan is instituted; and finally, cognitive and/or psychiatric impairment also does not automatically signify incompetency.[209] In addition to the traditional formulation for testamentary capacity, these factors are

---

[203]Marson DC et al. (2004), pp. 87–88.
[204]Marson DC and Hebert K (2005), pp. 367–368.
[205]Shulman KI et al. (2007), pp. 724–725.
[206]Ibid.
[207]Ibid.
[208]Ibid.
[209]Marson DC et al. (2004), pp. 82–83.

relevant to both legal and health professionals when making determinations. In fact, certain circumstances will require both professions to satisfactorily address these factors when assessing capacity. The development of an instrument which is able to perform a satisfactory clinical assessment of testamentary capacity within the appropriate legal framework will be a major innovation incorporating the need to assess key functional abilities for specific legal capacities.[210] In the meantime, employing standardised guidelines may enable the courts to adopt a more consistent approach to adjudicating applications regarding an individual's legal capacity.[211]

Evidence should also be sought in connection with: the presence of any illness affecting testamentary capacity; severe behavioural changes; the context, both psychological and environmental, in which the testator exists including an understanding by the testator of any conflicts; of any suspicious relationship(s) and circumstances; inconsistency in expressed wishes; and any other indicators of vulnerability and undue influence being exerted over the testator.[212] Reminiscent of Marson's suggestion of an interview, Shulman et al. propose a series of questions which could be asked in an assessment.[213] The multitude of potential assessment paradigms demonstrates that it would indeed be prudent to establish guidelines and general principles for legal and health professionals faced with the need to assess testamentary capacity. Any such guidelines should include directions to health professionals that when they diagnose a disease which can impact capacity the health professional should consider suggesting that the individual seek legal advice regarding wills, enduring powers of attorney and advance care directives.

8 Conclusion

The doctrine of testamentary capacity stagnated in the twentieth century. This must not be allowed to continue in the twenty-first century.[214] The test for testamentary capacity is well established. It is the assessment of testamentary capacity, however, which is only going to increase in both complexity and frequency. The elements from the traditional formulation of testamentary capacity although rightfully being interrogated, are adequate. It is the application of these elements through the assessment process which is in need of attention.[215] The assessment paradigm should facilitate substantiated determinations resulting from a transparent, authenticated and reliable process. This requires an interdisciplinary approach utilising the skills and knowledge of both legal and health professionals. Clear assessment

---

[210]Ibid.

[211]Champine P (2006), p. 93; Shulman KI et al. (2009), p. 438.

[212]Shulman KI et al. (2007), p. 722.

[213]Ibid 725.

[214]Champine P (2006), p. 93.

[215]Purser K (2015).

processes based upon guidelines and supporting principles will assist to counter any miscommunication and misunderstanding that can exist between the legal and health professions, especially with respect to discipline specific vocabularies. Contemporaneous assessment should be promoted, where possible, in an attempt to protect a testator's wishes. Additionally, there is a need for further education and information sharing between the legal and health professions, as well as with the community, to promote the importance of undertaking estate planning whilst people are still capable of doing so.

References

British Medical Association and the Law Society (2015) Assessment of mental capacity: guidance for doctors and lawyers, 4th edn. Law Society Publishing, London

Burns FR (2005) Elders and testamentary undue influence in Australia. Univ New South Wales Law J 28:145

Champine P (2003) Dealing with mental disability in trust & estate law practice: a Sanist will. N Y Law School J Int Comp Law 22:195

Champine P (2006) Expertise and instinct in the assessment of testamentary capacity. Villanova Law Rev 51:25

Croucher RF (2009) Towards uniform succession in Australia. Aust Law J 83:728

Falk E, Hoffman N (2014) The role of capacity assessments in elder abuse investigations and guardianships. Clin Geriatr Med 30(4):851–868

Finkel SI (2003) The matter of wills can your cognitively impaired older patient execute a new will? Geriatrics 58(1):65

Frost M, Lawson S, Jacoby R (2015) Testamentary capacity law, practice, and medicine. Oxford University Press, Oxford

Green MD Premise' (1943–1944) proof of mental incompetency and the unexpressed major. Yale Law J 53(2):271–311

Hamilton B, Cockburn T (2008) Capacity to make a will and enduring power of attorney: issues new and old. December Queensland Law Society Journal

Heinik J, Werner P, Lin R (1999) How do cognitively impaired elderly patients define "testament": reliability and validity of the testament definition scale. Isr J Psychiatry Relat Sci 36(1):23

Jacoby R, Steer P (2007) How to assess capacity to make a will. Br Med J 335:155–157

Jovanovic AA et al (2008) Medical reasons for retrospective challenges of testamentary capacity. Psychiatria Danubia 20(4):485–493

Kapp M (2015) Evaluating decision making capacity in older individuals: does the law give a clue? Laws 4(2):164–172

Marson DC, Hebert K (2005) Assessing civil competencies in older adults with dementia: consent capacity, financial capacity, and testamentary capacity. In: Larrabee GJ (ed) Forensic neuropsychology. Oxford University Press, Oxford

Marson DC, Huthwaite JS, Hebert K (2004) Testamentary capacity and undue influence in the elderly: a jurisprudent therapy perspective. Law Psychol Rev 28:71

McBride C (2015) The capacity conundrum. STEP J 23(2):49

Moye J, Marson DC (2007) Assessment of decision-making capacity on older adults: an emerging area of practice and research. J Gerontol B Psychol Sci Soc Sci 62(1):3–11

Moye J, Marson DC, Edelstein B (2013) Assessment of capacity in an aging society. Am Psychol 68(3):158–171

Mullins D (2006) Testamentary Capacity and Undue Influence Paper. In: Queensland Law Society Succession Law Conference, Brisbane, 27 October 2006

Myers P (2014) An increase in mental capacity claims and challenges to wills. Br J Neurosci Nurs 10(1):44–45

O'Neill N, Peisah C (2011) Capacity and the law. Sydney University Press, Sydney

Peisah C (2005) Reflections on changes in defining testamentary capacity. Int Psychogeriatr 17 (4):709–712

Peisah C et al (2009) The wills of older people: risk factors for undue influence. Int Psychogeriatr 21(1):7–15

Peisah C et al (2014) Deathbed wills: assessing testamentary capacity in the dying patient. Int Psychogeriatr 26(2):209–216

Peisah C, Brodaty H (1994) Dementia and the will-making process: the role of the medical practitioner. Med J Aust 161(6):381–384

Perlin ML et al (2008) Competence in the law: from legal theory to clinical application. Wiley, New York

Posener HD, Jacoby R (2008) Testamentary capacity. In: Jacoby R et al (eds) Oxford textbook of old age psychiatry. Oxford University Press, Oxford

Purser K (2015) Assessing testamentary capacity in the 21st century: is Banks v Goodfellow still relevant? Univ New South Wales Law J 38(3):854

Purser K, Rosenfeld T (2016) Too ill to will? Deathbed wills: assessing testamentary capacity near the end of life. Age Ageing 45(3):334–336

Regan WM, Gordon SM (1997) Assessing testamentary capacity in elderly people. South Med J 90 (1):13–15

Roked F, Patel A (2008) Which aspects of cognitive function are best associated with testamentary capacity in patients with Alzheimer's disease? Int J Geriatr Psychiatry 23(5):552–553

Shulman KI et al (2007) Assessment of testamentary capacity and vulnerability to undue influence. Am J Psychiatr 164(5):722–727

Shulman KI et al (2009) Contemporaneous assessment of testamentary capacity. Int Psychogeriatr 21(3):433–439

Shulman KI et al (2015) Cognitive fluctuations and the lucid interval in dementia: implications for testamentary capacity. J Am Acad Psychiatry Law 43(3):287–292

Shulman KI, Cohen CA, Hull I (2005) Psychiatric issues in retrospective challenges of testamentary capacity. Int J Geriatr Psychiatry 20(1):63–69

Sinyor M et al (2015) Last wills and testaments in a large sample of suicide notes: implications for testamentary capacity. Br J Psychiatry 206(1):72–76

Sousa LB et al (2014) Financial and testamentary capacity evaluations: procedures and assessment instruments underneath a functional approach. Int Psychogeriatr 26(2):217–228

Spar JE, Garb AS (1992) Assessing competency to make a will. Am J Psychiatr 149(2):169

Spaulding WJ (1985) Testamentary competency reconciling doctrine with the role of the expert witness. Law Hum Behav 9(2):113

Sprehe DJ, Kerr AL (1996) Use of legal terms in will contests: implications for psychiatrists. Bull Am Acad Psychiatr Law 24(2):255–265

Cases and Legislation

Application of J. R. Fenwick and Re Charles [2009] NSWSC 530

Astridge v Pepper [1970] 1 NSWLR 542

Bailey v Bailey (1924) 34 CLR 558

Banks v Goodfellow (1870) LR 5 QB 549

Bertoldo v Cordenos [2010] QSC 79

Bird v Luckie (1850) 68 ER 375

Boughton v Knight (1873) LR 3 P & D 64

Chapter 5
Substitute Decision-Making

1 Introduction

Decision-making autonomy is a right that accrues with legal majority but one that a person will lose if declared legally incompetent. However, individuals still need to be able to accomplish the tasks associated with everyday living such as paying bills, obtaining shelter, seeking medical treatment, buying food, purchasing presents for family and friends, and managing their finances. A paradigm shift occurred focusing on capacity and the retention of autonomy rather than the previously favoured disability labels and interventionist practises denounced by therapeutic jurisprudence.[1] This paradigm shift was generally representative of a movement away from a welfare based to a rights based model and resulted in the development of substitute decision-making schemes.[2] These schemes enabled the appointment of substitute decision-makers under enduring power of attorney and/or advance health directive documents to ensure that the types of tasks mentioned above can still be accomplished by a person or persons chosen by the individual when that individual is no longer able to discharge those tasks themselves. Indeed, there has recently been a further paradigm shift moving from the substitute model towards supported decision-making in line with the Convention on the Rights of Persons with Disabilities. Substitute decision-making, given its importance in the overarching contextual focus of estate planning, will be the focus here. Discussion will centre on the process of the assessment of capacity within this environment, rather than any jurisdictionally specific legislative and/or common law paradigms.

With respect to the process the point has been made, both here and elsewhere, that the relevant legal and medical standards determining the existence, or otherwise, of legal decision-making capacity need further exploration.[3] This is

---

[1]Standing Committee on Social Issues, Parliament of New South Wales (2010) 4, 37.
[2]Ibid.
[3]See also Collier B et al. (2005), p. v.

© Springer International Publishing AG 2017

K. Purser, *Capacity Assessment and the Law*, DOI 10.1007/978-3-319-54347-5_5

particularly the case with financial capacity. Aggravating the problem is the multitude of assessment models which can be modified by individual legal and/or health care professionals undertaking assessments to suit their own skills and knowledge.[4] Although outside the scope of this work, it is worth noting that the jurisdictional medley of legislative and common law substitute decision-making provisions only serves to further exacerbate this already challenging situation.[5] Inconsistencies in the relevant law impacts the usefulness of decided cases when undertaking legal capacity determinations which, importantly here, results in little guidance as to what constitutes best practice when assessing decision-making capacity.[6] This can also affect the instructions given to assessors if, for example, they receive such information from a legal practitioner in a different jurisdiction to the one in which they are accustomed to working. This is especially the case if those instructions are not as fulsome as they perhaps could be because the practitioner involved does not understand all the complexities involved in assessing the impact of a particular mentally disabling condition upon the specific capacity, such as that necessary to make financial decisions. Once again the existence of various sets of inconsistent guidelines mean that they are open to interpretation which, although well intentioned, result in insufficient protection of decision-making autonomy, especially when individual assessor preferences are then applied. This chapter seeks to examine capacity assessment in the substitute decision-making context and the principles underpinning such determinations. First, however, some comments specific to enduring documents.

2 Enduring Documents

Substitute decision-makers can generally be appointed in one of three ways which differ in formality. At one end of the scale support mechanisms can be put in place whereby family and friends informally assist the individual in question with the management of their own affairs. At the other end of the scale is formal intervention by the courts or relevant tribunals. In the middle are the 'pre-emptive' arrangements enabling the appointment of an enduring attorney and/or guardian utilising substitute decision-making provisions and enduring documents. These documents exemplify modern society's attempt to enable individuals to retain some degree of control or, at the very least, influence, over decision-making when the individual in question is no longer able to make his or her own choices. It is an attempt to recognise autonomy through safeguarding an individual's right to make his or her own legally recognised decisions while legally capable to do so, the decision in this

---

[4]Cockerill J et al. (2005), pp. 28–29.
[5]Kapp M (2015), p. 165.
[6]Cockerill J et al. (2005), p. 33.

case being the appointment of a financial and/or health attorney/guardian they trust to act in an appropriate manner.

There are two types of power of attorney documents, general and enduring.[7] The general power of attorney ceases to have effect upon the loss of legal capacity. The enduring power of attorney continues despite the loss of legal capacity.[8] Basically, enduring powers of attorney allow the appointment of an attorney to manage a person's ('the principal') finances or personal affairs, where the legislature has extended powers of attorney to cover both spheres, if they become unable to do so themselves. The powers contained within an enduring power of attorney can be limited and directions can be given as to the exercise of those powers.[9] Health or 'lifestyle' substitute decision-makers are generally appointed under an advance directive, which can also be referred to as an advance care directive or advance health directive (amongst other nomenclature). The label applied to the health substitute decision-maker will depend upon the jurisdiction in which the document was created.[10] 'Lifestyle' substitute decision-making can involve day-to-day decisions for an individual, for example, where to live and how to handle routine health care matters. It should be noted that the focus here is on the assessment of capacity in the designated estate planning context and not, for example, on the ability to consent to or refuse medical treatment or issues in relation to guardianship. Research has demonstrated that hospital policies rarely outline any criteria for labelling a patient as incapable.[11] Although this research was conducted in the context of not for resuscitation orders in Australian public hospitals, it is alarming that in the hospitals surveyed it was apparent that the policies were inadequate with respect to advance care directives and capacity determinations. Further, that there is no uniformity in the assessment processes adopted.[12] More research on this particular issue is desperately needed.

The nature and extent of the powers afforded to attorneys and guardians are immense: they are able to do anything that the principal lawfully authorises them to do; and the decisions made by substitute decision-makers have the same legal effect as if they were made by the person themselves.[13] This raises critical legal and ethical issues, amongst them, the dualistic notions of autonomy and protection which are so prevalent in this area. Additionally, there is the significant concern that the individual in question has lost legal capacity and is therefore unable to

---

[7]Standing Committee on Legal and Constitutional Affairs, Parliament of the Commonwealth of Australia (2007), p. 70.

[8]Ibid; Standing Committee on Social Issues, Parliament of New South Wales (2010), p. 10.

[9]Standing Committee on Social Issues, Parliament of New South Wales (2010), p. 10; O'Neill N and Peisah C (2011), p. 3.

[10]The Clinical, Technical and Ethical Principal Committee of the Australian Health Ministers' Advisory Council (2011), p. 9.

[11]Sidhu NS et al. (2007), pp. 73–74.

[12]Ibid 72.

[13]Standing Committee on Social Issues, Parliament of New South Wales (2010), p. 8.

monitor the use of the powers given to the substitute decision-maker. The relatively private nature of enduring documents means that they can be open to abuse, especially with respect to capacity determinations of vulnerable people.[14] This can be seen in a number of different avenues but most notably in financial abuse perpetrated by financial attorneys, the figures for which, although underreported, are growing exponentially.[15] For example, it is estimated that in middle to high income countries the rates of financial abuse are somewhere between 1% and 9.2%.[16] This is obviously an incredibly broad range but specific data is difficult to locate, again highlighting the desperate need for further research in this area. This can have flow on effects as well to, for instance, banks and external stakeholders who will be engaged in legal dealings with people acting under enduring documents. Such stakeholders need certainty that the principal has indeed lost the requisite capacity necessary to make his or her own financial decisions at law and that they are dealing with that person's correct legal representative.[17]

There is also scarce data in institutional settings such as hospitals, aged care facilities and nursing homes which have higher numbers of vulnerable people and arguably therefore abuse.[18] This leads to another, relatively unexplored, avenue of potential abuse which is in relation to euthanasia. This is topical given the currency of discussion around the legalisation of euthanasia in various countries around the world, for example recently in South Australia in Australia with the narrow defeat of the Voluntary Euthanasia Bill in late 2016.[19] One argument against voluntary euthanasia acknowledges that it may be used to perpetuate elder abuse, theorising that people lacking capacity as well as the aged, of which there can obviously be a considerable overlap, are both groups which can be especially vulnerable to euthanasia, and thus abuse, from health attorneys. Although abuse of the vulnerable resulting from a lack of capacity is outside the specific scope of this work, these are areas which need attention and further research is planned.

3 Relevant Principles

The recognition of the capacity to make decisions is one of the hallmarks of individual autonomy and personal sovereignty. It is founded on the presumption that every adult is legally competent until proven otherwise. A determination of total incapacity will mean a form of substitute decision-making will occur. In fact, a substitute decision cannot be made for an individual without first removing their

---

[14]Setterlund D et al. (2002), p. 128.
[15]World Health Organisation (2015).
[16]Ibid.
[17]Lock SL (2016), p. 18.
[18]World Health Organisation (2015).
[19]SBS (2016).

right to make that decision for themselves. This determination necessarily involves a third party stating that they know what is better for the individual than the individual does for themselves.[20] Given the importance placed upon individual autonomy, and therefore on an individual's ability to make decisions for him or her-self, the individual's approach to his or her affairs should be respected and continued where possible.[21] The loss of the ability to make decisions through a determination of legal incapacity and the process through which this decision is reached is therefore vital. There is very little guidance as to how to establish a satisfactory assessment process, or when to conduct the assessment. The 'processes' that do exist are further weakened by the ambiguity and confusion characterising the relationship between legal and health professionals in assessing capacity in the substitute decision-making context.

Attempting to achieve a balance between autonomy and protection is not only the obligation and responsibility of the legal and health professionals involved in the assessment. It is imperative that governments, policy-makers and other interested stakeholders such as insurance companies likewise devise adequate measures and earmark appropriate funding for research and development of satisfactory capacity assessment processes. Better educational programs are needed for which funding is a key component. However, as always, the funding for this serves as one of the major practical hurdles. The judiciary also needs to provide guidance on assessment processes which will then be adopted in practice by legal and health professionals as well as the other relevant stakeholders. Society in general and the local community similarly have an important role to play. Admittedly better education is needed, but members of society and the community need to take advantage of the information and mechanisms that currently exist, such as the enduring documents. On a more localised level, the role that family and friends of an individual with questionable capacity can play is vital. It is an individual's family and friends who have the means and opportunity to best assist with the maintenance of autonomy while attempting to protect the individual.[22] Individuals can often become dependent on those around them. Those closest to the individual in question are therefore frequently the ones best placed to help. This is clearly a position of immense power which not only promotes assistance and protection but can also expose the individual to abuse. Even well-intentioned infringement of the delicate balance between autonomy and protection is a risk. This dichotomy highlights the importance of the general principles which serve three main functions in this context: first, they represent the framework underpinning substitute decision-making regimes; second, they can help guide decision-makers; and third, they can offer guidance to assessors.[23] The principles are deliberately flexible with

---

[20] Ibid.

[21] Standing Committee on Legal and Constitutional Affairs (2007), pp. 70–71.

[22] Standing Committee on Social Issues, Parliament of New South Wales (2010), p. 3.

[23] Queensland Law Reform Commission (2010), p. 61.

the degree of specificity being dependent upon the principle and factual scenario in question.[24]

The principles vary being dependent on the particular jurisdiction which results in a lack of consistency. The lack of uniformity in even the general principles guiding capacity assessment, let alone the actual process, fundamentally undermines any attempt at reliability and transparency of process. However, general themes emerge when examining the varying principles. Not all of the themes are universally acknowledged. For example, in Australia, the Queensland model is the most thorough example encompassing all identified themes.[25] The United Kingdom, however, has fewer principles focusing on: the presumption of legal capacity; that no interference is to occur until all practical steps have been taken to assist the individual and those steps have failed; unwise decisions are not proof of legal incompetency; the best interests of the person should be paramount; and finally, the least restrictive alternative should be adopted.[26]

Interestingly, some of the general themes, as well as the specific principles, resonate with a therapeutic jurisprudence approach to assessment. Of particular note is the focus on the least restrictive option, normalisation and inclusion, recognition of the autonomy/protection dualism, and the promotion of self-reliance. The least restrictive alternative promotes an adult's right to make his or her own decisions where practicable and the ability to participate to the greatest extent possible in decisions affecting his or her life.[27] Any steps necessary to maximise the individual's participation in the decision-making process should be taken and third party decision-making should be undertaken in the least restrictive way. The least restrictive alternative values freedom of decision and freedom of action. Any formulation of the principle should also encourage maximum participation by the individual in the decision to be made.

The welfare and interests of the individual should be given paramount consideration and the views of the individual should be respected, even though others may not agree with the decision made. This is a matter fundamental to human dignity. Appropriateness to the circumstances can be relevant. There is a requirement that the individual's views actually be sought and taken into account, where possible, when making a decision.[28] That the substitute decision-maker take into account what an individual would want is more reflective of supported rather than substituted decision-making. This information helps maintain the balance between autonomy and protection by seeking to moderate the substituted decision with the individual's views. When seeking the views of the individual who lacks capacity,

---

[24]Ibid.

[25]Queensland Law Reform Commission (2010), lv.

[26]*Mental Capacity Act 2005* (UK) c 9s 1.

[27]*Powers of Attorney Act 1998* (Qld) schedule 1, part 1; *Guardianship and Administration Act 2000* (Qld) schedule 1, part 1 principle 7(1)–(2).

[28]See, for example, *Powers of Attorney Act 1998* (Qld) schedule 1, part 1; *Guardianship and Administration Act 2000* (Qld) schedule 1, part 1 principle 7(3)(b).

the views may be communicated in any manner possible for example, orally, in writing or through conduct. The principle of substitute judgment is often adopted, that is, where possible adopting what the individual in question has decided in similar or previous circumstances. The decision should be appropriate to the individual's characteristics and needs. Any formulation of a broad principle with respect to capacity assessment would need to acknowledge that the welfare and interests of the individual should be given paramount consideration and their views respected. It should be clear that this should be undertaken contextually to reflect the individual's circumstances.

Promotion of the best interests principle and supporting individual well-being is important in substitute decision-making.[29] The terminology used differs between jurisdictions, but is significant. For example, there are a variety of terms used in the Australian jurisdictions. In Victoria the focus is on promoting the best interests of a person with a 'disability' and the principles there generally adopt this language.[30] There is a danger that such a term could have a negative effect because the label 'disabled' would need to be imposed upon an individual. New South Wales refers to 'such persons' which again may be pejorative in tone. This is because the phrase tends to group a category of people together in a relatively negative manner. Although not specifically in relation to best interests and well-being, the Queensland principles generally adopt the more neutral terminology of 'the adult'. The *Mental Capacity Act 2005* (UK) has adopted the phrase 'a person'. This or the Queensland 'the adult' would be preferable as neither are pejorative terms especially within a therapeutic jurisprudence framework. However, 'the person' or 'the individual' would apply to everyone irrespective of age whereas 'the adult' is restricted to individuals aged 18 years and over. As every person aged 18 years and over is presumed to be legally competent they therefore have the ability to be *in*competent, hence the use of the term, 'the adult'. However, although capacity assessment predominantly occurs with respect to adults it can be relevant to those under the age of 18. Consequently, it is suggested that 'the person' or 'the individual' would be the best descriptor.

Respect for autonomy and basic human rights is a core concern of both the principles in substitute decision-making as well as therapeutic jurisprudence. Respect for an individual's autonomy arguably supports the proposition that, if the incapable individual can no longer make decisions for him or her-self, the substitute decision-maker should make the decision that the incapable individual would have made if he or she were able. This can be compared to the best interests principle which dictates making a decision based upon what represents the donor's best interests rather than the decision they would necessarily have made for themselves.[31] The dichotomy of approach in these two principles demonstrates

---

[29]*Guardianship Act 1987* (NSW) s 4(a); *NSW Trustee and Guardian Act 2009* (NSW) s 39(a); *Guardianship and Administration Act 1986* (Vic) s 4(2)(b).

[30]*Guardianship and Administration Act 1986* (Vic) s 4(2)(b).

[31]Queensland Law Reform Commission (2010), p. 36.

the flexibility that is necessary in substitute decision-making while maintaining integrity of process.

Therapeutic jurisprudence also discusses the concepts of normalisation and inclusion which are generally adopted throughout substitute decision-making principles. This recognises the individual's valued role as a member of society and encourages the adult to undertake social roles, as well as supporting the adult to live and participate in the general community while promoting the need for the community to respond in kind. Closely connected is the promotion of self-reliance with respect to personal, domestic and financial affairs as far as is practicable. Self-reliance is inherently linked to the notion of individual autonomy. Consequently, express recognition and encouragement of self-reliance should be incorporated into any principles guiding capacity assessment. The general principles are also intended to protect individuals from exploitation and abuse. Specifically acknowledging that the individual's care and protection should be paramount while prohibiting neglect, abuse and exploitation is a fundamental tenet of guiding principles in this context.

The importance of preserving and facilitating supportive relationships with family and friends, as well as cultural and linguistic differences is also generally recognised. This is imperative, provided these are relationships of support and not exploitation and/or abuse. Family and friends have a vital role to play in the maintenance of an individual's autonomy and in providing protection where necessary. It will be an individual's family and friends who are able to assist that person retain their decision-making autonomy for as long as possible by helping them with mobility, and providing care and support. The maintenance of cultural and linguistic environments is also to be promoted. For example, the Queensland principles specifically note the importance of maintaining the individual's values expressly recognising Aboriginal or Torres Strait Islander heritage.[32] Any capacity assessment principles would also need to recognise an individual's values, as well as their cultural and linguistic environments. This is an important element which contributes to making a person who they are and can be significant in decision-making, potentially impacting perceptions about that person as well as the assessment of capacity.

The general principles ideally provide the universal and necessarily fluid framework within which to make capacity determinations. They should provide a source of information and assistance to both legal and health professionals when assessing capacity. However, there needs to be consistency as to which principles are adopted. Further, there is little research on how widespread the use of these principles is—in either the assessment or the decision-making process—thus calling into question their practical utility distinct from their role as the philosophical cornerstone of substitute decision-making.

---

[32]*Powers of Attorney Act 1998* (Qld) schedule 1, part 1; *Guardianship and Administration Act 2000* (Qld) schedule 1, part 1 principle 9.

4 The United Nations Convention on the Rights of Persons with Disabilities

The United Nations *Convention on the Rights of People with Disabilities* ('CRPD') aims to recognise the rights of people with disabilities, seeking to reverse the stigmatisation which has resulted in authoritarian and repressive approaches.[33] Although supported decision-making is outside the scope of this work, some comment needs to be made in relation to the significance of the CRPD. The CRPD promotes a paradigm incorporating supported (which is sometimes referred to as assisted) decision-making emphasising the importance of the presumption of capacity and the principle of least restriction.[34] This promotes a landmark paradigmatic shift from substitute to supported decision-making.[35] In connection to this the word 'ability' is often used in the context of the CRPD rather than capacity.[36] Supported decision-making contrasts with substitute decision-making as a less invasive scheme which enables the individual in question to retain a level of autonomy. This is because the decision-maker (the 'supported decision-maker') has a role which is to 'support' or 'assist' rather than to make the decision in substitution for the subject individual.[37] Various support options can be employed to give primacy to the will and preferences of the individual which respect that individual's human rights.[38] That is, the decision-making should 'mirror' how an adult would make his, or her, own decisions. This is achieved through the decision-maker seeking the advice, input and information from a variety of sources, for example, friends, family and professionals.[39] Arguably, supported decision-making should be given precedence over substitute decision-making where suitable. This is because supported decision-making is more in line with the presumption of capacity and the principle of least restriction. It also enables the individual in question to maintain autonomy for as long as possible while establishing safeguards for his or her protection.

Importantly, legal capacity under the CRPD comprises two aspects: firstly, legal standing which is the ability to hold legal rights and duties; and secondly, legal agency, which is the ability to exercise such rights and duties resulting in legal recognition and potentially consequences.[40] It has been noted that while lacking capacity at law, an individual may still be able to exercise legal agency if adequate supports are put in place to facilitate that person recognising and expressing their

---

[33]*United Nations Convention on the Rights of Persons with Disabilities*, opened for signature 30 March 2007 (entered into force 3 May 2008); Perlin ML (2013), p. 1175.

[34]Perlin ML (2013), pp. 1176–1177.

[35]*Nicholson v Knaggs* (2009) VSC 64; Perlin ML (2013), p. 1179.

[36]Australian Law Reform Commission (2014a), p. 38.

[37]Standing Committee on Social Issues, Parliament of New South Wales (2010), p. 49.

[38]Australian Law Reform Commission (2013), p. 30.

[39]Blanck P and Martinis JG (2015), p. 26.

[40]Australian Law Reform Commission (2013), p. 28.

preferences.[41] It incorporates a request that all individuals, including people with a disability, experience legal capacity on an equal basis.[42] The CRPD implies that the generally favoured functional approach to capacity assessment may be in contravention of article 12 if the testing methods are discriminatory or disproportionately impact the ability of people with a disability to interact with the law.[43] The interrelation of individuals with the law and ensuring that, where possible, the law has a positive impact on those individuals, is again promoting a therapeutic jurisprudence approach. Thus, it can be seen that even though not expressly acknowledged, the principles of therapeutic jurisprudence are already playing a role in the promotion of a sound paradigm for capacity assessments, not only in the substituted but also in the supported decision-making model.

This paradigmatic shift obviously has significant implications for estate planning generally, and capacity assessment in particular. Much has been written about the utility of supported decision-making and how to best go about implementing the 'ideal' model.[44] Governments in Australia, the United Kingdom, the United States of America, Canada, Germany, Ireland and Sweden have all introduced mechanisms to assist with supported decision-making.[45] For example, a National Resource Center for Supported Decision-Making has been introduced in the United States of America which conducts research, and develops educational programs as well as interdisciplinary best practices with a view to positively impacting policy to establish supported decision-making as a viable alternative to guardianship.[46] Pilot programs have also been created in a number of jurisdictions worldwide, for instance, in Texas.[47]

In Australia, the Australian Law Reform Commission has recommended the development of a new model, 'the Commonwealth decision-making model' which incorporates the terms 'supporter' and 'representative' in an attempt to cultivate a new attitude evidenced by the terminology used.[48] The importance of terminology has also been recognised in Alberta, Canada where decision-making capacity is defined 'as the ability to understand the information that is relevant to a decision or the failure to make a decision and to appreciate its reasonably foreseeable consequences'.[49] The Alberta model provides that a subject individual can nominate up to three people to assist him or her to make decisions. The supported decision-maker would be able to collect information that would help the subject individual to

[41]Gooding P (2013), p. 437.
[42]Australian Law Reform Commission (2013), p. 36.
[43]Ibid 37.
[44]See, for example, Parker M (2016).
[45]Blanck P and Martinis JG (2015), p. 26.
[46]Ibid 24, 28.
[47]Ibid 27.
[48]Australian Law Reform Commission (2014b), p. 9.
[49]*Adult Guardianship and Trusteeship Act SA* 2008 cA-4.2, s 1.

make a decision. Any decisions made with the help of the supported decision-maker are treated as if they were decisions of the individual in question.[50]

Of particular importance are articles 5 and 12 of the CRPD. Article 5 is concerned with ensuring equality before the law and non-discrimination.[51] Article 12 is referred to as being at the centre of the Convention because it is representative of the paradigmatic shift that is occurring from substitute towards supported decision-making.[52] Article 12 focuses on equal recognition before the law, in particular that signatories shall ensure that measures for assessing legal capacity will provide necessary safeguards to prevent abuse in accordance with international human rights provisions. The safeguards are to be proportional and suited to the individual's circumstances and should ensure respect for the individual's rights, wishes and preferences. There should be no conflict of interest and no undue influence. Any measures should only be implemented for the shortest period of time necessary and be regularly reviewed by an impartial third party.[53] Article 12 is especially relevant to capacity assessment. This is because the development of a consistent and transparent capacity assessment paradigm is fundamental to adequately respecting the 'rights, will and preferences' of the individual as well as identifying safeguards proportional to the needs of the individual. Pursuant to the Convention, deficits in mental capacity will not be able to be utilised to establish legal incapacity.[54] Accordingly, going forward, any assessment process will need to have reference to the CRPD.

A number of challenging issues have been identified with the implementation of a supported decision-making paradigm including the need to reconsider and potentially revise guardianship regimes, setting standards of practice for the decision-makers, as well as preventing abuse and the exercise of undue influence whilst maintaining respect for legal capacity.[55] It is this last point which is most important here. As stated, it is not intended to examine supported decision-making other than to highlight that the existence of a supported decision-making paradigm only serves to further emphasise the need for accurate, authenticated and rigorous capacity assessments on an international level. It is also important to recognise that assessments of deficits in decision-making capacity in this context are undertaken with a view to determining adequate supports which can be put in place to support decision-making.[56] Nevertheless, it will be necessary to ensure that the subject

---

[50]*Adult Guardianship and Trusteeship Act SA* 2008 cA-4.2, ss 4(1), 6(1); Standing Committee on Social Issues, Parliament of New South Wales (2010), pp. 20–21.

[51]*United Nations Convention on the Rights of Persons with Disabilities*, opened for signature 30 March 2007 (entered into force 3 May 2008) art 5.

[52]Standing Committee on Social Issues, Parliament of New South Wales (2010), pp. 58–59.

[53]*United Nations Convention on the Rights of Persons with Disabilities*, opened for signature 30 March 2007 (entered into force 3 May 2008) art 12.

[54]Australian Law Reform Commission (2013), p. 29.

[55]Blanck P and Martinis JG (2015), p. 27.

[56]Gooding P (2013), p. 438.

individual's level of legal capacity is able to be satisfactorily determined in a precise manner as the individual in question will potentially be able to retain decision-making autonomy longer with the supported, as opposed to the substituted, decision-making paradigm. This is provided the necessary supports are put in place. Such supports could include assistive technologies, for example, voice recognition software.[57] The role of such technologies, as well as medical advancements, cannot be underestimated in capacity assessments as well as in the promotion of, not only capacity, but also of a positive interaction between the individual and the legal system.

5   Capacity to Make Enduring Documents at Law

Capacity is often defined to include 'elements' examining, for example: whether a person is capable of understanding the nature and effect of his or her making or not making (that is weighing up) the decision about the specific matter in question; retaining information pertinent to the decision and using that information in the decision; whether the decision is being made freely and voluntarily; and whether he or she is able to communicate his or her decision in some way. For example, s 3 (1) of the *Mental Capacity Act 2005* (UK) states that an individual has the necessary capacity to make a decision if he or she has the ability 'to understand the information relevant to making the decision; the ability to retain the relevant information; the ability to weigh up the relevant information; and the ability to communicate the decision in some way'.[58] In Australia, Queensland is the only jurisdiction to have adopted a statutory test for the capacity necessary to make an enduring power of attorney. The Queensland legislation generally is considered to contain some of the widest statutory powers in Australia.[59] Care is generally taken to ensure that the individual understands the power and trust that they are placing in the hands of the person that they are appointing as attorney.

That the individual understands the nature and effect of the decision is reminiscent of the judicial discussion in the cases focussing on cognitive ability and communication.[60] Two main approaches to assessing capacity in this context have emerged, which are represented by the cases of *In re K; In re F ('Re K')*[61] and *Ranclaud v Cabban ('Ranclaud')*[62] respectively. In *Re K* it was held that: the principal needed to understand that the substitute decision-maker would have

---

[57]On this idea see: Gooding P et al. (2015).

[58]Law Reform Committee, Parliament of Victoria (2010), pp. 110–111.

[59]Standing Committee on Legal and Constitutional Affairs, Parliament of the Commonwealth of Australia (2007), p. 74.

[60]Cockerill J et al. (2005), pp. 27, 38–39; Parker M (2004), p. 486.

[61][1988] 1 Ch 310.

[62](1988) NSW ConvR 55-385.

complete authority over the individual's affairs when the power came into effect; they would be able to do anything that the individual could have done if the individual had legal competency; that an enduring power of attorney would continue despite the principal losing capacity; and that if the individual became incapable then he or she could not revoke the document.[63]

In *Ranclaud*, Young J stated that when determining whether an individual was capable of giving a power of attorney the court should consider whether the individual understood that they were authorising someone to look after their affairs. The court should also check that the individual giving the power of attorney understood the types of decisions the attorney could make without needing to have reference to the principal and what he or she wanted.[64] That is, while *Re K* requires that the principal understand the nature and effect of the act of making the document, *Ranclaud* requires not only that the principal understand that he or she is authorising the attorney to act on his or her behalf and the effect of that decision, but also that the attorney can exercise their power without further reference to the principal. It appears that the nature and extent of the estate should be considered, as should the decisions that the attorney may need to make on behalf of the principal when assessing capacity at common law. Thought should also be had for the attorney's ability to make those decisions without further reference to the principal.[65]

Important in the assessment of capacity is the question of whether the person in question can carry out the ordinary routine affairs of 'mankind' in a reasonably competent way. Generally, this examines whether the lack of capacity means that there is a genuine risk that the individual may be disadvantaged in the management of their affairs or that their assets may be 'dissipated or lost'.[66] The meaning of the phrase 'ordinary routine affairs of mankind' is more complicated than just going to the bank to withdraw money.[67] The skills required seem to fall somewhere between managing housekeeping money and conducting complex financial affairs, depending on the decision to be made and the circumstances in which it is to be made.[68] An ability to plan for the future, including providing for oneself and one's family by generating income and managing capital is necessary.[69] Two additional considerations to determining the 'ordinary affairs of mankind' are whether appropriate advice is sought and whether the individual is able to identify people who may be trying to unfairly influence them or seize control of their assets.[70] This last

---

[63]*Re Key* (1988) NSW ConvR 310, 316.

[64]*Ranclaud v Cabban* (1988) NSW ConvR 57-548.

[65]Ibid.

[66]*PY v RJS* [1982] 2 NSWLR 700; Standing Committee on Social Issues, Parliament of New South Wales (2010), p. 25.

[67]Standing Committee on Social Issues, Parliament of New South Wales (2010), p. 26.

[68]Ibid.

[69]Ibid.

[70]*Re GHI (a protected person)* [2005] NSWSC 581 [119] (Campbell J).

requirement obviously aims to prevent undue influence. There has been limited satisfactory exploration of what amounts to being 'incapable of dealing, in a reasonably competent fashion' with those affairs. It should be noted that the standard for the mental capacity necessary to make an advance care directive is generally reflective, if not a lower standard, than that required for an enduring power of attorney, with the donor's understanding being central.[71]

Returning then to the notion of an individual 'understanding the nature and effect' of the enduring power of attorney—this includes the individual in question appreciating that he or she can specify, limit or direct the power given to the attorney and when the document will come into effect. He or she also needs to understand that once the document does come into effect that the attorney will have full power to carry out the authorised decisions; that the document can be revoked provided the principal has legal competency and a new one made; and that the enduring power of attorney will continue if the individual loses capacity. Importantly, the individual must understand that if he or she cannot revoke the enduring power of attorney then he or she cannot effectively oversee the attorney's use of the power.[72]

A certificate signed and dated by a health professional certifying that the individual appeared to have the capacity necessary to make the document at the time of execution may be required.[73] This is dependent on the specific requirements of the jurisdiction in which the document is being prepared, but also on any conditions that may be contained in the enduring document itself. The existence of this 'requirement' again highlights several themes that emerge throughout this discussion: the problem with health care professionals certifying capacity when there is no clear definition of what constitutes the capacity in question; the instructions provided by the legal professional regarding the assessment to be undertaken may be inadequate; and that there is no clear distinction between the legal and medical notions of capacity nor how to assess the clinical concept within the legal framework.

The need for voluntariness is intended as a measure to combat undue influence.[74] The issue here is whether capacity should primarily be assessed by a cognitive test, in effect ignoring the question of whether the decision was voluntary and made of the person's own free will, or whether the issue of voluntariness is so inexplicably linked to capacity that it would be difficult to separate them.[75] One way to address this conundrum is to ostensibly separate the purely cognitive function from the willingness to make the decision by, for example, assessing the former through cognitive testing and the addressing the latter through the existence of guidelines.[76]

---

[71]Collier B and Coyne C (2005), p. 18.
[72]Cockerill J et al. (2005), pp. 32–33.
[73]See, for example: *Powers of Attorney Act 1998* (Qld) s 44(6).
[74]Queensland Law Reform Commission (2010), p. 290.
[75]Ibid 281–282.
[76]Ibid 285.

The benefit of including any such 'requirements' in guidelines rather than, say, legislation is the flexibility of guidelines to not only be adapted to individual circumstances but to also be changed.

An individual should likewise be able to communicate his or her decision as the decision in question. The issue then is around the nature of this communication as mentally disabling conditions may impact auditory comprehension which can, in turn, impact an individual's decision-making ability.[77] Communication can, and should, encompass a variety of modes which respond to the hearing and vision status of the individual in question. This may need to be assessed independently, and the use of non-verbal cognitive tests may need to be employed.[78] The recognition and adoption of methods to heighten communication and ultimately the capacity of an individual to participate in decision-making, thus resulting in the promotion of individual autonomy, is supported by the CRPD. For example, short, simple sentences focussed on one issue at a time should be used in a quiet environment with repetition of key points.[79] One suggestion to heighten communication is the use of speech and language pathologists, audiologists, orthoptists or occupational therapists.[80] This is not least because of the increased complexity of the documents and oral explanations about concepts which can differ from what the individual is ordinarily used to.[81] Consequently, the role of health care providers who are trained in the impact of language and communication disorders on cognition and, ultimately, legal capacity cannot be underestimated and should be further explored.

One question which arises is whether there should be a legislative definition of capacity. For example, in the United Kingdom 'a person lacks capacity in relation to a matter if at the material time he is unable to make a decision for himself in relation to the matter because of an impairment of, or a disturbance in the functioning of, the mind or brain'.[82] An individual is unable to make a decision for him or her-self if he or she is unable to '(a) understand the information relevant to the decision; (b) retain that information; (c) use or weight that information as part of the process of making the decision; or (d) communicate his decision (whether by talking, using sign language or any other means)'.[83] The fact that an individual is only able to retain the information relevant to the decision for a short period does not prevent him or her from being capable.[84] With specific reference to enduring powers of attorney, the individual must be able to understand that the attorney will be able to assume complete authority over the principal or donor's affairs, the

---

[77]Zuscak SJ et al. (2015), p. 4.
[78]Ibid 3–4.
[79]Ibid 5.
[80]Ibid 2–3.
[81]Ibid 3.
[82]*Mental Capacity Act 2005* (UK) s 2(1).
[83]*Mental Capacity Act 2005* (UK) s 3(1).
[84]*Mental Capacity Act 2005* (UK) s 3(3).

attorney will be able to do anything that the principal/donor could do if they had legal competency; the attorney's power will continue despite the principal/donor losing legal competency; and to revoke the power the principal/donor will need to be legally competent.[85] Another jurisdiction which has a legislative definition of capacity is Alberta where capacity is defined as 'the ability to understand the information that is relevant to the decision and to appreciate the reasonably foreseeable consequences of (i) a decision, and (ii) a failure to make a decision'.[86] It is interesting to note the more stringent requirements of the test adopted in the United Kingdom. In Alberta the test requires an understanding and appreciation of making a decision or failing to make a decision. This is compared to the position in the United Kingdom whereby understanding is still a requirement, but an individual must also retain and use the information when making the decision and be able to communicate the decision. This is similar to the definition contained in Queensland, although Queensland also has a voluntariness requirement.

Closely connected to this is the follow on question of whether, if the definition of capacity is legislatively enshrined, should the test for capacity be as well?[87] If a definition and test for capacity were to be included in legislation, the level of understanding the principal is required to have to make an enduring document would need to be able to be more clearly stated. Additionally, the communication requirement would also need to be improved by, for example, providing examples of methods of communication. There should be no opportunity to construe any legislative definition of capacity as directly affecting a specific test for either an enduring power of attorney or an advance care directive unless specifically provided for in the relevant legislation.

A clear and consistent approach to decision-making capacity assessment will help address the confusion created by the complex jurisdictional based approaches to capacity which can vary within, let alone between, countries. The legal tests as they stand vary, are uncertain and, at times, can be incompatible, leading to confusion in their application. This is especially evident when the health profession is increasingly being asked to participate in capacity assessments with, often, little to no guidance from the legal profession as to what the legal standards actually are.

---

[85]O'Neill N and Peisah C (2011), p. 4. See also *Re K* [1988] Ch 310, 316; *Re W* [2000] Ch 343; *Re W* [2001] Ch 609 [20].

[86]Adult Guardianship and Trusteeship Act SA 2008 Part 1(1).

[87]For example, the New South Wales Standing Committee recommended that there be a legislative definition of capacity in New South Wales which should acknowledge that capacity is decision and time specific. Standing Committee on Social Issues, Parliament of New South Wales (2010), p. 35.

6 Witnessing Provisions and Capacity Assessment

Witnessing provisions for enduring documents vary between jurisdictions but may require the witness to certify not only that the principal understood the nature and effect of the enduring document, that is that the principal had the legal capacity necessary to make the document, but that the witness explained the impact and potential consequences of the document to the principal. Often however, requirements that the witness certify that the principal appeared to have the capacity necessary to make the enduring document fail to offer any useful guidance on how to actually determine whether the principal does, in fact, have the requisite capacity to understand the nature and effect of the enduring document. This is highlighted by the lack of a suitable, agreed upon definition of capacity, the numerous and varying types of capacity relevant to different decisions, and the multitude of ways in which to assess capacity. This is not to forget, however, the, at times, tenuous relationship between the legal and, where involved, health professionals conducting the assessments.

Who is considered an eligible witness is another problem. Often prescribed legislation will list a pool of professions from which the prescribed witnesses can be drawn, for example, a barrister or solicitor, or a licensed conveyancer.[88] This is problematic because while each of the prescribed witnesses will have training and qualifications regarding the valid execution of legal documents, they may not with respect to the assessment of legal capacity. Legal and health professionals are arguably ill-trained to undertake the task of attesting the capacity or otherwise of an individual. Other witnesses that can be listed are generally less qualified with fewer resources at their disposal to be able to satisfactorily carry out the assessment of capacity. However, although this is not an attempt to make the execution of these documents more difficult or expensive by forcing individuals to see a legal or health professional, it will have this result, and without the guarantee that the legal and/or health professional is able to satisfactorily assess their capacity in any event. The concern is to ensure that where capacity is at risk that the assessment is undertaken by a person knowledgeable in the intricacies and nuances that impact capacity.

7 Evidencing the Loss of Legal Capacity

Consideration also needs to be given to the evidence necessary to prove a lack of capacity. For example, medical certificates can be used as proof of an individual's lack of capacity or, alternatively, that the individual in question had the capacity to make the enduring document.[89] The argument against including a medical certification as to the existence, or lack of, capacity is that to do so overly complicates the

---

[88]See, for example: *Powers of Attorney Act 2003* (NSW) s 19(2).

[89]See, for example: *Powers of Attorney Act 1998* (Qld) s 33(5), s 44(6).

process. Further, such certifications can be time-consuming, expensive, and may act as deterrents to those considering the use of enduring documents.

It is tempting to state that a medical certificate should be required as a prerequisite to the loss of capacity and any enduring document coming into effect. However, an informal approach to seeking a medical opinion is consistent with the general principles, making the process less formal and arguably more accessible. Further, there may be circumstances which do not warrant seeking a medical opinion, where it is not possible to obtain a medical opinion, or obtaining a medical opinion is unaffordable. Attempts to ensure the accuracy, consistency and transparency of the capacity assessment process should not become prohibitive in the execution of these important future planning documents. Additionally, making a medical certificate a requirement may confuse and further complicate the role of the health professional in assessing capacity. It potentially elevates the opinion of the health professional to a determination as to the existence of legal capacity. It is questionable whether it would be appropriate for a health professional to adopt this role because the task of assessing capacity for an enduring document requires knowledge and skill in the execution of legal documents. Rather, it may be preferable for a medical opinion to be sought if there is an issue about an individual's capacity. The fundamental issue is, however, that capacity assessment should not be left to untrained people and, further, that there should at least be guidance on when to obtain such evidence, as well as what constitutes satisfactory evidence to demonstrate incapacity.

While legislation in this area may be too prescriptive and education of stakeholders—professional and in the community more broadly—is paramount, the view that this is only an educative issue which should be addressed in professional development and training programs is somewhat naive. This is currently not succeeding in ensuring a rigorous assessment process and, ultimately, the protection (where appropriate) of individual legal capacity. In addition to this, there are few incentives for this situation to change in the future given the problems facing capacity assessment. Added to this is the problem of ensuring that education programs are accessible and the standard of training is appropriate. Merely stating it is an educative issue is not enough. Programs need to be developed, implemented and attended for both legal and health professionals, as well as members of the community.

8 Conclusion

As people live longer it is clear that capacity assessments will become increasingly important in an attempt to retain control over decisions made—either by substitute decision-makers or through a supported decision-making process. This is, however, especially significant in the context of substitute decision-making, as although people are living longer, it is potentially without the legal competency to continue to make their own financial and/or health and lifestyle decisions. The current approach to assessments is beleaguered by the inherent challenges presented by both adequately defining, and assessing, the fluid concept of decision-making capacity, especially given the nebulous notion of financial capacity. Consequently, it is imperative that governments, policy makers, ethicists, the law and legal actors, health care professionals, and society generally attempt to maintain the delicate balance between autonomy and protection.

References

Australian Law Reform Commission (2013) Equality, Capacity and Disability in Commonwealth Laws, Issues Paper 44

Australian Law Reform Commission (2014a) Equality, Capacity and Disability in Commonwealth Laws, Discussion Paper 81

Australian Law Reform Commission (2014b) Equality, Capacity and Disability in Commonwealth Laws, Summary Report 124

Blanck P, Martinis JG (2015) "The Right to Make Choice": the national resource center for supported decision-making. Inclusion 3(1):24–33

Cockerill J, Collier B, Maxwell K (2005) Legal requirements and current practices. In: Collier B, Coyne C, Sullivan K (eds) Mental capacity powers of attorney and advance health directives. Federation Press, Leichhardt

Collier B, Coyne C (2005) An overview of the relevant legal principles. In: Collier B, Coyne C, Sullivan K (eds) Mental capacity powers of attorney and advance health directives. Federation Press, Leichhardt

Collier B, Coyne C, Sullivan K (2005) Preface. In: Collier B, Coyne C, Sullivan K (eds) Mental capacity powers of attorney and advance health directives. Federation Press, Leichhardt

Gooding P (2013) Supported decision-making: a rights-based disability concept and its implications for mental health law. Psychiatry Psychol Law 20(3):431–451

Gooding P, Arstein-Kerslake A, Flynn E (2015) Assistive technology as support for the exercise of legal capacity. Int Rev Law Comp Technol 29(2–3):245–265

Kapp M (2015) Evaluating decision making capacity in older individuals: does the law give a clue? Laws 4(2):164–172

Law Reform Committee, Parliament of Victoria (2010) Inquiry into Powers of Attorney Final Report of the Victorian Law Reform Committee

Lock SL (2016) Age-friendly banking: how We can help get it right before things go wrong. Public Policy Aging Rep 26(1):18–22

O'Neill N, Peisah C (2011) Capacity and the law. Sydney University Press, Sydney

Parker M (2004) Judging capacity: paternalism and the risk-related standard. J Law Med 11 (4):482–491

Parker M (2016) Getting the balance right: conceptual considerations concerning legal capacity and supported decision-making. Bioeth Inq 13(3):381–393

Perlin ML (2013) "striking for the guardians and protectors of the mind": the convention on the rights of persons with mental disabilities and the future of guardianship law. Penn State Law Rev 117(4)

Queensland Law Reform Commission (2010) A review of Queensland's guardianship Laws, Report No 67, Volume 1

SBS (2016) South Australia's latest attempt to pass voluntary euthanasia laws has fallen short but advocate Andrew Denton says the issue isn't going away. http://www.sbs.com.au/news/article/2016/11/17/euthanasia-bill-fails-sa-one-vote. Accessed 1 Nov 2016

Setterlund D, Tilse C, Wilson J (2002) Older people and substitute decision making legislation: limits to informed choice. Australas J Ageing 21(3):128

Sidhu NS, Dunkley MR, Egan MJ (2007) "Not-for-Resuscitation" orders in australian public hospitals: policies, standardised order forms and patient information leaflets. Med J Aust 186 (2):72–75

Standing Committee on Legal and Constitutional Affairs, Parliament of the Commonwealth of Australia (2007) Older People and the Law

Standing Committee on Social Issues, Parliament of New South Wales (2010) Substitute Decision-Making for People Lacking Capacity

The Clinical, Technical and Ethical Principal Committee of the Australian Health Ministers' Advisory Council (2011) A National Framework for Advance Care Directives

United Nations Convention on the Rights of Persons with Disabilities, opened for signature 30 March 2007 (entered into force 3 May 2008)

World Health Organisation (WHO) (2015) Elder Abuse: Fact Sheet No.357. http://www.who.int/ mediacentre/factsheets/fs357/en/. Accessed 1 Nov 2016

Zuscak SJ, Peisah C, Ferguson A (2015) A collaborative approach to supporting communication in the assessment of decision-making capacity. Disabil Rehabil 38(11):1107–1114

Cases and Legislation

Adult Guardianship and Trusteeship Act SA
Guardianship Act 1987 (NSW)
Guardianship and Administration Act 1986 (Vic)
Guardianship and Administration Act 2000 (Qld)
In re K; In re F ('Re K') [1988] 1 Ch 310
Mental Capacity Act 2005 (UK)
Nicholson v Knaggs (2009) VSC 64
NSW Trustee and Guardian Act 2009 (NSW)
Powers of Attorney Act 1998 (Qld)
Powers of Attorney Act 2003 (NSW)
PY v RJS [1982] 2 NSWLR 700
Ranclaud v Cabban (1988) NSW ConvR 55–385
Re GHI (a protected person) [2005] NSWSC 581
Re K [1988] Ch 310
Re W [2000] Ch 343
Re W [2001] Ch 609

Chapter 6
Capacity Assessment: An International Problem

1 Introduction

Increased life expectancy as a result of medical advances, changes in health and lifestyle, and the ageing population mean that capacity and its assessment has become a significantly more pressing problem worldwide in recent years, a problem which is only going to continue to escalate. Although age is not indicative of incapacity, abuse of the vulnerabilities arising from both ageing and impaired capacity are well documented, including the proliferation of elder abuse, in all its forms. This dilemma extends beyond national borders. The question therefore arises, we are living longer, but are we living well? Further, how can we live longer, better? The answer to these questions requires consideration of, amongst many contributing factors, retention of the ability to be able to make our own, legally recognised decisions. In response, the current general premise, transnationally, is founded in respect for the continued right to be able to make one's own decisions, which are recognised at law, for as long as possible. Underpinning this is the need to have a capacity assessment regime that supports, respects and facilitates this aim.

How then to achieve this? One method is through the development, use and functionality of the assessment process itself—attempting to ensure that it is as unassailable as possible, and that it provides useful guidance on assessing capacity, whilst retaining the flexibility so vital in this area. As has been seen, many problems confront and confound those involved with capacity determinations. Nation States are now global citizens. The moveability of people both within, and between, countries raises issues around the validity of estate planning documents such as wills, enduring powers of attorney and advance health directives in jurisdictions other than those in which the documents were executed. It also gives rise to questions about how the capacity of an individual was assessed, if the assessment was conducted in another jurisdiction. Such problems are not experienced in isolation. It is therefore useful to assess the utility of guidelines in different

© Springer International Publishing AG 2017
K. Purser, *Capacity Assessment and the Law*, DOI 10.1007/978-3-319-54347-5_6

jurisdictions worldwide when considering what a best practice framework can, and should, look like. Given the ad hoc and individualistic nature of capacity assessments, it is almost impossible to systematically review each and every proposed capacity assessment model nationally, let alone internationally. However, what is able to be collated and reviewed are some of the most notable 'best practice' guides. These guidelines will now be considered with a view to making some proposed suggestions in the next chapter based upon the 'best' approach. A transnational comparison is possible because this is restricted to an exploration of the assessment paradigm and methodology generally. It is not intended to discuss the specific legal regimes which exist internationally.

2   Assessment Guidelines: Some International Examples

There are some very useful publications emerging from a number of jurisdictions around the world with respect to capacity assessment processes. Select guidelines from Australia, the United Kingdom and the United States of America will be examined here.

2.1   Australia

There are no national capacity assessment guidelines in Australia. This is despite a clear call for Australia-wide parameters to be implemented to help facilitate transparency and consistency of the assessment process.[1] Instead, government departments, law societies, medical associations, insurance companies and other interested stakeholders each develop their own 'ideal' version of what 'best practice' looks like. Although similarities exist between the different models, there is a proliferation of differences in practice and approach arising both from, and in, an exponentially increasing number of guidelines. This only serves to further confuse an already complex area of practice, for both legal and health professionals, resulting in the issue of which guidelines should be used. Further, the question is, why cannot the various suggested paradigms be synthesised and contained within a single model that is easily accessible, and understandable, to all the professions engaged in capacity assessments? Practically, this has an impact not only on the individual who is the subject of the assessment but also potentially on the practitioners involved in carrying out the assessment given increasing issues of professional liability. The guidelines in Queensland and New South Wales will be examined here as they have both recently been reviewed.

---

[1] Standing Committee on Legal and Constitutional Affairs (2007), p. 88.

In Queensland, the Australian state with the fastest ageing population, the Queensland Law Society, in conjunction with Allens Linklaters and Queensland Advocacy Incorporated, has recently produced updated guidelines for legal practitioners on legal capacity.[2] The aim of the guidelines, which is fostering the 'belief that if lawyers better understand issues of capacity, and are presented with specific steps to undertake in certain circumstances where the capacity of a client seems likely to be called into question, there will be fewer instances in which lawyers refuse to act out of fear that the clients lacks capacity',[3] is to be commended and the guidelines are a very good starting point. However, there are some concerns, both generally and specifically, in relation to these guidelines. Generally, this is yet another set of guidelines which differ in detail from all the other existing guidelines. It is argued that in Australia the best approach is to have one set of consistent, national best practice guidelines which accord with international best practice. Given the necessarily general nature of guidelines, it is difficult to see why guidelines cannot all be developed using a transnational approach which can then be modified as necessary to jurisdictional idiosyncrasies. The first step, however, is achieving national uniformity.

Specifically, the Queensland guidelines clearly define capacity as 'a reference to legal capacity'. Whilst correct, this is done without acknowledging the other, very relevant, context in which capacity assessments can occur and in which these guidelines will be used—in a clinical setting.[4] Merely stating 'legal capacity' is insufficient in light of the significant problems which can arise as a result of the existing terminological challenges. Contained within the very useful step by step diagrammatic representation of a conceptual framework are the statements, 'conduct a preliminary assessment of capacity' and 'does the medical professional's report, when considered along with all of the other available evidence, indicate the client has capacity?'[5] However, for junior lawyers, and/or legal practitioners not familiar with how capacity assessments should ideally be conducted, further guidance on *how* to conduct a preliminary assessment would be of great assistance.

An attempt at such 'guidance' comes later in the guidelines where the process of how to assess a client's capacity is explained, and a list of questions that a lawyer should ask a client supplied.[6] One of the questions mentions determining the cognitive ability of the client to utilise the information to make an informed decision. One issue is: how many legal professionals are trained to be able to assess the cognitive ability of a client? This section references the use of standardised tests, including the familiar warnings about the Mini-Mental State Examination (MMSE), but no reference is made to the necessity of involving health professionals in assessments in appropriate circumstances. Nor is mention made as to how

---

[2] Queensland Law Society, Allens Linklaters and Queensland Advocacy Incorporated (2014).
[3] Ibid 6.
[4] Ibid 5.
[5] Ibid 9.
[6] Ibid 33–34.

this can be effectively accomplished whilst attempting to maximise the decision-making ability of the individual.[7] Reference is, however, made to seeking a second opinion from another *lawyer*.[8] While this may indeed prove useful, it demonstrates the legal-centric position of these guidelines, raising the question, what mechanisms exist to assist the health professionals who are increasingly being asked to participate in legal capacity assessments? Tension already exists between the legal and health professions which will be exacerbated by such heavily legally concentrated guidelines. This is not to say that the guidelines should not contain a legal focus, indeed they must. It should not, however, be at the expense of recognising, facilitating and supporting the growing need for an interdisciplinary approach to assessments, and how this can be achieved. Guidelines must address this and to do so satisfactorily will require such guidelines to be aimed not only at the legal professionals conducting the assessments, but also at the health professionals who are asked to participate in them.

The guidelines do contain a useful, albeit introductory, section on reports from health professionals, including a precedent referral letter.[9] However, whilst identifying that a health professional should prepare a report, the guidelines arguably offer limited assistance as to what should be included in such a report. This can then result in insufficient evidence being available if a document or the assessment is contested. The guidelines do not indicate that individuals should have the opportunity to be reassessed if there are steps that can be taken to increase the likelihood of a positive finding of capacity after the clinical, as well as the preliminary assessments are conducted. The issue of funding is loosely addressed but it is noted that the responsibility for funding assessments remains uncertain.[10] The issue of finance is especially important because in Australia, as discussed previously, assessments are not covered by Medicare meaning that, theoretically at least, individuals will have to pay out of pocket for any assessment undertaken.

Basically, to comply with the guidelines a legal professional should consider: whether the client has the capacity to proceed according to the relevant legal test; undertake a 'thorough and honest assessment' of whether the client has the capability to instruct the lawyer; and produce a 'detailed record of the assessment process, the lawyer's reasoning and their ultimate conclusions'.[11] Again, the issue is that there is no detail given around the nature of the assessment process to be conducted—to ascertain either the capacity to make the particular legal decision or to give instructions—or about the nature of the report. The nature of the report is less a problem for the legal professionals than the health professionals, provided there is clear guidance from the legal professional to the health professional about the nature of the assessment process to be undertaken and the report. Whilst these

---

[7] Ibid 34.
[8] Ibid 34.
[9] Ibid 43–45.
[10] Ibid 54–55.
[11] Ibid 17.

guidelines are much better than the predecessors, they still do not go far enough. Consequently, they will not, and arguably cannot, address the multi-faceted challenges that exist when assessing capacity, especially the issues arising from the medico-legal relationship.

The New South Wales Law Society has also recently updated its professional guidelines for assessing capacity.[12] The new guidelines are far superior to what was in place previously demonstrating that progress is definitely being made. They follow much the same ground as those in Queensland. One notable difference is that the New South Wales guidelines extensively reference the Handbook for Lawyers from the American Bar Association and the American Psychological Association.[13] This includes the capacity worksheet for lawyers and techniques legal professionals can employ to enhance a client's mental capacity.[14] This is a welcome addition. The guidelines also reference the 2008 New South Wales Attorney General's Capacity Toolkit.[15] As with Queensland, there are both general and specific issues with the New South Wales guidelines. Generally, the concern is the perpetuation of different guidelines covering substantially similar, but still different, ground which only serves to further confuse an already complex and challenging area. For example, the use of the American Handbook for Lawyers in New South Wales, a welcome step forward, but not in Queensland.

Specifically, although including a section devoted to when and how to refer to a health professional, the guidelines do not discuss when a referral to a general practitioner may be preferred to a specialist, for example, if there is a longstanding relationship where the general practitioner is better placed to be able to ascertain if there have been any cognitive changes over time.[16] Decisions from Australian courts have demonstrated that this type of evidence can sometimes be preferred to that of an expert who has never met with the individual in person.[17] Further, although an appropriate legal professional may be located, what of geographical problems presented by the lack of specialist health professionals in regional, rural and remote areas? The guidelines likewise do not state what information should be given to the health professional to assist in both the assessment and the preparation of the report. This again assumes that the health professional is either already familiar with the relevant legal standards or, alternatively, places an obligation on them to become so, often with little guidance from the legal professional involved. Unlike the Queensland guidelines there is notably no recognition of the significant issue of cost, including who should fund the assessment—an ongoing issue to which there is no easy answer.

---

[12] Law Society of New South Wales (2016).

[13] American Bar Association Commission on Law and Aging, American Psychological Association Assessment of Capacity in Older Adults Project Working Group (2005).

[14] Law Society of New South Wales (2016), p. 16, 19.

[15] Attorney General's Department of New South Wales (2008).

[16] Law Society of New South Wales (2016), p. 9.

[17] See, for example, *Sargent & Anor v Brangwin* [2013] QSC 306.

Neither set of Australian guidelines examined discuss what should happen if the capacity assessment is urgent. For example, in the case of a deathbed will do legal professionals attending hospitals preparing both wills and enduring documents for patients who lack the requisite capacity refer to the treating physician or health care staff? This can obviously cause friction between the professions. Significantly, it can likewise be detrimental to the individual in question because they may be under the influence of not only the illness and any comorbidities, but also the pharmacological effects of any medications. The Australian guidelines are silent on the situation where the legal and health professionals reach different conclusions as to capacity. Noting the requisite duties in this area, for example the duty to make a will, presumably the legal professional will follow his or her assessment not least because the determination of the existence of legal capacity or otherwise is ultimately a decision for a court to make. It must be remembered that whilst correct, often these types of matters do not reach the stage of formal adjudication. This is one of the many reasons why an adequate assessment paradigm is vital. Consequently, a form of dispute resolution when conflicting evidence is received and court proceedings are not on foot may prove beneficial in resolving any conflicting assessments. This also acknowledges the growing attention that elder mediation more generally is garnering. Australian guidelines are also silent on the challenges and benefits of conducting contemporaneous and retrospective assessments.

The term 'medical professional' is also used. Although arguably 'merely' a relatively minor terminological issue, this reduces the important role that the wider health professionals have to play in conducting assessments, for example, neuropsychiatrists. Significantly, both sets of guidelines do not make reference to supported decision-making, only to substituted decision-making, not even to state that the former is outside the purview of the guidelines. This, in effect, ignores the significant impact of the paradigmatic shift but also the important role that accurate, transparent and consistent capacity assessments will play in both substituted and supported decision-making regimes. The language used reinforces that these guidelines are legal–centric, begging the question, what information should be furnished to the health professionals when they are asked to assist in the assessment of the contextually specific *legal* capacity—about both the assessment and the nature of the report. Such an oversight could prove to be to the detriment of the assessment process as well as the evidence available as a result of the assessment. There are also the increasing plethora of guidelines. These, as stated, only serve to create inconsistency of process both within and between the different professions, professional organisations and individual practitioners, who then further add to the problem by modifying the guidelines to create their own idiosyncratic assessment paradigms.

2.2   The United Kingdom

As with Australia, many sets of guidelines also exist in the United Kingdom. However, it is the collaboration between the British Medical Association and the Law Society which is of interest. This is because of the interdisciplinary approach adopted to both develop *and* assess capacity.[18] To this end, the guidelines make the position clear that capacity is a legal issue decided, ultimately, by a court of law.[19] However, what the guidelines do well is to identify and acknowledge that it is not only legal professionals who will be in need of assistance with assessing capacity, but also health professionals.

Structurally, the guidelines work through introductory material, as well as professional and ethical issues arising from the assessment of mental capacity, before clearly outlining the general and legal principles, including evidential concerns. Identifying the evidential issues is not something that the Australian guidelines address, which is a significant oversight. Part of the purpose of any set of guidelines is to help ensure accuracy, consistency and transparency of the assessment process that accords with the best known practice. This is with a view to not only ensuring protection for the autonomy of the individual and protection for the practitioner if there are allegations of unsatisfactory conduct, but also that the best evidence possible is placed before the court if the matter goes that far. It also serves to promote a positive interaction between the individual who is having their capacity assessed and the legal system within which that assessment is taking place. The provision of checklists and tips for health, as well as legal, professionals is a simple, yet effective and, importantly, practical tool to try and assist with the continuous development and implementation of best practice in the capacity assessment context.[20]

Significantly, there is practical guidance for health professionals which includes discussion, albeit briefly, on the fact that capacity is a legal determination, recording the assessment, and a systematic approach to the assessment process. Arguably this information could be more fulsome but was probably condensed in the interests of time and space, but also in not over-burdening the practitioner with too much information. The guidelines mention assessment tools for capacity generally but only really discuss the MacArthur Competence Assessment Tool for Treatment (MacCAT-T). It is unfortunate that the utility of other tests was not critically examined in light of the legal requirements, especially given the questionable importance attached to the MMSE in capacity assessments. Although, again, the issues of time, space and information overload would have a role to play.

Similarly to health professionals, there is also practical guidance for legal professionals which discusses who should assess the person (giving useful summaries of relevant disciplines), information on psychiatric disorders, and medical

---

[18]British Medical Association and the Law Society (2015).
[19]Ibid 203.
[20]See, for example: Ibid 91.

assessment of mental conditions. The draft letter provided here for legal professionals to first send to the health professional they are asking to be involved in the
assessment is a very good example of the detail necessary to help combat the
terminological problems and tension that can exist between the two professions
when conducting assessments.[21] The information about what the report should
contain is particularly useful. This is in contrast to the New South Wales guidelines
examined which did not provide a draft letter, and those in Queensland which,
although providing a draft letter, was not as detailed or informative.

The legal tests of capacity are then examined in a number of areas extending
beyond the estate planning context, before examining practical aspects of the
assessment of capacity. Significantly, this section is divided into information for
health and legal professionals. Setting out the legal principles not only serves as a
reminder to legal professionals but can also serve as an introduction for health
professionals to the relevant legal test for the specific capacity being assessed. As
noted above, this is something that is missing from the Australian guidelines.
Moreover, this addresses the issue of guidelines not being inclusive of health
professionals, in either content or language. By doing this, it is not only enhancing
the relationship between the legal and health professionals involved in the assessment, but also their interaction with, and consequently the experience of, the
individual who is having his or her capacity assessed.

2.3   The United States of America

It has been noted that in the United States of America the law itself supplies limited
useful guidance for adequate, accurate and consistent capacity determinations.[22]
Consequently, there is a need for guidance around how to best assess capacity.
Legal practice generally is governed by the American Bar Association Model Rules
of Professional Conduct.[23] Significantly, and as mentioned above, the American
Bar Association (ABA) has joined with the American Psychological Association
(APA) to produce handbooks on the assessment of older adults with diminished
capacity.[24] This has been accurately acknowledged as a major first step in
synthesising the material on assessing capacity and providing guidance as to best

---

[21] Ibid 304–306.

[22] Kapp M (2015), p. 169.

[23] Ibid.

[24] American Bar Association Commission on Law and Aging, American Psychological Associa-
tion Assessment of Capacity in Older Adults Project Working Group (2005); American Bar
Association Commission on Law and Aging, American Psychological Association and National
College of Probate Judges (2006); American Bar Association Commission on Law and Aging,
American Psychological Association Assessment of Capacity in Older Adults Project Working
Group (2008).

practice when conducting such determinations.[25] The guidelines emphasise that a clinical determination about capacity should rest on an underlying foundation consisting of the legal standard and the health professional's understanding of the context specific standard.[26] The guidelines build upon elements of Grisso's work, being expanded to nine-steps including: legal, functional diagnostic, cognitive, psychiatric or emotional, values, risks, means to enhance capacity, and finally, clinical judgment.[27] These handbooks, distinct from the interdisciplinary collaboration in the United Kingdom which produced a combined handbook for both legal and health professionals, have been specifically tailored for lawyers,[28] judges[29] and psychologists.[30] However, similarly to the guidelines examined from the United Kingdom, these handbooks take the approach of: examining the importance of the assessments; setting out the legal standards as well as the clinical models; discussing how capacity can best be assessed, including worksheets and ethical concerns; detailing techniques which can enhance capacity; and, particularising the best process to refer individuals for assessments.

With regard to legal professionals, the handbook notes that there are three levels of involvement in capacity screening. The first is 'preliminary screening', followed by 'professional consultation' (if necessary), before reaching the third level of involvement which is the making of the legal determination as to whether the requisite capacity exists or not.[31] In particular, the capacity worksheets for lawyers are valuable.[32] They detail observational signs for cognitive, emotional and behavioural functioning, including any qualifying reasons for the observed behaviour, which can impact capacity. The worksheet then proceeds to identify the relevant legal capacity, highlighting the importance of the client's understanding, appreciation and/or functioning with direct reference to the particular standard of legal capacity in question.[33] The handbook for psychologists is similarly set out with information on how to work with legal professionals and courts. The handbook for judges is limited to guardianship proceedings which is obviously restrictive in application. This is, however, understandable given that the handbook is set out in

---

[25]Falk E and Hoffman N (2014), p. 855. See also Moye J, Marson DC, Edelstein B (2013) for a discussion of the guidelines.

[26]Falk E and Hoffman N (2014), p. 856.

[27]Moye J et al. (2013), p. 164.

[28]American Bar Association Commission on Law and Aging, American Psychological Association Assessment of Capacity in Older Adults Project Working Group (2005).

[29]American Bar Association Commission on Law and Aging, American Psychological Association and National College of Probate Judges (2006).

[30]American Bar Association Commission on Law and Aging, American Psychological Association Assessment of Capacity in Older Adults Project Working Group (2008).

[31]American Bar Association Commission on Law and Aging, American Psychological Association Assessment of Capacity in Older Adults Project Working Group (2005), p. 3.

[32]Ibid 23.

[33]Ibid 25. It is this worksheet that has been adopted by The Law Society of New South Wales in those guidelines: Law Society of New South Wales (2016), p. 16.

far more detail and focuses on a specific area in order to offer more detailed and context specific guidance. As this is the approach taken, it would be useful to have guidelines prepared for other areas of capacity which are commonly disputed such as testamentary capacity, but also, going beyond the estate planning context, driving.

These handbooks, in effect, promote a hybrid approach to capacity assessment seeking to balance diagnostic and functional elements, that is, the status and the functional approaches to capacity assessment.[34] The handbooks, however, take the assessment approach further noting that while these factors have to be balanced against each other, they also have to be balanced against the potential risk and values preferences of the individual who is having his or her capacity assessed.[35] This is not novel but it is best achieved in these handbooks and those in the United Kingdom. Explicit recognition of the need to understand the relevant legal standard is also made.

Falk and Hoffman have adapted a useful table from the guidelines which details what is identified by the authors as the framework element, potential sources of information, and limited specific resources which may be available to better assess capacity.[36] So, for example, for the framework element of the legal standard, they have identified that the potential sources of information are discussion with the referring legal professional, hospital counsel and local public guardian. Although more detail would be useful, this could prove to be an invaluable resource offering guidance as to other repositories of information that could be utilised in the accurate assessment of an individual's capacity. Moreover, this incorporates elements of the guidelines from the United Kingdom. For instance, being specific about both the legal capacity and the standard for each decision and/or transaction, such as testamentary capacity, or the financial capacity necessary to make an enduring power of attorney. Adding to the utility is information about where the type and standard of capacity can be located at law, that is, case law or through statutory provisions. This will also help remove any ambiguity, where possible, as to the applicable legal standards, although obviously would need to be jurisdiction specific. It would also be useful for professionals—both legal and health—practising across multiple jurisdictions to know the requirements, and to be familiar with the best practice process. Another element that would supplement this idea is to include the legal standard followed by the types of clinical capacity it may relate to and suggestions as to appropriate testing processes. For example, Falk and Hoffman have for the cognitive underpinnings, the framework action, clinical interviews and mental status examinations as the potential sources of information.[37] What would be even more beneficial is clarifying which clinical examinations are best suited to assessing which types of legal capacity in connection to which type of mentally disabling condition and, additionally, which health professional(s) would be best

---

[34]Falk E and Hoffman N (2014), pp. 856–858.

[35]Ibid.

[36]Ibid 857–858.

[37]Ibid.

involved in the assessment process. This builds on similar approaches not only in the APA and ABA handbooks but also the guidelines in the United Kingdom.

Importantly, the ABA and APA handbooks emphasise that a clinical determination about capacity should rest on an underlying legal foundation which takes into account the health professional's understanding of the context specific legal standard.[38] This is also reflected in the United Kingdom guidelines, and to a lesser extent, those examined from the Australian jurisdictions. It is, however, *a step*. The APA and ABA guidelines were first developed approximately a decade ago and a great deal of research has been conducted since then which also needs to be synthesised and included in any best practice guidelines. The United Kingdom guidelines are recent, with new editions regularly becoming available. Similarly, however, there needs to be a synthesis of all material, including the different guidelines that are consistently being developed by various stakeholders, but particularly by the professional organisations and government departments.

Whilst there is no one arbiter of best practice, taking the best elements from all the guidelines and building upon the current research seems the *next logical step* in ensuring consistent, transparent and, arguably most importantly, accurate assessments of legal capacity. The interdisciplinary approach adopted in both the United States of America and the United Kingdom in preparing the respective sets of guidelines is to be admired and replicated—any set of guidelines must have the input of both legal *and* health professionals, although this should be broader than one particular health discipline, as well as incorporating ethical principles. It is worthwhile considering which other stakeholders may be useful in including in the development of any guidelines, such as professional bodies and potentially insurers as well as advocacy groups to ensure that the voice of the people who are being assessed is heard. One issue, in addition to the plethora already faced in this area, will be communication about the existence of guidelines. Insurance companies could be one way in which to ensure that the message is heard—especially with increasing concerns about professional liability in relation to capacity assessments.

It is clear that the guidelines or handbooks, depending on the terminology adopted from the United Kingdom or the United States of America, are superior to those in Australia. This is despite those from the United States of America being originally developed approximately a decade ago. The United Kingdom and the United States of America guides are relatively similar. One of the major differences, however, is how they have been framed for the intended audience. Whilst one consolidated volume was developed in the United Kingdom aimed at legal professionals and the wider health professions, handbooks for specific professions were developed in the United States of America. On the one hand the specificity of the American guidelines is beneficial because it targets the concerns particular to the specific discipline. The problem with this, however, is that capacity assessments can arise in any legal context and the guidelines, therefore, have to be generic enough to offer a starting base from which to assess capacity more broadly.

---

[38]Ibid 856.

Alternatively, handbooks need to be developed for every, or at least the most common, scenarios in which questions about capacity can arise. Further, health professionals more broadly, rather than just psychologists, are being involved in capacity assessments and so may feel excluded by the targeted nature of the titles of these handbooks. Consequently, having a more general approach to the types of capacity discussed is ideal, but the approach of then targeting the guides to specific issues faced by different professions is useful, provided it does not have the unintended consequence of excluding wider health professionals who may also become involved in assessments.

3 Challenges

Capacity assessment and attempting to develop a set of guidelines aimed at assisting in the improvement of the assessment process is clearly plagued by a variety of challenges. With a view to progressing the discussion in this area, further research needs to be had examining the actual impact of existing guidelines in each of the jurisdictions to ascertain whether there is any utility to the different approaches adopted and which, if any, are the most useful in promoting best practice. Further, are the guidelines actually referred to in disciplinary proceedings and can, as well as, does anything happen to practitioners who fail to act in accordance with them? This raises the question of what is the point of having such guidelines if they are not able to be used in establishing, maintaining, developing, and perhaps even 'enforcing' best practice standards. This last point raises difficult questions. Guidelines are just that, guidelines. So, referring to them in disciplinary proceedings could be overstretching what they are designed to do and giving them greater significance than what they were meant to have. Having said this, any guidelines are intended as a best practice starting point from which practitioners, both legal and health, are able to deviate if required by the particular facts at hand, but they do offer that consistent and transparent starting point from which practitioners should commence—important information for all practitioners, but particularly those who are inexperienced in assessing capacity in a particular jurisdiction. Consequently, guidelines should be able to be used in professional misconduct cases if they have been based on rigorous transdisciplinary research encompassing both traditional doctrinal as well as empirical research exploring relevant stakeholders' views and best practice.

A further, fundamental question then, in connection to the consideration of whether guidelines should be used in disciplinary proceedings and what they should contain, is do legal and health practitioners even know about them, let alone actually use them? If they do know about them, what is the knowledge? Is it, for example, limited to the guidelines in their respective jurisdictions, which while better than nothing, in the case of, for example, New South Wales or Queensland in Australia, can be seen as inferior to the guidelines used in the United Kingdom or the United States of America. This also raises questions of access to 'quality' advice, and how to ensure that assessments are being conducted by 'assessors' knowledgeable in the process they are an integral part of. This consists, in part, of not causing harm to the individual who is having his or her capacity assessed, that is, the assessor, or neutral third party, having a role which prevents the law from having an anti-therapeutic impact on the lives of individuals through the use of best practice.

This also links to education and communication both within and between the legal and health professions, and with the community more generally. What is the point in continuing to do what has been done when it is not being successful? Individual practitioners continue to employ their own unique methodologies which perpetuates the outcome of ad hoc, inconsistent, opaque and potentially inaccurate assessments. Again, further empirical research is required to ascertain whether the guidelines are utilised and if so, to what extent. Alternatively, if not, why not?

Another challenge is that of advancing technologies and innovation in the medical field and various disciplines. Can and do guidelines adequately take into consideration advances in medicine and health related sciences? Can and do they adequately utilise developing disciplines? One example is the use of neuroscience and standardised testing to assess capacity. The use of this discipline is still relatively new with questions being raised over how to best employ the techniques it makes available when assessing capacity, for example, can this be satisfactorily extended to the determination of a specific legal capacity and the requisite standard in relation to a particular decision and/or transaction, such as, for example, testamentary capacity.

There are also problems with witnessing enduring documents where attesting to the donor's capacity is a requirement. There is sometimes a failure on the part of the witnesses to consider questions about capacity. This is not to mention that, even if they did ask relevant questions, would the witnesses be in a position to assess the answers in light of whether the individual has or does not have the requisite capacity. Therefore, even with the development of satisfactory guidelines challenges will persist which will require not only adequate training in assessment methodologies but also effective communication—within and between professions, and with the stakeholders and society in general. The combination of guidelines, training, communication and education, ideally, will help develop an assessment paradigm in which the law can have a therapeutic rather than an anti-therapeutic impact on the lives of individuals who are potentially experiencing one of the most traumatic experiences of their lives—the loss of the ability to make their own decisions, the loss of self.

4 Conclusion

As can be seen, there are numerous guidelines being developed around the world demonstrating not only the magnitude of the capacity assessment problem but also the dedication being shown to try and address it. There are a range of legal and health professionals involved in capacity assessments—ranging from experts who conduct assessments regularly to those who only need to assess capacity on an infrequent basis. Consequently, it is clear that something which is readily accessible and easily understood is needed in an attempt to benchmark what 'best practice' looks like in this context. Guidelines are the most prudent and workable way to proceed as anything 'stronger', such as legislative provisions mandating how assessments should be conducted, would be too prescriptive in an area where the need for flexibility remains a paramount consideration.

Obviously guidelines also have their drawbacks and, although well intentioned, the multitude of guidelines being developed and already existing are, in fact, only serving to exacerbate the problem. This is because it is not only (understandably) the law that is being varied in each set of guidelines, as is jurisdictionally relevant, but also the language used; the triggers; the provision of precedents such as letters to health professionals regarding, for example, the assessment of testamentary capacity; and ultimately the very assessment process itself. These disparities are only further exacerbated by the fact that each individual legal and health practitioner will then further modify the guidelines to suit his or her own individual skill set and knowledge base. There is also the connected problem of how many practitioners first, know of, and secondly, use the guidelines. Further, if using them, which ones are they using and why? Is it one particular set of guidelines or a combination of different ones given that some are lacking? How much are practitioners modifying the guidelines being used, either through choice or necessity? What impact, if any, are such guidelines having on the evidence being provided in court, and are they having any impact in professional liability matters? Empirical research is desperately needed in this area providing an evidence base establishing which sets of guidelines are being utilised, why, and how they could be improved upon to inform a consistent approach to best practice.

Nevertheless, guidelines still present the best opportunity to provide information to and model best practice for both legal and health practitioners. This is obviously as a starting point because any set of guidelines has to retain the flexibility necessary to enable adaptation to each individual set of circumstances. It is refining the content of those guidelines, as well as the education about their existence, substance, and application that is necessary. With respect to the subject matter, as discussed above, there are a variety of different approaches having been adopted around the world. Those interdisciplinary guidelines adopted in the United Kingdom and the United States of America being the best. Those adopted in Australia are inconsistent and are not as robust as those in the other two jurisdictions examined. While the guidelines in the United Kingdom have been consolidated into one work, those in the United States of America are designated for particular professions. As discussed above, there are obviously advantages and disadvantages to each approach, with possibly the single volume being the most inclusive to all professions who can potentially become involved in the assessment process. Even so, there does need to be dedicated guidance and support given to each specific profession where required. For example, while guidelines for legal professionals need suggestions as to whom from the health profession to involve, guidelines for the health profession will obviously not need such information, instead potentially benefitting from a more detailed explanation of the legal principles. Education is especially important if the guidelines are going to have optimal effect—education not only as to existence and import of the guidelines, but also of the need to modify them, where necessary, as the *matter* requires, not to suit the skill, experience, expectation and comfort of the legal and/or health professional(s) using them.

References

American Bar Association Commission on Law, Aging, American Psychological Association (2005) Assessment of Older Adults with Diminished Capacity: A Handbook for Lawyers. https://www.apa.org/pi/aging/resources/guides/diminished-capacity.pdf. Accessed 1 Nov 2016

American Bar Association Commission on Law and Aging, American Psychological Association (2008) Assessment of Capacity in Older Adults Project Working Group, Assessment of Older Adults with Diminished Capacity: A Handbook for Psychologists. https://www.apa.org/pi/aging/programs/assessment/capacity-psychologist-handbook.pdf. Accessed 1 Nov 2016

American Bar Association Commission on Law and Aging, American Psychological Association, National College of Probate Judges (2006) Judicial Determination of Capacity of Older Adults in Guardianship Proceedings: A Handbook for Judges. https://www.apa.org/pi/aging/resources/guides/judges-diminished.pdf. Accessed 1 Nov 2016

Attorney General's Department of New South Wales (2008) Capacity Toolkit. http://www.justice.nsw.gov.au/diversityservices/Documents/capacity_toolkit0609.pdf. Accessed 1 Nov 2016

British Medical Association and the Law Society (2015) Assessment of mental capacity: guidance for doctors and lawyers, 4th edn. Law Society Publishing, London

Falk E, Hoffman N (2014) The role of capacity assessments in elder abuse investigations and guardianships. Clin Geriatr Med 30(4):851–868

Kapp M (2015) Evaluating decision making capacity in older individuals: does the law give a clue? Laws 4(2):164–172

Law Society of New South Wales (2016) When A Client's Mental Capacity is in Doubt A Practical Guide for Solicitors. http://www.lawsociety.com.au/cs/groups/public/documents/internetcontent/1191977.pdf. Accessed 1 Nov 2016

Moye J, Marson DC, Edelstein B (2013) Assessment of capacity in an aging society. Am Psychol 68(3):158–171

Queensland Law Society, Allens Linklaters, Queensland Advocacy Incorporated (2014) Queensland Handbook for Practitioners on Legal Capacity

Standing Committee on Legal and Constitutional Affairs (2007) Older People and the Law (2007) Parliament of the Commonwealth of Australia

Cases

Sargent & Anor v Brangwin [2013] QSC 306

Chapter 7
Some Proposed Suggestions

1 Introduction

It is clear, the assessment of capacity is currently an individualistic process under-taken in a haphazard way without a rigorous paradigm underpinning the approach. One argument is to leave the current 'system' as is—that it would be too difficult to ensure adequate, consistent and transparent assessment methodologies are employed, and the approach thus far has worked reasonably well.[1] This argument, however, centres more on the changing of legislation. That is not what is proposed here. Instead, it is the use of guidelines that is suggested as the next step in progressing the discourse in this area. This is because ensuring the satisfactory assessment of testamentary and decision-making capacity through the development of an appropriate assessment paradigm is of vital importance given the increase in mentally disabling conditions which will impact an individual's ability to make his or her own legally recognised decisions. Determining a set 'score' to establish capacity, or incapacity, at law is implausible and would not allow for the inherent flexibility and individualistic—task and decision specific—nature of legal capacity. The ultimate goal is to have a robust idea of what sufficient performance, including cognitive assessment, of the specific functional tasks required to establish a partic-ular legal capacity would look like in the requisite legal framework.[2] This is a problem that transcends disciplinary boundaries.

The challenge for those involved in assessing capacity is to recognise the impact of the underlying mentally disabling condition on the relevant legal capacity.[3] As discussed, legal professionals can fail to understand the impact of such presenting conditions, any comorbidities, as well as medications on legal capacity. This can be for a number of reasons including education, training, or a client deliberately or

---

[1]Kapp M (2015), p. 170.
[2]Moye J et al. (2013), p. 167.
[3]Falk E and Hoffman N (2014), p. 856.

© Springer International Publishing AG 2017
K. Purser, *Capacity Assessment and the Law*, DOI 10.1007/978-3-319-54347-5_7

unintentionally misrepresenting conditions which would impact their capacity. One approach to redress this situation has been the increasing inclusion of health professionals in the assessment of capacity. This has inevitably, and beneficially, exposed the assessment process to wider, interdisciplinary investigation. Such external scrutiny has revealed that not only can legal knowledge and application of appropriate assessment methods be lacking, but this is not always effectively countered by blindly including other professionals, which has generally been the approach to date.

The adoption of an interdisciplinary approach can bring its own set of challenges, for example: the quality of the instructions provided to the health professionals can be inadequate; the relationship between the legal and health professions can be influenced by an underlying tension which is aggravated by miscommunication and misunderstandings; absent standardised assessment methodologies and tools, the process is dependent upon individual experience and knowledge; the understanding of the appropriate legal test for, and standard of, capacity for the specific decision to be made may be incorrect or misinterpreted; what is the 'best' evidence about capacity, especially if the health and legal assessments conflict; who should be providing the health evidence; and despite the best of intentions, the actual assessment process itself may not be undertaken in a satisfactory manner to ensure the accuracy of results which does, and will, continue to impact individual autonomy and personal sovereignty. Each problem can negatively contribute to the others and are generally exacerbated by the lack of guidance—in both the professional and academic literature—about the intersection between clinical assessments and legal concepts. For example, how do notions of cognitive decline experienced in Alzheimer's disease align with the four limb test to establish testamentary capacity? These problems are only going to escalate.

Consequently, discussions around standardised and consistent assessment paradigms need to be had, on an international and transdisciplinary scale given the magnitude of the problem. Suggested guidelines and general principles will be made here which draw upon the models examined previously. In addition to the assessment process and principles, included in any discussion to this effect will necessarily be the terminology used as well as the relationship between the legal and health professionals. It is by no means an easy or foolproof exercise, but rather the furtherance of discussion centred on developing an approach to the rigorous assessment of capacity in the context of testamentary and substitute decision-making. Any such guidelines will necessarily be transdisciplinary, recognising the importance of managing capacity assessment processes in both the legal and health settings, and utilising the skills of legal and health professionals.[4] Uniquely, it is proposed that a satisfactory assessment paradigm should be positioned within an overarching framework of therapeutic jurisprudence. This will provide a novel lens through which to conduct these assessments while taking into account many of the ethical and practical concerns that exist. This is one step in attempting to

---

[4]Collier B et al. (2005a), p. 161.

re-imagine capacity assessments and further the dialogue in this area. The development of any suitable guidelines and principles, and the surrounding discussion, will require detailed and considered input from all the various stakeholders including the legal and health professions, as well as government, insurers, advocacy groups, financial bodies, and community organisations.

2   Defining Legal Capacity

A lack of clarity in terminology has been clearly identified as one of the fundamental challenges confronting capacity assessment. This inevitably leads to a lack of dependability and clarity of process. As noted, there is some discussion as to the separation of capacity as a medical and competency as a legal construct. This is not borne out in practice, nor in the more recent literature.[5] Consequently, any attempted demarcation into discipline-specific terms would be arbitrary in nature and a poor investment of time exemplifying an academic exercise in futility.[6] This is not, however, to deny the need for consistent and clear definitions in assessments. For example, determining whether it is *legal* competency/capacity or *medical* competency/capacity which is to be assessed. Everyone involved needs to understand what it is they are assessing and to what standard—unequivocal terminology is essential to accomplish this. For terminological clarity to exist, the first thing that must occur is a consistent and accepted definition of what the relevant legal capacity to be assessed is. One idea is that such definitions should be included in legislation.[7] This is because a legislative definition offers some certainty when informing the approach adopted by legal and health professionals. Although the lure of certainty is one reason for legislatively determining the definition of capacity, the downside is the rigidity of such an approach which is contrary to the flexibility required in this area. Statutory inclusion of any guidelines and/or principles would be prohibitive, not allowing for the fluidity necessary to address individual situations.[8]

It would be ineffectual to attempt to define capacity in clinical terms only. There must be reference to the relevant legal standard. However, it would also be counter-productive to define capacity in a purely legal sense as the assessment process increasingly requires the involvement of the health profession. For example, reference to advances in neuroscience may be invaluable in adequately defining and assessing notions of legal capacity given that neuroscience examines the structure and purpose of the brain and nervous system, and their connection to behaviour which can inform an individual's capacity.[9] Practically, advancements in

---

[5]See for example: Purser K and Rosenfeld T (2014); Sousa LB et al. (2014).

[6]See also for example Kershaw MM and Webber LS (2004).

[7]Darzins P et al. (2000), p. 139.

[8]Queensland Law Reform Commission (2010), p. 279.

[9]Marson D (2016), p. 13.

neuroscience in the assessment of cognition may lead to the refinement of imaging studies (which are still in their infancy) of financial capacity and direct links between, for example: brain activity, networks and structure; and cognition as well as function. Such imaging can be applied to 'normal' individuals not experiencing cognitive loss but also to those people suffering from neurodegenerative diseases.[10] Hypotheses can then be made as to how the structure and function in the particular brain networks and regions can lead to impairment of functional that is, for instance financial, capacity.[11] This can provide a more definite cognitive assessment which must then be understood within the relevant legal framework and particular individual's circumstances in order to satisfactorily assess the specific legal capacity in question.

It is generally acknowledged that the outcome and status approaches are insufficient to define capacity. The definition should therefore have reference to the functional approach recognising that capacity is time as well as task specific, and that it can fluctuate. Although generally inappropriate, it is worthwhile considering the inclusion of a diagnostic element connecting the assessment to the stage and severity of the disability or illness.[12] This would help avoid the constant assessment for every task which is a risk when the functional approach is taken to extremes. However, the potential effects of labelling on individuals and on their autonomy, as identified when applying a therapeutic jurisprudence lens, cannot be ignored. Consequently, although the stage and severity of an illness or disability is relevant in the assessment process, this cannot be determinative of capacity, and the test itself should be functional concentrating upon whether the individual: understands the issue and what he or she is talking about; can communicate the information; knows the consequences of making positive and negative decisions; and is capable of expressing a consistent choice.

3 The Relationship Between Legal and Health Professionals

Facilitating clear communication, and thus the relationship, between legal and health professionals is of critical importance to ensuring a rigorous assessment process. It is vital that any guidelines and general principles aid legal and health care participation to ensure that all professionals involved know what capacity is being assessed, the standard required to have the requisite legal capacity, how the assessment is to be conducted, and by whom. This section will explore some recommendations to strengthen an interdisciplinary approach whilst recognising the role of education in improving the medico-legal relationship in this context.

---

[10]Ibid.

[11]Ibid.

[12]Bennett H and Hallen P (2005), p. 486.

An interdisciplinary approach is ideal when assessing testamentary and decision-making capacity in increasingly complex situations. Legal professionals are not trained to assess the effect of medical conditions, such as advanced dementia, on legal capacity. Health care professionals are not trained to assess the notion of legal capacity and may not understand the law informing the requisite capacity. Conducting cognitive assessments within a legal framework is extraordinarily difficult given all the factors at play. However, the professions together possess the skills necessary to accomplish this. Consequently, there needs to be effective interaction and involvement between them. An interdisciplinary approach, as well as an educational campaign and training, could help counter some of the miscommunication, as well as the misunderstandings, that each profession can develop about the other. This could specifically target the fear of liability that seems prevalent amongst the health profession, which is where support from medical associations and insurers would be beneficial.

A tangential issue is that of the evidence given by legal and health professionals and which, if any, is preferred by the courts. There is a current preference for evidence from legal professionals. This may change given the increasing need for medical assessments of cognitive capacity and advances in, for example, neuroscience in assessing the impact of cognitive decline on questions of capacity.[13] Ideally, health care professionals would be able to provide contextually specific cognitive evidence including assessments of the major domains of cognition including memory, language and spatial skills, orientation, ability to pay attention, as well as the higher executive functions such as analysis and judgment.[14] These are especially pertinent when assessing financial capacity. However, one of the problems which will need to be overcome is the apparent reluctance of health professionals to become involved in legal matters.

Absent periodic 'legal check-ups', it is possible that health professionals could have a role in disseminating information about future planning, particularly supported and substitute decision-making as well as advance care planning.[15] This may be particularly pertinent if there has been a diagnosis of a mentally disabling condition which will impact an individual's decision-making ability.[16] Arguably, this would be valuable because individuals see their health care professional more frequently than a legal professional. Individuals also generally regard their health care professional without the negative connotations that can be attached to attending a legal appointment, that is, they tend to trust them more. The extent of such advice might be limited given the health care profession's apparent wish to remain disengaged, and indeed should be limited to information as to where to locate legal advice. Further, issues also exist regarding the ability of members of the health care professions to explain legal processes and clearly this would, and indeed

---

[13]Ibid 485.

[14]Ibid 486.

[15]Finkel SI (2003), p. 418.

[16]Marson DC (2013), p. 386.

should, not amount to the giving of legal advice.[17] Perhaps knowing that they cannot provide legal advice would make health care professionals feel more comfortable with suggesting future planning.

The timing would also need to be carefully considered. When approached through a therapeutic jurisprudence lens, the diagnosis of a mentally disabling condition combined with the provision of a plethora of information about not only treatment options, but also legal considerations, would not be in the interests of the patient and may, indeed, have an anti-therapeutic effect. Consequently, discussions of this nature should be dependent on the individual circumstances and what is most beneficial to the person in question. Nevertheless, there is arguably value in health care practitioners, particularly general practitioners, informing their patients of the existence of testamentary and enduring documents, and suggesting that it may be worthwhile seeking legal advice.

The increasing value of medical evidence in legal proceedings also demonstrates the importance of contemporaneous assessments of capacity. If capacity is in question and an assessment is conducted contemporaneously with the signing of the testamentary or enduring document then the issue of capacity should be supported by both legal and medical evidence. Although this may give notice that legal competency is an issue, any determination of legal competency or incompetency would be supported by evidence. Legal tactics and manoeuvring should not be allowed to trump what is in the best interests of the individual.

4   Education and Communication

Education for, and communication between, legal and health care professionals has been identified as fundamental to the progression of the capacity assessment dialogue.[18] Legal and health care professionals need more continuing professional development.[19] The education programs should be conducted both within and between the professions. Legal professionals should be more familiar with and be able to recognise the effect that a disability, illness and/or medications can have upon an individual's legal capacity. Health care professionals involved in capacity assessments need to be more familiar with the relevant legal standards or have access to relevant knowledge and materials.[20] Members of the legal profession need to assume some responsibility for generally educating, as well as providing situation-specific information, to the relevant health care professionals.[21] Members

---

[17]Ellison S et al. (2004).

[18]Law Reform Committee, Parliament of Victoria (2010), p. 131. See also Collier B et al. (eds) (2005b).

[19]Parker M and Cartwright C (2005), pp. 88–89.

[20]Parker M (2008), p. 34.

[21]Cockerill J et al. (2005), p. 55.

of the health care professions also need to be confident and informed enough to know when they require more information about the legal issues to request such information from the particular legal professional. Any education program should include a discussion about the assessment paradigm, guidelines, general principles, and definition of capacity. This would demonstrate what is being assessed and how it should be assessed at a common level with scope for flexibility depending upon individual circumstances. It should also address the relationship between the professions.

It seems unlikely that any such educational programs would fit within either the legal or medical undergraduate curriculums, although some medico-legal tutorials are currently conducted, for example at Monash University in Melbourne, Australia. However, the Monash approach seems to be the exception rather than the rule. An introduction to the issues would be beneficial at the undergraduate stage but it appears impractical with both the legal and medical curricula already full. Another option is having the education as the subject of a legal and health postgraduate offering. However, the success of the dissemination of the information would be reliant upon the specific professionals enrolling in postgraduate degrees, and then the particular unit. It is also unlikely that tertiary institutions would be able to offer such specialised programs, especially considering the need to provide appropriately qualified individuals to deliver the material.

An alternative to tertiary education, and arguably the most feasible of the educational options available, is the inclusion of education campaigns in continuing legal and medical education. For example, the Rush University Medical Centre offers training courses in Assessing Decisional Capacity which contains the following learning outcomes: properly evaluating capacities; discussing capacity with patients; requesting a more thorough assessment, where required, including a referral; and using appropriate terminology and methodologies when working with courts regarding guardianship proceedings.[22] It should be noted that guardianship regimes differ markedly between the United States of America and for example, Australia and the United Kingdom. Further, an examination of these systems is outside this work. The point is, that the problems presented by the satisfactory assessment of capacity transcend jurisdictional, discipline and national borders.

It is worthwhile considering whether such education campaigns should be compulsory for legal and health care professionals who encounter issues concerning capacity assessment in their practice. If compulsory education is adopted, a percentage of practice conducted in this area should be identified, for example 50%, before legal and/or health care professionals attract the mandatory education requirements so as not to make them too onerous. Again, the question of cost also arises—should practitioners be forced to pay for further education in this area? Should there be subsidies given the significance of the accompanying social issues (loss of autonomy, the ageing society, increases in mentally disabling

---

[22]See Rush University Medical Centre (2016).

conditions)? As with the actual assessment of capacity, there are no easy answers to these difficult questions. What is clear, however, is that thought must be given to these problems as solutions are going to need to be provided at some time in the not too distant future.

Building on the idea of continuing professional education is the notion of mentor/mentee relationships to develop and pass on skills in assessing capacity. This could occur both within and between the legal and the health care professions as a kind of 'public service'. That is, it is done on a voluntary basis to better inform the legal and health actors involved in the assessment process. For example, demarcated geographical areas could have access to a mentor(s) who is experienced in capacity assessment. So, if a legal professional in a regional community has to assess capacity, the assessment could be recorded and then sent to the mentor for that 'area' for comment, or to work through any issues which have resulted from, or during, the assessment process.[23] With modern technology, it would be far easier to have such a 'program' have real impact.

Impediments obviously exist to establishing a potential mentor/mentee relationship. Obtaining the agreement of potential mentors to sacrifice their time to participate in the mentoring process could pose a problem, as could obtaining the agreement of legal and/or health care professionals to subject themselves to such a 'review' process—even if the outcome is to improve their practice. Although ideally such a mentor/mentee system would be conducted on a voluntary basis, cost will nevertheless feature as the assessment itself will still need to be paid for. Perhaps even, a 'mentoring' fee can be built into the cost to the individual, especially if a system is established whereby assessments are subsidised by the government. Given the reluctance of people to participate in assessments now, any additional costs are likely to only reinforce this attitude. Nevertheless, a mentor/mentee system is something which practically has the potential to have a significant impact on the quality of the assessments being conducted in real time. It is a proposal which should be explored in further detail to see if the theoretical utility is borne out in practice.

Education for, and clear communication with, the community about testamentary and substitute decision-making as well as capacity assessment is also vital. This would inform the community about the nature, the effect, and the advantages of executing testamentary and substitute decision-making documents. Further research is required to identify at what time, including in what age bracket, such communication would be most effective and possibly what is the best age for individuals to consider engaging in future planning.[24] Although there is obviously no single point at which an individual loses capacity, especially as capacity is decision and time specific, there may be evidence regarding when people start to decline in their cognitive skills which could provide an impetus to encourage individuals to engage in estate planning if they have not already done so.

---

[23]See, for example, Kennedy KM (2012), p. 193.
[24]Monash University and the University of Tasmania (2010), p. 7.

It is important for legal and health care professionals to be trained in employing effective communication methods with ageing and cognitively impaired clients as this may heighten the chances of a positive finding with respect to capacity. This is especially important as legal professionals are not trained to critically evaluate how age related cognitive decline can impact a client's ability to relay important information, as well as his or her memory, attention, learning, cognitive control, function, risk taking and perception, any and all of which could influence both the nature and the quality of decisions that are made—a problem which may, in part, be able to be addressed by adopting effective communication techniques for use with older individuals.[25] Further, legal professionals may not understand that a significant number of older people make decisions based, not on the facts before them, but rather on the experiences which have informed their lives.[26] Thus, the implementation of an unyielding legal standard risks not only stereotyping and generalising the ageing process but also ignoring important factors which inform individual decision-making. Increased knowledge and understanding about the impact of such factors on individuals and their capacity is one way in which to begin to redress such issues. Further, employing effective communication methods will heighten individual interactions with legal actors and the legal system as advocated by the principles of therapeutic jurisprudence. What is important is that individuals understand why it is important for them to not only execute a future plan but to also review any estate planning on the happening of any major life event, or at least every 3 to 5 years.

5 Guiding Principles

The need for guiding principles underpinning capacity assessment has been previously discussed. Importantly, therapeutic jurisprudence principles are already increasingly apparent in the testamentary and substitute decision-making context, for example, the concepts of autonomy, labelling and self-fulfilling prophecies, as well as the least restrictive principle. It therefore follows that the development of capacity assessment guidelines and general principles, which are imperative to the development of a consistent and transparent assessment model, should be informed by relevant therapeutic jurisprudence principles which can be used to guide capacity assessors.[27] Therapeutic jurisprudence offers an innovative and cogent framework within which to reassess testamentary and decision-making capacity assessments.

---

[25]Moye J et al. (2013), p. 167; McNeal MH (2013), p. 1083.
[26]Moye J et al. (2013), p. 167.
[27]Queensland Law Reform Commission (2010), p. 61.

The (rebuttable) presumption of capacity should underpin any set of capacity assessment principles.[28] Recognition of the following, at the very least, should likewise occur:

1. respect for basic human rights, including the right to be free of discrimination and any ageist stereotypes;
2. protection and respect for the welfare and best interests of the individual including protection from neglect, abuse and exploitation;
3. respect for autonomy and individual sovereignty;
4. freedom of decision, and the morality of the choice as judged by other people should not determine incapacity;
5. normalisation and inclusion;
6. the least restrictive alternative;
7. respect for the individual's wishes and value as a human being;
8. importance of preserving familial and supportive relationships;
9. promotion of self-reliance;
10. encouragement of the community to know and apply the principles;
11. encouragement of the individual to participate in their community as a valued member of society;
12. respect for cultural and linguistic differences;
13. promotion of maximum participation, minimal limitations and substituted judgment;
14. maintenance of the individual's environment and values;
15. consideration of the individual's circumstances for any supported or substituted decision, including any change in capacity; and
16. respect for confidentiality.[29]

These principles are in harmony with the CRPD.[30] Points 1 and 2 also signpost the significance of the development and implementation of any international pronouncements and/or conventions in relation to older people and the issues faced by the ageing population. On this point, the negative experiences of older people represent violations of their human rights. It is therefore essential that the economic, social, cultural, civil and political rights of older people are protected, especially if they are vulnerable as a result of a lack of capacity. Older people are entitled to the same rights as all other individuals and are protected by the major international human rights instruments, such as the International Covenant on Economic, Social and Cultural Rights and the International Covenant on Civil and Political Rights. Nonetheless, older people have particular needs, and experience unique forms of abuse and exploitation which warrant specific protection. The

---

[28] See also British Medical Association and the Law Society (2015), p. 11.

[29] American Bar Association Commission on Law and Aging, American Psychological Association Assessment of Capacity in Older Adults Project Working Group (2005), p. 13.

[30] *United Nations Convention on the Rights of Persons with Disabilities*, opened for signature 30 March 2007, (entered into force 3 May 2008).

abuse of the human rights of older people cannot be allowed to continue to blanket our ageing population in a cloak of invisibility impacting the quality of life able to be led. The identification of individual autonomy in decision-making as a fundamental principle which ought to underpin all laws affecting older people is thus paramount, as demonstrated by its application in the law relating to, for example, key areas of driving, housing, the provision of health care, and financial management.

Although outside the scope of this work, it is suggested that supported decision-making should ideally underpin capacity assessment. This would not remove the substitute decision-making model, instead co-existing with it. What this approach attempts to do, is to ensure the retention of individual autonomy while still making provision for decisions to be made for individuals who have completely lost legal capacity.

6 Assessment of Capacity

The most significant step towards the rigorous assessment of capacity is the development of guidelines or a general code of practice and ethical standards. Certainly from the perspective of both legal and health practitioners, it is the process adopted which determines whether they have adequately realised their legal and ethical obligations.[31] This would likewise help combat the inconsistent and unpredictable assessment of capacity which currently exists. Guidelines could also help counter inadequate definitions of capacity by ensuring consistency of procedure. What is important is the uniform adoption of generally consistent guidelines to offer assistance with terminological, definitional and methodological inconsistencies. As stated, it is suggested that the guidelines should not be codified as to do so would remove the flexibility necessary to adapt them to individual situations.

In contemplating the assessment of capacity, it is also important to recognise that decision-making is not always a rational process, with decisions often being influenced by bias or irrationality. The impact of emotion on decision-making cannot be underestimated.[32] The ageing process can also result in deficits in 'attention, memory, learning, cognitive control, and risk taking' which may have an impact on the nature and quality of people's decisions.[33] Further, older individuals are more likely to take experience into consideration when making a decision rather than relying solely on the available facts.[34] This section will discuss a general framework of the proposed guidelines in the context of testamentary and decision-

---

[31]*Ruskey-Fleming v Cook* [2013] QSC 142; *Sharp v Adam* [2006] EWCA Civ 449.
[32]Moye J et al. (2013), p. 167.
[33]Ibid.
[34]Ibid.

making capacity assessment. As stated, any set of guidelines would need to have the input of all relevant stakeholders. It is therefore intended that this help progress the capacity assessment dialogue.

6.1   General Framework

At the outset, a clear definition of capacity is imperative in any set of guidelines. The general principles should also be outlined, as should: the triggers; the need to obtain consent for the assessment to take occur; and the importance of educating the individual about the process, including some exemplars as to how to undertake this. For estate planning purposes, the guidelines should then be focussed on either testamentary or decision-making capacity, with financial and health/personal matters being sub-categories of the latter. It is perhaps judicious when developing these sub-categories to have a further profession-specific division for legal and health professionals. These sections should include the information that is necessary to be provided to the other profession when assessing context specific capacity and examples of the format of that information as well as the structure of any assessment report. Establishing the format is significant because otherwise legal and health professionals will tailor the reports and the information provided to their own experiences and skills, as has been occurring, rather than necessarily focusing on the best practice assessment processes. It is these processes which can be used to inform the quality of evidence if court proceedings eventuate, as well as ensuring the protection of individual autonomy.

The guidelines should take into account the individual's circumstances including their behaviour; the presence of any relevant medical factors and medical history;[35] and considerations such as values, gender, lifestyle, as well as social and cultural factors in which decisions are to be made.[36] Although age, in and of itself, is not an automatic indicator of a lack of legal capacity, legal and health care professionals should be more knowledgeable about the ageing process and the impact it can have on individuals, especially on their cognition if, for example, they are over the age of 80 years when their capacity is being assessed.[37] Any pressures on the individual should be acknowledged including an assessment of how the individual meets these pressures. If there is an issue as to capacity, the assessment should consider the individual's ability to understand, appreciate, reason, and communicate choices and reasons with respect to the decision he or she is making.[38] This last point raises the abilities necessary to be determined as legally capable. Adequately assessing these abilities involves weighing the individual's ability to receive, understand, retain and

---

[35]Cockerill J et al. (2005), pp. 39–41.

[36]Pinsker DM et al. (2010), p. 338.

[37]McNeal MH, (2013), p. 1083.

[38]Capacity Assessment Office Ontario Ministry of the Attorney General (2005), II.6.

recall relevant information; select between options; understand the reasons for the decision; apply the information received to the individual's circumstances; evaluate the benefits and risks of the choice; communicate the choice; and then persevere with that choice, at least until the decision is acted upon.[39]

In addition to the issue of understanding, which is vital when assessing legal capacity, the above criteria demonstrate the importance of appreciating the effect of the decision, as well as being able to justify and communicate that decision. The decision should be made free from any undue influence. These criteria would be designed to reduce the ability of the individual to simply repeat the information which they have been given about the documents. The individual should be able to demonstrate an appreciation of the information and how it impacts their particular circumstances.[40] Guidelines should not be too specific, instead containing only core information. However, references to more detailed resources should be included, for example, detailing the cognitive levels necessary to understand the specific legal decision and how this should be taken into consideration in the assessment.[41] The guidelines should provide practical advice and best practice examples, and be reviewed regularly.[42]

The content of the guidelines ideally would be modelled upon a combination of the guides examined. The handbooks prepared for lawyers,[43] judges[44] and psychologists[45] by the American Bar Association Commission on Law and Aging and the American Psychological Association, as well as the handbook produced by the British Medical Association and the Law Society are significant in such a modelling exercise.[46] These resources are invaluable when considering what should be considered in any set of guidelines, as well as providing an example of the benefits of an interdisciplinary approach to the development of satisfactory guidelines. For example, the British Medical Association and the Law Society have included 'Assessment of Capacity and Guidance Notes', a form which sets out specific information to be gathered in the assessment of capacity. Such information should include the qualifications of the legal and/or health care professional conducting the assessment; the nature and length of the disability/illness; the effect of the disability/illness; whether the individual in question is able to make the specific decision and if not, why not; on what grounds the opinion is made; whether there is an issue

---

[39]Cockerill J et al. (2005), pp. 38–39. See also Darzins P et al. (2000), p. 16.

[40]Capacity Assessment Office Ontario Ministry of the Attorney General (2005), p. II5.

[41]Queensland Law Reform Commission (2010), p. 279.

[42]Ibid 272.

[43]American Bar Association Commission on Law and Aging, American Psychological Association Assessment of Capacity in Older Adults Project Working Group (2005).

[44]American Bar Association Commission on Law and Aging, American Psychological Association and National College of Probate Judges (2006).

[45]American Bar Association Commission on Law and Aging, American Psychological Association Assessment of Capacity in Older Adults Project Working Group (2008).

[46]British Medical Association and the Law Society (2015).

of undue influence; whether there is a possibility of the individual regaining capacity; if there are different opinions regarding the existence of capacity, why that is; and whether there is any conflict of interest.[47]

The critical issue is how a legal professional, perhaps in conjunction with a health professional, reaches the conclusion that an individual has lost legal capacity.[48] Ideally, there will be three stages of investigation. First, an initial assessment undertaken by the legal professional; second, the involvement of and clinical assessment conducted by a health care professional (if necessary); and finally, a determination as to whether the individual has the requisite legal capacity or not for the specific task in question.[49] Of primary importance to any assessment is taking into account the decision and time specific nature of capacity. The relevant legal standards need to be clearly established, including what the individual must be able to understand for them to be considered legally capable.[50] Thought must likewise be given to the clinical models available for assessment, with the benefits and disadvantages of those model(s) being taken into consideration, for example, the limitations of the MMSE.[51] It is also necessary to consider the triggers indicating that capacity is an issue, for example, is the individual exhibiting emotional, behavioural or cognitive symptoms such as difficulty with comprehension or communication, memory loss, deficiency in mental acumen including problems with performing calculations and/or disorientation.[52] Alternatively, is the individual experiencing significant emotional distress, delusions, hallucinations and/or poor hygiene, or displaying inappropriate behaviour?[53] Any of these can serve as warnings indicating that there may be issues with capacity which warrant further exploration.

Consideration must be given as to who should assess capacity, when the assessment should take place, and how, including when an interdisciplinary approach is warranted.[54] The legal professional may proceed as 'normal' when there is little to no evidence of a loss of legal capacity. If there are minor problems, which can be evidenced by a loss of capacity which is insufficient to conclude that the individual cannot make the decision in question, the legal professional can proceed but should consider seeking the opinion of a health care professional. If there is evidence of a loss of capacity the legal professional should proceed with caution. The legal

---

[47]Ibid 289.

[48]American Bar Association Commission on Law and Aging, American Psychological Association Assessment of Capacity in Older Adults Project Working Group (2005), p. v.

[49]Ibid 3. See also British Medical Association and the Law Society (2015), pp. 22–24.

[50]American Bar Association Commission on Law and Aging, American Psychological Association Assessment of Capacity in Older Adults Project Working Group (2005), pp. v–vi.

[51]Ibid v.

[52]Ibid 14–15.

[53]Ibid 15–16.

[54]British Medical Association and the Law Society (2015), pp. 23–24, 222.

professional should consult with, upon obtaining an authority from the client, or refer the individual to an appropriate health care professional. For instance, this could be any one of the local general practitioner, a geriatrician, psychologist, neuropsychologist or psychiatrist, depending on the disability or illness.[55] A formal capacity assessment should be undertaken if there are acute problems wherein the individual clearly lacks capacity.[56] If a medical assessment is sought, the information that the referral letter should contain must be established, including: the individual's background; why the individual saw the legal professional; is the individual a new or an existing client; why the legal professional is referring the individual to the health care professional; any known medical information about the individual, especially that pertinent to the issue of capacity; the legal capacity in question; the standard of that capacity; the environment, social and familial circumstances of the individual; and any known values or preferences.[57]

It should not be assumed that all health care professionals are familiar with capacity assessments. Health professionals should feel comfortable to refuse to assess capacity unless there is adequate information and they feel they are possessed of the skill necessary to do so.[58] Connected to this is the obligation on the legal professional to clearly explain the role of the health professional. This would also represent an attempt to allay any fears about potential involvement in litigation. Further, there should be a discussion between the legal and health professionals prior to the production of a written report from the health professional to determine if the report would be useful and what the report should focus on.[59] An example of a general format for the report should be included containing, for example: demographic information, the history of the referral, the questions asked on referral, an authority consenting to the referral and the assessment, any behavioural observations, medical history—both generally and relevant to the (alleged) loss of capacity, tests administered, the results, an evaluation of the results including their validity and reliability, a diagnosis and/or opinion as to the individual's capacity to undertake the task at hand with reference to the appropriate legal framework, and recommendations for actions to treat the symptoms and to improve capacity.[60] As flagged, consideration has to be given to issues of consent. Consent from the individual is needed, provided that the individual is capable of giving consent, before the referral and the assessment can occur. An appropriate form should be included in any assessment guidelines which is able to be modified as the situation requires.[61] Potentially a system of information gathering could be developed

---

[55] American Bar Association Commission on Law and Aging, American Psychological Association Assessment of Capacity in Older Adults Project Working Group (2005), p. vii.

[56] Ibid vi–vii, 21.

[57] Ibid vii. See also British Medical Association and the Law Society (2015), pp. 52–54.

[58] British Medical Association and the Law Society (2015), p. 52–54.

[59] American Bar Association Commission on Law and Aging, American Psychological Association Assessment of Capacity in Older Adults Project Working Group (2005), p. vii.

[60] Ibid.

[61] British Medical Association and the Law Society (2015), p. 19.

which may include speaking to family members and/or friends, again upon an authority being firstly obtained. There are questions around whether this information should be stored electronically, and possibly nationally, to ensure ease of access if the individual relocates to another area within the same country.

Any circumstances potentially impacting an individual's capacity such as stress, grief, depression, treatable medical conditions, effects of medications, hearing or vision impairment, educational, socio-economic, cultural, or linguistic factors also need to be identified and taken into account in the assessment process.[62] The actual assessment process itself should focus on the elements contained in the definition of capacity and context specific level required rather than the agreeability or cooperativeness of the individual, including the perceived morality or 'correctness' of his or her decision.[63] A bank of sample questions should be developed which can be used in the assessment process. The questions have the potential to guide the assessor as to what information he or she should be seeking and how he or she should attempt to attain the information.

Assessment guidelines should include measures about how to enhance capacity, for example, building trust, educating the individual about the process, and/or accommodating any sensory (including hearing) impediments, as well as cultural and linguistic differences.[64] The recording of the assessment process is important, as are the mechanisms used for this purpose such as extensive file notes and potentially recording the assessment process.[65] Clearly the consent of the individual involved will be required before any recording can take place. Recording is something that should be given serious thought—would recording the person giving instructions and the assessment process, if one were deemed necessary, make it clear that capacity was not in issue, thus offering clear evidence as to any potential future allegations of incapacity? Alternatively, would recording the assessment process place additional stress on the individual thus having a negative impact? Practitioners involved may likewise be reluctant to be involved in recording as, again, it could feed into issues of professional liability. However, this does not have to be in a negative sense—recording the process could offer some level of protection against any such claims, especially if the assessment was carried out in accordance with best practice—which it is suggested here that guidelines should be developed, and consequently recognised, to comprise.

Careful deliberation should occur as to whether medical assessment is necessary. This is in recognition of the fact that this could concede that capacity is an issue if a third party wants to contest the validity of a testamentary or enduring document. Assessments can also be undertaken in anticipation of future legal proceedings

---

[62]Ibid 23–24; American Bar Association Commission on Law and Aging, American Psychological Association Assessment of Capacity in Older Adults Project Working Group (2005), pp. vi, 16–17.

[63]American Bar Association Commission on Law and Aging, American Psychological Association Assessment of Capacity in Older Adults Project Working Group (2005), p. 13.

[64]Ibid vi; British Medical Association and the Law Society (2015), pp. 17–19.

[65]British Medical Association and the Law Society (2015), p. 211.

questioning an individual's legal capacity and either the outcome of the assessment or the process itself, or perhaps both. This raises the concern of the professional liability involved in assessing capacity, or not assessing it, as the case may be. Any ethical issues, both professionally and regarding the actual assessment process itself, must also be kept to the front of the assessor's mind. This will include investigating whether the decision in question is consistent with the individual's long-term values and beliefs and if it is not, why not.[66] Finally, as stated, the guidelines should promote an interdisciplinary approach acknowledging that although the determination of capacity is ultimately a legal question, that medical evidence should be considered where appropriate, which involves putting in place mechanisms such as those discussed above to try and ensure that the evidence available is the best evidence possible.[67]

Care must be taken to retain flexibility and to avoid 'setting the bar too high' in assessing capacity.[68] Consideration must also be had for the expense and disruption to an individual with regards to seeking a medical assessment of testamentary or decision-making capacity.[69] This is not to mention the fear that could be felt by an individual who is being told that he or she may no longer possess the ability necessary to make legally recognised decisions—a fear which could impact on the outcome of the assessment process as recognised by the question of whether the law is having a therapeutic or anti-therapeutic effect on the individual who has come into contact with the law and legal actors. Consequently, the involvement of a health care professional should not be undertaken lightly, especially as it is important to ensure that the law itself is not having a detrimental impact on the individual's capacity. Nevertheless, a formal assessment can be invaluable in clarifying questions about a loss of capacity, obtaining advice on methods to enhance capacity, identifying where protections may be needed, and providing evidence in court proceedings.[70] It is possible, and should not be forgotten, that an informal conversation between legal and health care professionals wherein the individual is de-identified may also be useful as a preliminary investigative tool.[71]

As can be seen throughout the above discussion, guidelines are also significant as issues surrounding legal practitioner liability arise and will increasingly continue to do so. It has been suggested that the assessment of capacity goes beyond a legal requirement to comprise an actual duty. With testamentary and decision-making capacity assessments growing in complexity, it is possible that issues surrounding practitioner liability and the assessment process itself will increase. Legal

---

[66] American Bar Association Commission on Law and Aging, American Psychological Association Assessment of Capacity in Older Adults Project Working Group (2005), vi.

[67] Ibid vii.

[68] Queensland Law Reform Commission (2010), p. 277.

[69] American Bar Association Commission on Law and Aging, American Psychological Association Assessment of Capacity in Older Adults Project Working Group (2005), vi.

[70] Ibid.

[71] Ibid vii.

professionals need to be aware of circumstances which give rise to issues of capacity assessment.[72] Consequently, if guidelines exist establishing a base standard and a legal and/or health care professional is able to explain the reasons for deviating from this standard, this may help address issues of practitioner liability. What is also significant then is the question of whether these guidelines are referred to in disciplinary proceedings.

6.2 Testamentary Capacity

The fundamental elements established in the test for testamentary capacity must be taken into account in any guidelines dealing with the ability to be able to make, alter or revoke testamentary instruments.[73] Although the test itself does not need to be substantially updated, there is an issue about its application which requires better education of the professionals involved in assessments about best practice, as well as the unfair expectation that health care professionals ought to know and understand the relevant legal standards. Developing interdisciplinary guidelines establishing the procedure to be followed, and the information which should be both given and sought when an assessment is to occur will assist with the better application of the test for testamentary capacity.

It is suggested that when assessing testamentary capacity, including the application of the traditional elements, that the testator should understand the nature and effect of making a will. This incorporates the testator having an appreciation of the persons who are natural beneficiaries and the testator's obligations to provide for people who are dependent upon him or her. The testator should realise the effect of the testamentary provision that he or she is making and the consequences of the will on family and friends. There would also need to be clinical guidelines relevant to assessments being undertaken by health professionals including information about what content any report should contain. The information should go further than merely regurgitating the elements for testamentary capacity established in *Banks*, instead demonstrating engagement with the concepts raised by each element with respect to the individual's ability to give effect to his or her testamentary intentions. The development of clinical guidelines would require consultation with appropriate, especially medical, stakeholders.[74] The legal profession has a responsibility to ensure that the health care professions have adequate information to be able to participate in, and report on, an assessment to determine an individual's capacity to execute testamentary instruments.

---

[72]See, for example, *Legal Services Commissioner v Ford* [2008] LPT 12.
[73](1870) LR 5 QB 549.
[74]Pinsker DM et al. (2010), pp. 332, 341.

6.3   Decision-Making Capacity

Decision-making capacity should be distinguished from testamentary capacity as the legal tests differ, especially for enduring powers of attorney which require a higher standard. For enduring powers of attorney the concept of understanding will also include the individual comprehending the powers to be given; that the individual can state or restrict those powers; when the power given under the enduring document commences; that once the power comes into effect, the attorney will be able to use and will have full authority over the powers given to him, her or them; that the individual may revoke the enduring power of attorney at any time provided that he or she is capable; that an enduring power of attorney continues despite the individual losing capacity; and that an individual who has lost capacity is unable to oversee the attorney or revoke the power.[75] As stated, there is no accepted clinical model to assess financial capacity, although further research is being conducted into this and advances are being made, especially in the role that neuroscience has to play in the assessment of legal capacity. However, any such model cannot be developed independently of the legal requirements, again demonstrating the importance of fostering the relationship between legal and health professionals.

6.4   The Role of the Health Professional

The health professions are also recognising the need for consistent, accurate and transparent capacity assessment paradigms. The role that the health care professional is assuming and, alternatively, is being asked to assume, by the legal profession in the determination of an individual's legal capacity needs to be made clear. This involvement can take one of five personas, that of education, detection of an issue, assessment, supporting individual autonomy, and/or referral.[76] The potential role of a health professional in the education of individuals about the utility of wills and substitute decision-making documents was discussed above. This connects with the early detection of an issue which could later impair or eliminate capacity. By providing the individual with this knowledge the health professional is, in effect, supporting individual autonomy and ensuring that his or her interaction with not only the legal system is therapeutic but also his or her interaction with the medical profession as well. If the health professional in question does not have, or does not feel that he or she has, the expertise to undertake any of the previous roles then there is always the option of a referral. Each is a vital role that the health professions have to play in the assessment of capacity. However, not all of these 'hats' will be worn at once, and it must be understood what is being

---

[75]O'Neill N and Peisah C (2011), pp. 8–9.
[76]Marson DC (2013), p. 385.

asked of the particular health professional who is involved in the situation specific assessment. Clear guidelines would assist with this.

Guidelines would be especially useful in emergency situations or at the end of life where time is of the essence.[77] Typical of the medical literature is the statement that 'the legal standards [as well as the methods] for capacity vary, so health professionals should be aware of the standard for each jurisdiction...'.[78] The problem is that there is often little to no guidance from the legal profession as to how to assess legal capacity when a health professional is requested to do so. Alternatively, health professionals can assume a knowledge and familiarity with the law based on an incorrect understanding which may then impact the outcome of any assessment. Both professions need to understand their limitations and the health professional's role should be defined as much as possible to offer certainty to both professions as to who has the responsibility for what aspect of the assessment to ensure that miscommunications and misunderstandings are kept to a minimum.[79] Further, in considering the actual development of a tool to assess legal capacity, it is arguable that instead of an elusive 'capacimeter' against which capacity can be measured, energies should be directed towards establishing, refining and disseminating suitable clinical parameters.[80] However, whilst it may be difficult, if not impossible, to develop a clinical assessment tool, certainly in the near future, it is very possible to develop a set of guidelines to establish the appropriate method to be adopted by legal and health professionals, which is understandable by both, when assessing capacity.[81]

In providing evidence, health professionals would be best placed to give evidence about the individual's medical condition and any comorbidities as disclosed by the individual's medical history and relevant diagnostic evidence, as well as what, if any, effects such conditions had on the cognitive functioning of the testator. For example what and how severe are the cognitive impairments; whether the cognitive impairments affect the individual's daily functioning or activities and if yes, what ones and how; and finally, whether the individual's ability to make personal and/or financial decisions is affected by the cognitive impairments and, if they are, what evidence supports this conclusion.[82] They would also be able to (potentially) describe how apparent these effects are, that is, whether they would be evident to anyone or only to people with specialised training? This includes consideration of the legal 'terms of art' such as insane delusions and lucid intervals. Further, health professionals would be able to provide evidence on: what, if any, medications the individual was taking; what effects the medications—individually and as a whole—would likely have on the person's ability to make the contextually

---

[77]Parker M and Cartwright C (2005), p. 89.

[78]Bennett H and Hallen P (2005), p. 486.

[79]British Medical Association and the Law Society (2015), pp. 132–133.

[80]Kapp MB and Mossman D (1996), p. 73.

[81]Moye J et al. (2007), p. 592.

[82]Bennett H and Hallen P (2005), pp. 201–218.

specific decision; whether these effects were evident at the requisite time, for example, signing the will; whether the effects would have impacted the person's ability to understand and communicate his or decision; and whether there any processes that could be put in place to combat this, for example, lowering the dosage of medication to increase cognition at the relevant time? This information then needs to be contextually examined with reference to the relevant legal test and the four elements discussed—how do the mentally disabling condition and/or the medication(s) (both prescribed and illegal) impact on the individual's ability to meet that standard at the requisite time? The health professional also needs to have an awareness, if possible, of the social, familial, educational and cultural circumstances which may influence the assessment, as well as being able to access information about previous decision-making such as prior wills and/or enduring documents.[83]

Giving consideration to such issues can help identify the evidence that the 'expert' is capable of providing by directly identifying the area in which the professional is an 'expert'. It provides a clear foundation as to why the expert is qualified to provide evidence in the matter at hand and ideally improves the quality of the evidence that is being adduced in court. Even if the matter does not make it that far, giving thought to such questions can assist with the assessment through the identification of who is the best person to conduct it and matters to which he, she or they ought to be turning their minds. Opinions should, however, be restricted to facts in existence rather than to those which have been assumed—the latter of which offers no foundation upon which to base an opinion. Although, this is not to say that reports cannot consider different factual scenarios—such scenarios just need to be grounded in the established and verifiable facts. Expert opinions should likewise take into account all relevant lay evidence that is available—does this impact the 'expert's' opinion and if so, why and in what way?

It is acknowledged that a standard approach may be too rigid, discouraging new initiatives from being developed. However, it is not intended that the proposed guidelines and supporting principles remove the flexibility that is undeniably essential in this area. They would instead establish a standard, yet flexible, process to underpin testamentary and decision-making capacity assessment. Such a paradigm would create both transparency and consistency of approach, as well as establishing a 'baseline' for good practice to promote satisfactory assessments. The guidelines and general principles should be reviewed at regular intervals ensuring that they reflect current best practice and advancements in both the medical and legal disciplines with respect to adequately assessing capacity. Further, any such guidelines are not intended to replace diagnostic tools. It is when these diagnostic means are used in conjunction with the skills of the legal profession in a systemised way that clarity and uniformity of process should ideally occur. Guidelines would only serve to facilitate this process. The test for capacity is undisputedly

---

[83]O'Neill N and Peisah C (2011), 1.4. See also *Simon v Byford & Ors (Re Rose (Deceased))* [2013] EWHC 1490 (Ch).

a legal test. However, the complexities of the human mind and body, as well as new and developing medical knowledge require the increasing involvement of health professionals in capacity assessments.

6.5 A National Body/Specialist Assessors

The concept of national bodies of assessors has emerged as one method through which to attempt to ensure the consistent, transparent and accurate assessment of legal capacity. This body would implement and monitor capacity assessments, potentially taking the form of a memory assessment clinic. It is suggested that this may offer a feasible structure in which to satisfactorily assess capacity.[84] Such clinics may be able to provide specialist assessors and/or legal and health care specialists. There are systems, for example in Canada, in which capacity assessors are used and guidelines have been developed for the assessor to follow.[85] In particular, the potential adaptability of the Quebecois tutorship council is of interest. Briefly, this 'council' comprises one legal professional, one health professional and an ethics officer to cast a deciding vote in the case of a deadlock. The presence of both a legal and a health professional would ensure that both disciplines would be represented and the ethics officer would safeguard the fundamental importance of the concept of individual autonomy. The role and relationship of the legal and health professionals would need to be closely scrutinised to determine whether such an approach would be successful.

An alternative to a specialist body would be individual professionals specifically trained to assess capacity in the testamentary and/or decision-making context. Additionally, there may be a different form of team-based approach which still incorporates legal and health professionals but which takes on the role of a cognitive assessment clinic.[86] This would be more interactive and less formal, providing the opportunity to work with individuals to potentially increase their capacity through avenues such as education rather than having a purely determinative role. While this may be a possibility in metropolitan areas it is difficult to see how this would work in rural communities with limited access to specialist legal and health care services.

People in need of assistance could also potentially be identified through cognitive screening procedures. For example, in the United States of America, the new 'annual wellness examination' available for Medicare patients provides an opportunity for capacity screening and community education on planning for the loss of financial and/or health care decision-making ability.[87] Using this, or a similar

---

[84]New South Wales Department of Lands (2009), p. 6.
[85]Cockerill J et al. (2005), p. 49.
[86]Collier B et al. (2005a), p. 162.
[87]Sabatino CP (2011), p. 707.

system, as a means to assess capacity may be one way in which to ensure consistency and transparency of process as well as providing funding for the assessment process to ensure that health care professionals are adequately remunerated for any assessments conducted.

The loss of capacity is stressful enough without people being forced into foreign environments for such assessments.[88] To have qualified people make the determinations in an environment familiar to the individual in question could serve to heighten their ability to retain capacity.[89] However, the practicalities of developing such a body would be significant, not least with questions of funding, training and implementation needing to be addressed. It may be something that is worth further investigation, however, especially with the move towards a supported decision-making paradigm where the assessment of capacity and the stage the person is at may become even more critical.

7 Witnessing Requirements

Witnessing requirements for testamentary and enduring documents likewise need consideration. This is especially the case depending on the approach that is adopted with respect to the paradigm shift from substitute to supported decision-making. Witnessing testamentary documents is also important—if both a legal and a health care professional attest to the testator's capacity then this is useful evidence in the event of any alleged incapacity. It also accords with the golden rule in the United Kingdom, and good practice in Australia and the United States of America. It could also serve to provide a counter check if, for example, the legal professional involved has missed an issue as to capacity.

While the concerns regarding the ability of health professionals with respect to witnessing documents of this type and, in particular, enduring documents are noted if, for example, justices of the peace (who receive no specific training regarding legal capacity assessment) are able to witness enduring documents then the question arises, why are health professionals any less qualified to assess capacity for enduring documents? However, the question is, do health professionals even want to become involved in witnessing testamentary and enduring documents? This leads to questions of involvement in litigation raising concerns about professional liability. What is clear is the need to implement adequate safeguards which are designed to not only protect and promote the individual's wishes, but to also try and avoid unnecessary and expensive litigation or tribunal applications. Gathering the best contemporaneous evidence possible can help achieve this. It can also signal if a more complete assessment is required. Consequently, the witnessing requirements are fundamental and need to be given detailed consideration, and strengthened in

---

[88]British Medical Association and the Law Society (2015), pp. 17–19.

[89]Darzins P et al. (2000), pp. 14–18.

the case of enduring documents, as this will assist in providing contemporaneous evidence if and when issues of incapacity arise.

8 Registration

A system of registration arguably may assist in verifying the existence and formality of testamentary and enduring documents.[90] Although it must be acknowledged that registration would not necessarily ensure the validity of the document in question. The use of registration could, however, assist with assessment to see what processes have been adopted. It could also address the problem that these documents may remain hidden in the proverbial 'desk drawer'. E-records could be utilised as a central register for the documents, although privacy concerns and ensuring the integrity of the system would clearly be an issue.[91] Registration could be used to acknowledge issues of abuse and third party liability enabling a third party, such as a bank, to verify that an enduring document has come into effect. Alternatively however, and depending upon the response to the issues around the protection of privacy, such a registration scheme may inadvertently open vulnerable individuals up to abuse. For example, child two becomes aware that child one has their mother's enduring power of attorney and subsequently pressures the mother to alter the document.

Registration, particularly if it is compulsory, arguably also infringes upon individual autonomy running contrary to one of the reasons for encouraging the uptake of estate planning documents. A national register for wills currently exists in Australia, although it is not compulsory and is not Government controlled.[92] Consequently, legitimacy issues do exist. Nevertheless, a centrally operated system of registration should at least be considered for both testamentary and enduring documents given the opportunities presented by such a system, principally ensuring ease of location of such documents. As with this area more broadly the practical considerations as to who would pay, for which there are no easy answers, again feature.

Connected to this is the question of whether a system of annual reporting for decision-makers could or should be implemented. This would present an opportunity to hold third party decision-makers accountable, particularly for financial decisions. This, however, also has its challenges, principally that potential decision-makers may refuse to take on the role if it is seen to be even more onerous than it already is.

---

[90]Standing Committee on Legal and Constitutional Affairs, Parliament of the Commonwealth of Australia (2007), xlvi, xlvii, ch 8.

[91]Monash University and the University of Tasmania (2010), p. 7.

[92]See The Will Registry (2009).

9   Hindrances and Hurdles

Any proposed guidelines and general principles are potentially of relatively limited effect. Problems resulting from the subjectivity inherent in capacity assessment exist in addition to the issue of attaining jurisdictional cooperation.[93] These difficulties include financial cost as well as the enormous investment of time necessary to develop, refine and implement any guidelines and general principles. Provision would also need to be made for a period of adjustment during which time there would be inefficiency.[94] Legal and health professionals may also be resistant to changes in their practice. However, the discord between theory and practical implementation cannot be allowed to continue. The current ad hoc approaches must be replaced with one balancing regulation and practicality while safeguarding vulnerable individuals but also having regard to the practitioners involved in conducting the assessments.[95] The guidelines and general principles need to be opened for discussion amongst the various stakeholders including the legal and health professions, relevant government departments, insurers, advocacy groups, and community interest organisations. The input of such a variety of organisations will only serve to strengthen any suggested paradigm.

As signposted throughout this work, this area is one requiring extensive further research. There is scope for further research to be conducted in a number of related areas. This includes the existence of specialist capacity assessors and a review of the capacity assessment protocols implemented in hospital and aged care facilities. This would involve an assessment of relevant policies to examine what the procedures are if a person presents with an enduring document or is in need of one, or a will, being prepared. The capacity assessment protocols surrounding emergency situations also need to be examined.[96] Whether capacity is assessed differently depending on the individual's geographical location, that is metropolitan or rural, likewise warrants further research. Exploration should occur regarding whether individuals in regional areas lack access to the resources that individuals in the metropolitan centres have when their capacity is at issue.

10   Concluding Remarks

The need for capacity assessments in the context of testamentary and substitute decision-making is growing in importance and frequency as society ages and rates of mentally disabling conditions increase. Capacity assessments are inherently connected with the dualistic nature of autonomy and protection signalling the

---

[93]Kapp MB (2002), p. 415.

[94]Ibid.

[95]Ibid 417.

[96]Parker M and Cartwright C (2005), p. 89.

importance of accurate assessments conducted within a rigorous, consistent and transparent methodology. This work is novel in the approach taken to the issue of capacity assessment in this context. First, it builds upon the significant research investigating capacity in areas such as consent to and/or refusal of medical treatment by conducting an analysis of the methods utilised to assess capacity in the testamentary and substitute decision-making contexts, and the legal framework within which the assessments are, and should be, conducted. Secondly, the doctrinal analysis conducted revealed a dearth of research into assessing financial capacity, a key component when assessing testamentary and enduring power of attorney documents. This research explored the assessment of financial capacity from a medico-legal interface. Thirdly, there has been no comprehensive international doctrinal exploration of testamentary and decision-making capacity assessment tools, including guides and handbooks, resulting in the development of one set of proposed guidelines and general principles. This will ideally provide for a more rigorous assessment paradigm promoting consistency and transparency of process which is currently lacking. Such guidelines will augment the existing test for testamentary capacity, an acknowledgment of the health profession's call for the legal discipline to reassess testamentary capacity in light of twenty-first century concerns. A call which is reasonable in the application of the legal test given varying factors such as the ageing population, recognition of mentally disabling conditions, and the increasing requests for medical involvement in capacity assessments. The adoption of an interdisciplinary approach can also be utilised to address the misunderstanding and miscommunication which exists between the legal and health professions through the promotion and development of common communication and educational tools. Finally, therapeutic jurisprudence has been used as an innovative lens through which to examine the approaches to capacity assessment in this context.

What is clear is that any assessment model must be consistent and transparent, giving due respect to individual autonomy. This is not to deny the importance of retaining flexibility of process but there remains a distinct lack of precision, consistency and rigour both at law and in the assessment paradigms adopted, which are dependent upon both jurisdiction and practitioner. This is unacceptable when capacity and autonomy are so closely interconnected. There is an increasing acknowledgement of the need for, and movement towards, an interdisciplinary approach to assessing capacity incorporating the skills of both legal and health professionals. A focused education campaign amongst the relevant professions, as well as the general community, will be necessary. This is not to deny that problems exist with the development of such a paradigm, but with the growing frequency and import of capacity assessments in the testamentary and decision-making context, especially given the ageing demographic, it is a worthwhile investment of time and funds on behalf of all the relevant stakeholders. The capacity assessment dialogue cannot be allowed to stall. Action needs to occur.

References

American Bar Association Commission on Law, Aging, American Psychological Association (2005) Assessment of Older Adults with Diminished Capacity: A Handbook for Lawyers. https://www.apa.org/pi/aging/resources/guides/diminished-capacity.pdf. Accessed 1 Nov 2016

American Bar Association Commission on Law and Aging, American Psychological Association (2008) Assessment of Capacity in Older Adults Project Working Group, Assessment of Older Adults with Diminished Capacity: A Handbook for Psychologists. https://www.apa.org/pi/aging/programs/assessment/capacity-psychologist-handbook.pdf. Accessed 1 Nov 2016

American Bar Association Commission on Law and Aging, American Psychological Association, National College of Probate Judges (2006) Judicial Determination of Capacity of Older Adults in Guardianship Proceedings: A Handbook for Judges. https://www.apa.org/pi/aging/resources/guides/judges-diminished.pdf. Accessed 1 Nov 2016

Bennett H, Hallen P (2005) Guardianship and financial management legislation: what doctors in aged care need to know. Intern Med J 35(8):482–487

British Medical Association and the Law Society (2015) Assessment of mental capacity: guidance for doctors and lawyers, 4th edn. Law Society Publishing, London

Capacity Assessment Office Ontario Ministry of the Attorney General (2005) Guidelines for Conducting Assessments of Capacity. http://www.attorneygeneral.jus.gov.on.ca/english/family/pgt/capacity/2005-06/guide-0505.pdf. Accessed 1 Nov 2016

Cockerill J, Collier B, Maxwell K (2005) Legal requirements and current practices. In: Collier B, Coyne C, Sullivan K (eds) Mental capacity, powers of attorney and advance health directives. Federation Press, Leichhardt

Collier B, Coyne C, Sullivan K (2005a) Conclusion. In: Collier B, Coyne C, Sullivan K (eds) Mental capacity, powers of attorney and advance health directives. Federation Press, Leichhardt

Collier B, Coyne C, Sullivan K (eds) (2005b) Mental capacity, powers of attorney and advance health directives. Federation Press, Leichhardt

Darzins P, Molloy DW, Strang D (eds) (2000) Who can decide? The six step capacity assessment process. Memory Australia Press, Adelaide

Ellison S et al (2004) The legal needs of older people in NSW. Law and Justice Foundation of NSW. http://www.lawfoundation.net.au/ljf/site/articleids/6ffeb98d3c8d21f1ca25707e0024d3eb/$file/older_law_report.pdf. Accessed 1 Nov 2016

Falk E, Hoffman N (2014) The role of capacity assessments in elder abuse investigations and guardianships. Clin Geriatr Med 30(4):851–868

Finkel SI (2003) The matter of wills can your cognitively impaired older patient execute a new will? Geriatrics 58(1):65–76

Kapp MB (2002) Decisional capacity in theory and practice: legal process versus "bumbling through". Aging Ment Health 6(4):413–417

Kapp MB (2015) Evaluating decision making capacity in older individuals: does the law give a clue? Laws 4(2):164–172

Kapp MB, Mossman D (1996) Measuring decisional capacity: cautions on the construction of a "Capacimeter". Psychol Public Policy Law 2(1):73–95

Kennedy KM (2012) Testamentary capacity: a practical guide to assessment of ability to make a valid will. J Forensic Legal Med 19(4):191–195

Kershaw MM, Webber LS (2004) Dimensions of financial competence. Psychiatry Psychol Law 11(2):338–349

Law Reform Committee, Parliament of Victoria (2010) Inquiry into Powers of Attorney Final Report of the Victorian Law Reform Committee. http://www.parliament.vic.gov.au/images/stories/committees/lawrefrom/powers_of_attorney/Report_24-08-2010.pdf. Accessed 1 Nov 2016

Marson D (2016) Commentary: a role for neuroscience in preventing financial elder abuse. Public Policy Aging Rep 26(1):12–14

Marson DC (2013) Clinical and ethical aspects of financial capacity in dementia: a commentary. Am J Geriatr Psychiatry 21(4):382–390

McNeal MH (2013) Slow lawyering: representing seniors in light of cognitive changes accompanying aging. Penn State Law Rev 117(4):1081

Monash University, the University of Tasmania (2010) The right for an individual choice: advance care planning. A Submission to the Productivity Commission Inquiry into Caring for Older Australians

Moye J et al (2007) A conceptual model and assessment template for capacity evaluation in adult guardianship. The Gerontologist 47(5):591–603

Moye J, Marson DC, Edelstein B (2013) Assessment of capacity in an aging society. Am Psychol 68(3):158–171

New South Wales Department of Lands (2009) Review of the Powers of Attorney Act 2003 Issue Paper. http://www.lpi.nsw.gov.au/__data/assets/pdf_file/0014/106322/Power_attorney_final. pdf. Accessed 1 Nov 2016

O'Neill N, Peisah C (2011) Capacity and the law. Sydney University Press, Sydney

Parker M (2008) Patient competence and professional incompetence: disagreements in capacity assessments in one Australian jurisdiction, and their educational implications. J Law Med 16 (1):25–35

Parker M, Cartwright C (2005) Mental capacity in medical practice and advance care planning: clinical, ethical and legal issues. In: Collier B, Coyne C, Sullivan K (eds) Mental capacity, powers of attorney and advance health Directives. Federation Press, Leichardt

Perlin ML (1999–2000) A law of healing. Univ Cincinnati Law Rev 68:407

Pinsker DM et al (2010) Financial capacity in older Adults: a review of clinical assessment approaches and considerations. Clin Gerontol 33(4):332–346

Purser K, Rosenfeld T (2014) Evaluation of legal capacity by doctors and lawyers: the need for collaborative assessment. Med J Aust 201(8):483–485

Queensland Law Reform Commission (2010) A review of Queensland's guardianship Laws, Report No 67, Volume 1. http://www.qlrc.qld.gov.au/__data/assets/pdf_file/0003/372540/ r67_vol_1.pdf. Accessed 1 Nov 2016

Rush University Medical Centre (2016) Assessing Decisional Capacity. https://www.rush.edu/ services-treatments/geriatric-services-older-adult-care/assessing-decisional-capacity-curricu lum. Accessed 1 Nov 2016

Sabatino CP (2011) Damage prevention and control for financial incapacity. J Am Med Assoc 305 (7):707–708

Sousa LB et al (2014) Financial and testamentary capacity evaluations: procedures and assessment instruments underneath a functional approach. Int Psychogeriatr 26(2):217–228

Standing Committee on Legal and Constitutional Affairs, Parliament of the Commonwealth of Australia (2007) Older People and the Law

The Will Registry (2009) Welcome to The Will Registry. http://www.thewillregistry.com.au. Accessed 1 Nov 2016

United Nations Convention on the Rights of Persons with Disabilities, opened for signature 30 March 2007, (entered into force 3 May 2008)

Cases

Banks v Goodfellow (1870) LR 5 QB 549

Legal Services Commissioner v Ford [2008] LPT 12

Ruskey-Fleming v Cook [2013] QSC 142

Sharp v Adam [2006] EWCA Civ 449

Simon v Byford & Ors (Re Rose (Deceased)) [2013] EWHC 1490 (Ch)

Index

© Springer International Publishing AG 2017
K. Purser, *Capacity Assessment and the Law*, DOI 10.1007/978-3-319-54347-5